FOOTFALLS

The Author,1952.

FOOTFALLS

Echoes of the Life of My Time
1895 - 1985

Frances Broene Rogers

Sunstone Press
Santa Fe, New Mexico

COVER PHOTOGRAPH: Beginning of a ten-mile hike. Frances (R) and friends. Lake Michigan, 1914.

First Edition
Printed in the United States of America

Library of Congress Cataloging-in-Publication Data:
    Rogers, Frances Broene, 1895-
        Footfalls: echoes of the life of my time, 1895-1985 / Frances
    Broene Rogers. —1st ed.
        p. cm.
        ISBN 0-86534-164-8: $12.95
        1. Rogers, Frances Broene, 1895-   2.Michigan—Biography.
    I. Title
    CT275.R7545A3   1991
    977.4' 04' 092—dc20
        [B]   91-27665
                                                  CIP

Published in 1992 by SUNSTONE PRESS
            Post Office Box 2321
            Santa Fe, NM 87504-2321 / USA

for my cousin Charlene

ACKNOWLEDGMENTS

I had no idea when I undertook to write this book how much the generosity of others would contribute to the making of it. My thanks to my cousin Charlene Stoltz, a great granddaughter of my Aunt Kate, for insisting that I had a story to tell; to Robert Bart, tutor and sometime dean of students of St. John's College in Santa Fe, and to J. Burchenal Ault, until recently provost of the college, for encouragement and advice; to Robert J. Ferrera, superintendent of schools, and Gordon Olson, city historian, of Grand Rapids, Michigan, and to Karen M. Mason, assistant reference archivist of Bentley Historical Library at the University of Michigan, Ann Arbor, for supplying or confirming information; to Daniel Bell, who word-processed the manuscript, for his personal interest in the project and for unflagging care and patience; to Konstantin Sutt for skillful reproduction of old photographs; to my publisher, James Clois Smith Jr., and Vicki Ahl, the designer, with whom it has been a pleasure to work; and to Robert Rogers, my husband and best friend, who lent me his eyes and his ears and was patient with me on days when my mind was adrift in "other worlds and other seas."

I regret that a number of friends as dear to me as any others have no place in this book. Condensing the experiences of ninety years into a couple of hundred pages is a highly selective process, which, if the book is to be readable, must focus on a few principal themes. Omissions are inevitableTo all, hail and farewell.

CONTENTS

PREFACE

The year is 1900. I am holding Mama's hand very tight on this fine, fresh September morning as we walk purposefully along Thomas Street in Grand Rapids, Michigan. My mind is in a tumult of anticipation and dread. Mama answers my questions reassuringly but without conviction. Her mind is elsewhere. This is a momentous day for her as well as for me, her firstborn. It is to be my first day at school. Of our arrival and leavetaking I remember nothing. We would have clung to each other wordlessly for a moment and then, abruptly, I would have been alone in the world for the first time.

From now on, for part of every day, I shall have to fend for myself, learning to be independent. I have been launched as a member of society just eight months after the new century was ushered in—with bells and whistles and assorted happy noises I do not doubt, for America is riding high. In this sense I am a child of the century, my thinking life almost coincident with it.

Actually, the Twentieth Century as we have come to know it and as history will remember it was scarcely a speck on the horizon. Victoria, queen since 1837, still sat enthroned in London, and the social order to which her name has become attached persisted throughout my childhood. Underlying and supporting it, in the United States of America, was the assured feeling that all was well.

Rumblings there were of quarrels overseas, a few "muckraking" writers were beginning to find faults in this best of all possible worlds, but the man in the street was not listening. Even the guns of August, fourteen years later, were too far away to cause serious concern. When this country became involved, the purpose, as most people saw it, was to get this foreign foolishness over with quickly and get on with Progress. Only when our troop ships turned homeward did we begin to realize vaguely that everything had changed somehow. Still, it was nothing you could put your finger on; we had won a war and we felt good. So, some twenty years behind time, the Nineteenth Century slipped quietly into oblivion while we looked the other way.

For me, the passing of the old order was fortunate, for it was circumspect to a fault, with little tolerance for diversity, especially in a lady, which I was supposed to be. My parents' religious views imposed further restrictions. As a consequence, my childhood was stormy, and throughout most of my adult life my view of the society that nourished me was distorted. I could see only its limitations. Only very late did I begin to understand the benefits I had received.

However naïve, however complacent, however provincial and prejudiced society may have been at the turn of the century, it was stable and it was decent: self-respecting and responsible. The nation was young and confident. There was even some reason to hope that mankind was at last on its way to becoming civilized. A child could put down roots and feel secure.

In the event, I never belonged entirely to either world. What I wanted fundamentally was what I had been brought up to expect, marriage and children. When my life did not turn out that way, I was unprepared for independence. With no clear end in view, I took whatever path was open and abandoned it when I found it unsatisfying.

I cannot call those years wasted. I was learning and growing. What I missed in depth I gained in breadth. Yet in themselves those years were empty; they signified nothing. What was lacking was commitment. My heart was not in what I was doing.

The Depression of the Thirties hastened the inevitable decline of my fortunes. The future looked bleak when I married in 1938. My husband was little better off than I, but when we got on our feet again I was off to a fresh start at a time of life when many women thought of themselves as finished.

When I try to see myself clearly, as I have been obliged to do in writing this book, I realize that there is still much I do not understand. I have no more idea today than I had seventy years ago about what direction I should have taken. I have an uneasy feeling that I missed a cue somewhere along the line, that some door remains shut that should have been opened. But regret is idle. I have had those things that matter most in the end.

What I wanted most deeply, I think, was simply to keep on growing, and that I have done. I have loved and been loved. I have helped others when I could and been helped most generously. I have known the joy to be found between the covers of a book, and in music and the beautiful works of men's hands. I have known the joy of simply being alive in a world where every new day is a miracle.

> "Life is sweet, brother, . . . There's night and day, brother,
> both sweet things; sun, moon, and stars, brother, all sweet
> things; there's likewise a wind on the heath."[1]

It is enough.

Central Figures of my Early Years

MAMA, Cena Beneker, who made room for me to grow in

PAPA, Cornelius Broene (Broona), who loved me devotedly in his fashion

GRANDPA, Gerrit Beneker, Mama's father, valued member of the household, early companion and uncritical friend

ANNA, my little sister

AUNT KATE, Mama's older sister, impulsive and generous, always ready to help

AUNT LOUISE, Mama's younger sister, pious spinster, through whom, ironically, I first became acquainted with the ways of the world

COUSIN LEVINUS (Le-VEEN-us), Louis L. Beneker, Mama's cousin; urbane, humane, who expanded my horizons

COUSIN MATHILDA, Mathilda Boone (Bona) his wife; effortless charmer, everybody's favorite hostess

GRANDPA BROENE, Geert or George, who walked companionably with God and talked to him at family dinners while the turkey got cold

GRANDMA BROENE, Andina Harmsen, with the warm smile and the tireless knitting needles, about whom her numerous family revolved

Two ghostly presences:
GRANDMA BENEKER, Martina Verhorst, first and last, a lady
JOHN CALVIN of Geneva, whose shadow lay across my childhood

Off stage :
UNCLE BART, Bartel Beneker, Mother's brother, whom I scarcely knew, to my lasting regret

1

PROGENITORS

All of my grandparents were immigrants, and the available records are few. Everything I know about my maternal grandmother's family is contained in a brief genealogical record, painstakingly written in an elegant script by her father, Arie Albertus Verhorst, of Wissenkerke, Zeeland, the Netherlands, who identified himself as a Master Watchmaker. He was married in 1817 to Jannetje Geelhoed, who died in 1825 shortly after the birth and death of her fourth child. Eight months later, probably in desperate need of a mother for his three young children, he married Cornelia Huiszoon, my great-grandmother. My grandmother, Martina, and her sister Johanna, six years younger, were the only survivors among ten children by this marriage. Her childhood must have been gloomy. It is certain that she grew up markedly conventional and grimly religious and that she was homesick and unhappy after she was transplanted at the age of forty-four to a backwoods town in the American Midwest for which she was totally unsuited.

Her family appears to have been middle-middle class. Everything I know about her points to solid bourgeois standards and certain amenities. She had the concern for respectability and propriety that marks persons with a position to maintain. What little remained of her possessions when I was a child, a little quite charming jewelry that her father had made, a few pieces of china, bespoke a comfortable income. The house in which she was born appears, in a photograph, to dominate a block of small cottages with dormer windows in their second stories.

Her standards were deeply ingrained in my mother and were passed on to me: an appreciation of genuineness and quality in material things, that carried over into conduct. I was taught to settle for nothing but the best and to set myself high standards of behavior.

Nothing is known with certainty about the family of my grandfather, Gerrit Beneker, except that he and a younger brother were orphaned when they were very young. When Gerrit appears on the scene, he has learned the trades of carpentry and cabinet-making and is putting his brother through school to become a teacher. This was very unusual. Government scholarships were available to young men who wished to teach; but to qualify, it was necessary to have attended an expensive private preparatory school, usually affordable only by the upper classes. It was also unusual that the brother, in the course of acquiring an

11

education, also acquired heretical religious views. He became a Unitarian. If a predisposition to autonomy is an inherited characteristic, it must have come to me from the Benekers.

How Gerrit Beneker, a carpenter, came to marry Martina Verhorst, I do not know. It seems doubtful that such a marriage could have been arranged, but Martina would at least have needed her father's approval. I think that Gerrit may have been quite good-looking in his youth: tall, lean, fit, blond, and blue-eyed. When I knew him he was always clean, neat, well spoken and well mannered; and although he was inarticulate about his feelings he was loving and considerate.

He was forty-six years old when he uprooted himself and his family and brought them to Grand Rapids, Michigan, already known as a city of furniture factories, where his skills would be useful. A document labeled simply "Dutch Immigrations" gives the reason for this move as "economic improvement." I think he must have been concerned about his son Bart's future which, in the Old Country, would have been circumscribed by class barriers. Bart, now fourteen, had presumably finished school and would have to go to work. What Gerrit had done for his brother he was unable to do for his son. There were now six mouths to feed. Besides Bart, there were three little girls between four and eight years: Cornelia Klaasina (Kate), Klaasina Cornelia (Cena, my mother) and Johanna Catharina Louisa (Louise, named after Arie's mother).

The family came to this country along with that of Gerrit's lifelong friend, whom I never knew by any name other than Old Man Van Heulen (Hulen). He had three sons and three daughters. Jim, the one we knew best, was as happy and genial a man as I have ever known; and his wife, Mary, and daughters, Susie and Barbara, were easy-going, friendly people. They were friends and neighbors for many years.

Martina brought up her daughters with puritanical strictness. Her religious views appear to have been more like those of my father's sect than those of her own Dutch Reformed Church. My mother was required to do a stint of knitting after school every day that kept her occupied until supper time. Little hands must never be idle. She had to pray every night that her sins might be forgiven, so that she would not be damned if she died in the night. On one occasion her mother walked with her past a lighted hall where a dance was in progress and said, "I want you to look well at the fiddler; the devil is standing behind him." The effect on a small child may be imagined.

Kate was impetuous and apparently difficult—not strange, perhaps, since most of the housework fell upon her shoulders when her mother felt depressed. Louise was very tiny when she was born, perhaps prematurely, and remained fragile throughout her childhood. As a result, she was exempted from the tasks that would otherwise have been hers and grew up self-deprecating, timid, and ineffectual. All her life she leaned on Cena for support and advice. Religion was her only solace. She once told me that she had sometimes wished she had been born a Catholic so that she might have been a nun.

Cena was gentle and amenable and loved her mother devotedly, sympathizing deeply with her unhappiness. I think this left its mark on her. A strain of sadness overlaid her naturally happy disposition, and she was extremely vulnerable to the sorrows of others. There must have been something endearing about Martina to arouse such depths of childish affection.

Cena was sixteen years old when her mother died in 1880, and thereafter she took over the management of her father's household while working six days a week and Saturday evenings in Paul Steketee's drygoods store. For a few years, after Bart and Kate had married, the family was small; but in 1886 Kate, having been abandoned by her irresponsible husband, was home again with two babies, Martina (Mertie) and Louise. She went to work as a practical nurse, a live-in job, but the two children remained in my grandfather's house until Cena got married in 1894 and Grandpa went to live with her. Those years took a heavy toll of Cena's vitality, but she seems to have enjoyed them. She loved the children and she had many friends.

She was thirty and still unmarried when she met my father, Cornelius Broene, at work. She was probably superior in education and manners to most of the men she met. She had had no schooling beyond the eighth grade, but she was an avid reader. At the time she met my father she was engaged reluctantly to a dentist whom her friends had urged her to marry. He would provide her with a good living; a woman could not wait forever for a man exactly to her liking. That engagement was broken in short order. My parents were deeply in love with each other, and they were still in love when she died twenty-two years later.

At the time I was born and throughout my childhood, my paternal grandfather, Geert Broene (known in this country as George), was a minister of the Christian Reformed Church in Grand Rapids. He was an extraordinary person with a singularly beautiful nature, a Protestant St. Francis, radiant with the love of God and of all God's world. He was loved and esteemed by all who knew him, and his sons revered him. Family life revolved around the church. Any dissent from its doctrines was an insult to Grandpa as well as to God.

The Broene family had been freehold farmers for several generations in the tiny principality of Bentheim, now only a bulge in the western boundary of Germany, surrounded on three sides by the Netherlands. In speech and customs the family seems to have been more Dutch than German. My grandfather's grandfather, also named Geert, was a part-time lay preacher who had been active in establishing the Christian Reformed Church in his community.

The new sect had been founded by members of the established Reformed Church who deemed the latter not strict enough in its adherence to Calvinist principles. With the passage of time and the twin influences of new democratic and scientific concepts, the rigorous standards of conduct of early puritanism had fallen off lamentably. Worldliness had crept in. The Broenes were in the forefront of the movement to restore the old austerity.

The new church had been declared illegal, and the older Geert had served a term in prison for holding forbidden meetings in his home. This made him a hero in the eyes of his family, and they clung to their religion with the fervor of those who have known persecution. My grandfather grew up with a longing to emulate his honored forebear. He was a serious child, who worried about his sins from an early age through long, lonely hours tending the sheep. Let him speak for himself:

> Before I was nine years old I had to shepherd the sheep in the heather at some distance from the house. Often I was mortally afraid, especially after a thunderstorm threatened.... I would pray earnestly.... I was afraid I would be struck by lightning and then what? I would be forever lost. ... From my ninth to my twelfth year I was much engaged in prayer. I was never entirely at ease. I remember being in the field and thinking profoundly, considering my age, of the vast difference between the saved and the unsaved in the future life.

Harm Hendrik Broene, my great-grandfather, came to the United States in 1865, bringing with him his four sons and a daughter, and my grandfather's fiancée, Andina Harmsen. Geert and Andina were married the following spring. Geert, like his father, acquired a farm in Graafschaap, Michigan, near the city of Holland. For several years he and Andina endured all the hazards of life on the frontier: sickness, accidents, forest fire, debt. Then, just when they were beginning to prosper, Geert became convinced that the Lord wanted him to become a preacher.

The church was reluctant to consider it at first, but Geert was not to be deterred. In the end, they not only accepted him as a student for the ministry but offered to lend him any money he might need and assigned a full-time teacher to him. This was the beginning of Calvin Theological School, now associated with Calvin College; and my grandfather and one other man were the first graduates in 1877. In my time there has almost always been some member of the family teaching at the college, and my Uncle Johannes was the president during the late Twenties. Learning was highly respected, and these connections with the college gave the family high standing within the church community.

Throughout those years of trouble, Andina was the practical one, adapting herself to the changes, "making do," and looking after a growing family. She was a courageous and competent woman.

With respect to religion, Andina was convinced that her beliefs were the whole and the only truth. This made trouble when Cornelius told her of his engagement to a Dutch Reformed woman. "Why couldn't you have chosen one of the daughters of Israel?" she asked him; that is, one of the Lord's latter-day chosen people! My father, who was unable, ever, to hurt his parents, broke the engagement. For many bitter weeks or months, he and Cena were both miserable, but love won the day. After my mother's death I found a letter of reconciliation that Father had written her. He told her that he had often followed her at a distance, longing to speak to her but afraid of being rebuffed. It was so intimate, so intense and tender and anguished, that I felt as if I had committed sacrilege by reading it. I wanted no stranger's eyes to see it. In the first rush of emotion, I burned it.

They were married on December 6, 1894. As might have been expected, there was a coolness between Cena and her mother-in-law for some time. However, Cena joined her husband's church and was conciliatory, and the two women were soon on good terms. Nevertheless, the hurt remained, and Cena was never happy with her new church affiliation. She used to sputter occasionally about "those seceders."

"They think they are going to have their own little corner in heaven and I hope they do!"

My grandmother's misgivings, as the event proved, were fully justified from her point of view. However small might be the difference between my parents' religious beliefs, they did differ, as I observed at an early age. The truth, then, was not beyond question. The effects of that observation were far reaching.

2

THE GARDEN

I was born on the eighth of November, 1895, and christened Frances Martina. The beginning of my life was felicitous. I was the first baby in a household of three adults, all of whom loved babies, and this baby in particular. My mother was thirty-two when I was born, a late age for a first child. She must sometimes have wondered, when taking care of Mertie and Louise, whether she would ever have a child of her own. My father had a natural rapport with babies. I have seen wailing or screaming babies relax into smiles at his touch. Grandpa was able to let down his guard with them as he was never able to with older persons. A picture of me in my baptismal gown is the image of placidity.

This happy state of affairs was interrupted when I was three years old by my mother's long and nearly fatal illness. I was so distressed that I can still recall a number of incidents as if they had happened yesterday. To begin my account with these memories, however, would give a wrong impression. What is significant is the tenor of the first six years of my life, and they were happy ones.

My earliest recollections constitute a composite landscape that, over the years, evolves into a flow of time. I remember being held and gently rocked and sung to sleep, most often by Mama, but sometimes by Papa. I remember that Mama sometimes sang Isaac Watts' cradle hymn.

> Hush, my dear, lie still and slumber,
> Holy angels guard thy bed,
> Heavenly blessings without number
> Gently falling on thy head.
>
> How much better thou'rt attended
> Than the Son of God could be
> When from heaven he descended
> To become a child like thee.

Papa was more likely to sing:

> I'm Captain Jenks of the horse marines.
> I feed my horse on corn and beans
> And often live beyond my means.
> I'm Captain Jenks of the army.

Sitting on Grandpa's knee and playing games belongs to this same time. He would walk his fingers lightly up my chest, my chin, my lips, while reciting a Dutch nursery ditty.

Kribbeltje Krabbeltje komt geloopen naar de kleine meisje toe.
Piep!
Little Kribbel Krabbel comes walking towards the little girl. Peep!

With the "Peep!" he would tweak my nose. This was great fun. He taught me the Dutch alphabet long before I knew the English one, chanting it with a marked rhythm that made a kind of song out of it. To me, it was amusing nonsense.

There was always much singing at our house. Papa and Mama both had pleasant voices, baritone and contralto, and they played well enough to accompany themselves on the family organ in the parlor. Such singing was a customary Sunday evening pastime and a form of entertainment when there was company. Mama also sang all day about the house.

There were old songs like "Annie Laurie" and "The last rose of summer" and "The harp that once in Tara's halls . . ."; songs from light operas that it would have been sinful to go and see; a few from such operas as *Carmen* and *The Bohemian Girl*; others inspired (if that is the word) by the recent War with Spain; and hymns, of course, from the Moody and Sankey collection, a few from the Episcopalian hymnal.

The taste of the day was romantic and sentimental to a degree that we find incomprehensible. This was the generation that wept over Dickens' Little Nell. It may not be quite fair to pick out the most lugubrious song I know of, but I cannot resist.

> Oh, do you remember sweet Alice, Ben Bolt,
>   Sweet Alice whose hair was so brown,
> How she wept with delight when you gave her a smile
>   And trembled with fear at your frown?

There was one that I liked for its evocation of summer pleasures. I presume that "mill May" was the miller's daughter.

> The strawberries grow in the mowing, mill May,
>   And the bobolink sings on the lea.
> In the fields the ripe clover is blowing, mill May.
>   Oh, come to the meadow with me.

Summer and winter memories belong to different worlds. In winter, when the only heat in the house came from two stoves, warmth

17

was the most important concern and the ultimate pleasure, never taken for granted. When my day began, the kitchen was already warm, and the fire had burned down to glowing embers just right for toast. The comforting odor of a woodfire and the good smell of coffee and bacon filled the room. Since the sun had not yet got around to the windows, the glittering jungles painted by Jack Frost during the night were still intact on the cold panes. I could let my mind roam in them while I lingered over my oatmeal or my favorite rolled wheat.

The great pleasure of the day was the excursion with Grandpa, both of us wrapped up to our eyes: the crisp air, the creak of snow underfoot, the added creakiness of board sidewalks, the whole sparkling blue and white world. When I was very small I rode out in state in the sleigh that Grandpa had made for me. It was a boxy sleigh with sloping sides that curved up towards front and back, and it was painted sky blue outside and lined with white. Often we stopped at a neighborhood store to pick up some Dutch cheese with caraway seeds or a spool of thread for Mama or to renew Grandpa's store of tobacco.

At bedtime the scene shifted to the sitting room, lit now by kerosene lamps that cast massive shadows, making familiar objects seem strange. I was undressed beside the stove, where the glow of the fire through the isinglass panes gave visual comfort as well as heat. For a few moments I could hold my feet out towards the fire, soles tingling, little toes squirming with pleasure. But the moment of truth had to come: the trek into the cold hall and up the stairs after Mama, who went ahead with the lamp to an unheated bedroom.

As soon as I was in bed between cotton flannel sheets, blankets firmly tucked in, all was well. Outside there was complete silence except when a sleigh came by, sleigh-bells jingling. It was a cheerful sound. Sometimes the moon looked in through the window. The moon was beautiful, and it made the night-time world a wonderland, but I was a little afraid of it. It followed me on the rare occasions when I was out at night, for no reason that I could fathom. When Mama left with the lamp, the world was wiped out and I was alone in a great void. Still, Mama had tucked me in and kissed me, and Grandpa slept in the next room. There was not much, really, for a Big Girl to worry about.

Summer memories are nearly all of the outdoors, and mostly confined to our yard and garden. In spring the two big silver maples blossomed red before they leafed out. The woodbine began to cast its shadows on the porches. The wren built its eye-level nest in a vine, and the orioles flew off with the bright-colored embroidery floss that Mama snipped for them, to make their nest high up at the tip of a long branch. The bluebirds came back, and the redheaded woodpeckers, and the robins with their full-throated songs at sunset or after a rain. There were cherry and peach blossoms; and later, the fruit. The blackbirds that swarmed in the big white oak next door knew the exact moment when the cherries were ripe. About this time the croquet set came out, and Papa's bicycle.

Grandpa was busy in the garden. He always grew a few flowers along with the peas and beans and lettuces and radishes. I loved the sweet peas, with their delicate colors and light scent. Once Grandpa made a trench for marigolds and let me drop in the seeds. They grew, and it was a miracle. Unfortunately, this was my first and last lesson in gardening.

Most beloved of all was the cottonwood tree, into which I could climb by way of the rail fence beside it. It had a comfortable crotch where I could sit by the hour dreaming. The adjoining vacant lot was full of Scotch thistles, which one learned not to touch, and of milkweed, whose pods popped open to release thousands of miraculous, silky, winged seeds. The ground fell sharply away to Sherman Street far below. This was almost as good as being up in a balloon. Stevenson's *A Child's Garden of Verses,* with which I was not yet acquainted, perfectly reflects my mood. Sometimes I was a Gulliver among the little people. Sometimes I was one of the little people myself. At other times my thoughts were far across the sea.

> The children sing in far Japan,
> The children sing in Spain.
> The organ and the organ man
> Are singing in the rain.

There were also summer excursions with Grandpa. In summer we went farther afield. We might go together to spend the day at Van Heulen's, where Mattie and Jane, the old man's middle-aged daughters, made much of me. One old lady we visited used to give me cookies and a bouquet from her garden to take home with me.

I had one close friend, a boy with the rather unfortunate name of Jewell Henry. We were inseparable for three or four years. I don't know what we played at, except that we sometimes played we were married and set up housekeeping. As soon as everything was in place on the back porch, Jewell would say, "Well, I must go to work now," and he would be off. Such was wedded life.

This paradise was not completely cloudless. I was naughty at times, although I still think that most of my misdemeanors might more properly be called errors. I tried hard to be good, if only to keep out of trouble. Punishment was usually a scolding or banishment to my room. Lying called for more severe measures. I don't doubt that I told the lies all children tell: who started the quarrel or who ate the strawberry jam; but sometimes I simply didn't know whether the tale I told belonged to the outside world or the inside one. Punishment was to kneel beside Mama's bed and pray God to forgive my sin. I resented this. I had already learned that people were entitled to a certain amount of privacy. It was wrong to pry into things you had been told to keep out of. If God could see right through the roof and watched every single thing I did, it was too much. It wasn't fair.

There were days when, for some reason, I needed continual reassurance. I would tag Mama around, asking over and over, "Do you love me? Say you love me." She would reply, "Of course I do," or "You know I do." It must have got very tiresome. One day she said, "I love you more than tongue can tell." I was thunderstruck. *Who* was Tuncan Tell? How could I not have known of his existence? If Mama loved me *more,* then she loved him *some.* For months or years, I don't know which, I was haunted by my invisible competitor.

A few other incidents stand out, and through all of them runs a thread of frustration. I think this not unnatural. Young children are supreme egotists. Their response to disappointment or interference is far stronger than their response to gratification. The latter is pretty much taken for granted. A birthday party with ice cream and cake and presents, a Christmas tree with its brightly colored baubles and lovely candlelight: these are fine things but they stir no strong passions. And, being rituals, they tend to flow together in the memory.

The first of these events was the birth of my sister when I was not quite three. Papa deposited me one day, without explanation, with our next-door neighbors, the Zacharias family. It consisted, I believe, of two grown-up sisters and their father. I had never been in their house before, and they seemed not to know what to do with a small child. The morning passed slowly. We had lunch. I amused myself for a while looking at the world through the panes of colored glass that framed a window at the foot of the stairway, growing more and more bored and then furious. I told the assembled Zachariases what I thought of them and what I was going to tell Papa. I announced that I was going home. No way. At last Papa came for me. As we walked the short distance home he asked me how I would like a little sister. I was dying for a sister to play with. Then I was shown into the room where Mama was in bed with a *baby*! What good was a baby! What a day!

Then there was Mama's fifth wedding anniversary. I questioned her about it while she dusted the parlor for company in the evening. It seemed that an anniversary was a very special kind of party. It was to celebrate her wedding, which was something that occurred only once in a lifetime. I wanted to know whether I had been present on the great occasion and was offended when I learned that I had not been. I was very curious about all this.

The marriage of Papa's sister Alyda, shortly afterward, was seen as an opportunity to remedy my ignorance. Mama got out her wedding dress for the occasion, and we all went to Grandpa and Grandma Broene's house early in the day. There was a great stir of cooking and baking and last-minute straightening up, and then of getting dressed, everyone in his best. Left to my own devices, I sat on and slipped off from the horsehair chairs in the parlor and looked at the family album and fidgeted, while the excitement grew.

The marriage took place in the evening at Grandpa's church next door. It was the custom to precede the ceremony with a sermon, and no Dutch minister ever skimped a sermon. By the time Grandpa got around to the main business, I was asleep in Mama's arm. When she woke me up it was all over. My anger knew no bounds. I stormed. Quieted at length, I sulked. I refused a piece of the wedding cake until the bride herself knelt beside me and begged me to take it for her sake. Conscious now of being the center of attention, I grandly condescended to accept it.

A degree of enlightenment came with Mertie's wedding. Aunt Kate had taken a second husband, Lafayette Forbes, and now lived around the corner from us on Dolbee Street. Mertie was married at home in the afternoon in the presence of the family and a few friends. The bridal party moved into place before a minister with a book in his hand. He read from it for a little while, asked a few questions, and it was over. Nothing had happened. Nothing had changed. If this was getting married then one mystery remained: what was all the fuss about?

Kindergarten, I loved. We painted and cut out patterns in colored paper, and sometimes we sang and played games. I was so devoted to my teacher that I cried all the way home when I was promoted to first grade after one semester. Mama intervened, saying that I was very young, and learning could wait.

One day we were told that we were to go next day to Silver Creek, a mile or so out Madison Avenue, to see the pussywillows. This was very exciting. That night was just like waiting for Christmas. The next morning, just before we were to leave, we were told that we would proceed sedately by twos, hand in hand with an assigned partner. By sad mischance, I drew a boy whom I found repulsive. I don't know why. Nothing could have made me touch him, let alone hold his hand all morning. When we went for our wraps I seized mine on the run and headed rapidly for home.

Another trip left me much bedraggled. We had taken a streetcar to the soldiers' home, a little this side of North Park. It was situated in an open area, near a wood where spring wildflowers were in blossom. When we unexpectedly came upon a large patch of marsh marigolds with their sunny color, I lingered for a closer view. Before I realized what I was getting into, I had plunged into a bog and lost my footing. I emerged muddied and sobered. Life had a way of pulling one up short when one acted in ignorance.

I have one lovely memory of that year. On my way to school I passed a house that faced a cross street, and on the far side of the back yard a hedge of large old-fashioned rose bushes was in blossom. One day as I passed, a woman was cutting the flowers. I wanted some of them so bad that I couldn't move. When she turned around, she must have seen the hunger in my eyes. She came towards me with a smile, holding out the bouquet she had just picked, and asked, "Would you like these?" Her spontaneous generosity has stayed with me all my life.

The next year I had to go to Baxter Street School. I had had all I wanted of kindergarten and couldn't wait to learn to read. It was not to be. I was not yet six, and the school was unwilling to make any concession. Reading had to wait another semester.

When I got my chance it didn't take long. After the first day I burst into the house, shouting, "I can read, Mama! I can read!" By June I was reading my own quite advanced storybooks. Mama had bought them from the Mills's across the street, an elderly couple who were about to move. One of the books, *The Pansy Storybook,* had a series of stories about little princes and princesses, entitled, "Children of History." I was on my way to becoming a history buff. Another storybook, *The Chatterbox,* that had been my father's in his childhood, had a series about the Trojan War and another about the black-tulip craze in Holland, whetting my appetite for faraway places. In school we were still reading: "These are cherries. The cherries are red. See the red cherries." From this time on, I read my new school reader each year at odd moments during the first week and was bored for the next nine months.

That year I brought a dreadful retaliation upon myself. Every morning Miss Anna inspected our finger nails. We had to spread our hands out flat upon our desks so she could see them. One day, without warning, she ordered me to do the inspecting. I trembled, but orders were orders. Fortunately, most of the nails passed, but one boy's were just plain black, and I had been taught to tell the truth at all times. I tapped him on the head, the signal to stand up and be judged. He got his revenge. Every child, big or little, for blocks around, went coasting on Dolbee Street hill after school. He never failed to find me. Just as I was about to take off, he would sneak up behind me and give my sled a crooked steer. I did not dislike him for this; I did not complain. I understood that justice must be served. It was, nevertheless, extremely annoying; and worse, a hazard. For a moment I would be out of control and could have got in the way of a bobsled. I never told Mama.

One other incident of that year merits mention, I think. I had my first and last view of the theater for the next ten years. Theater was vanity at best, and often it was sinful. Actors were a race apart, without roots in the community, who earned their living frivolously and worked on Sunday. The theater was off limits. Mama made one exception that she would have regretted if she had known the consequences. The city schools put on a show of *Mother Goose* stories acted by school children. Surely this was harmless and worth supporting. She reckoned without the glamour. This was pure magic, Fairyland come alive. From that day,

I would have sold my soul to the devil for an occasional hour of such bliss.

This brings me to the two most important influences in my life, aside from the love I received: my early familiarity with the Bible and Greek mythology.

Our church believed in early indoctrination. I cannot remember a time when I did not attend Sunday service regularly. There I heard the Bible read in the King James version, the only English version in which the language is adequate to the concepts. At home the Bible was read aloud three times a day after meals; in Dutch when Grandpa was present and in English when he was away. (He used to spend one day a week at Uncle Bart's house and another at the Van Heulen's.) The Bible stories were also read to me on Sunday afternoons. I curled up in Mama's arm where I could see the pictures while she read to me from a paraphrased version, a well-known one with engravings by a German whose name I have forgotten. They were very well done and vivid.

This storehouse of literature, the great stories and the great poetry, the striving for righteousness became so much a part of me that I don't know how to speak of it without sounding inflated. It armored me for life against the tawdry and the inconsequential; and the language, its rhythms and cadences, became an integral part of the furnishings of my mind.

Confronted as I was with the demands of a theology alien to my nature, I found the Greek myths equally vitalizing. That other root of Western civilization was the counterbalance I needed.

The Greek stories were a Friday afternoon treat at school. I think Miss Anna told them to us. I seem to see her moving about, now at her desk and now near the windows. I cannot account for the impression they made on me unless they were told in a broad context of Greek nature lore. The stories in themselves were alarming: Perseus and the Gorgon's head, Theseus and the bed of Procrustes, Jason and the army he unwittingly sowed, Pandora, Persephone. Yet what remains with me is a sense of a silvery early-morning world in which waterfalls were alive and reeds were for piping, where the life of this world was seen as good, where one could breathe freely. I felt at home there.

The end of this period in my life was marked by our moving from Dunham Street at the end of that school year. My babyhood was over; my first garden, a memory.

*   *   *

Before we leave it behind us, however, I must relate the story of Mama's illness. It began in December, 1898. My sister had been born in July. I remember following Mama upstairs one day when she was carrying a big basket of freshly ironed linens. She was saying, more to herself than to me, "I am so tired. I am so tired."

Then Mama is sick in the bedroom off the sitting room, with the door shut. Anna's cradle has been moved into the sitting room near the stove. Miss Richards, a nurse, is living with us; she is on 24-hour duty. Dr. Hulst comes every day. Aunt Kate is there much of the time; sometimes, all night. I am not allowed in the bedroom. All my pleas are met with a firm no. My longing becomes despair. Mama has typhoid fever, soon complicated by peritonitis. Before she is out of danger, spinal meningitis sets in. She is in bed for months.

I sleep wherever I happen to be most out of the way. One night, I am on the couch in the parlor; another, on a cot in the sitting room or the kitchen. One night when I am in the kitchen with the light on all night, Aunt Kate moves continually between the kitchen and the bedroom, brushing past my cot. She is perhaps heating water on the kitchen stove. Another night I am in the sitting room. By the dim light from the stove, I can see that Papa is asleep in a chair. I wake him up to inquire how anybdy can sleep sitting up. He says, "Child, I could sleep on my feet."

At some point it becomes advisable to get me out of the way for a while if possible. I am taken to spend the day with one person or another, in the hope that I will stay over night. It never works. A day at the Henry's goes well enough till near supper time when my doll's head gets broken. I cry and want to go home. Mrs. Henry says she will make the doll a new head. I am doubtful but willing to give her a chance. She walks off with the doll and when she comes back she has painted a face of sorts on a salt sack. I am incensed, and out of the house in a flash.

Another day I am with Grandpa and Grandma Broene, contented until after supper, when I announce that it is time to go home. They try to persuade me to stay. It is impossible; my mother needs me. They try bribes, they cajole, to no purpose. Finally they give up. Uncle Dick will take me home. I will not have it. Grandpa must take me. But I am little and tired and must be carried the long way to the end of the streetcar line. At length I settle for Uncle Dick if Grandpa will go along, which he does.

These are people who are used to being obeyed. They are not accustomed to bargaining with infants. They must have understood my extremity. By day I can subdue my fears but at night I am overwhelmed. I must be near Mama, even with the door shut.

Mama told me long afterwards that there was a time when she was able neither to speak nor to move and she was thought to be unconscious. One day someone asked the doctor in her presence how much longer she might live, and he replied that it was a matter of days. She always credited this incident with saving her life. She said that she had resolved to live because she was determined that no one else should bring up her children.

Anna was too young to remember those days, but Papa and I were left with a lifelong fear of losing Mama. Papa's repeated admonition was, "Help your mother," "Be kind to your mother," "Don't hurt your mother." For many years I was consumed with anxiety every time Mama left the house without me. I was afraid she would never come back. After a time I realized that this was irrational, but the fear persisted. It was something I could not mention to anybody.

3

FIGS AND THISTLES

The move from Dunham Street came about indirectly as a result of Papa's ill health. For a year or more he had been having frequent, severe headaches and had felt generally indisposed. The cause was almost certainly anxiety. He was deep in debt for Mama's long illness, and he probably saw no way out of it. His doctor, unable to find anything definitely wrong, diagnosed lack of fresh air and recommended a change of occupation. Accordingly, Papa began to look around for something else to do and eventually bought a small grocery store on Jefferson Avenue at Fair Street.

The fresh air was to be supplied by making deliveries and by early-morning trips to market, in season, for fresh produce. Grand Rapids was surrounded by fertile, rolling terrain well suited to truck farming. Vegetables and fruit picked the day before were brought to market at night and went on sale at five o'clock in the morning. Their equal is no longer to be had except from home gardens.

Papa disliked the grocery business from the first, and the venture did not last long. His headaches disappeared, however, and he remained in good health almost to the end of his life.

For the first six months we lived above the store. I don't remember much about our quarters; the yard interested me more. It was large. Behind the store Grandpa had a big garden, and at the very back was the barn. Grandpa had made me a bow and arrow, and with the side of the barn for a target I could scarcely miss my aim. I soon felt quite proficient. The rest of the lot, beside the store, was in rough grass like the adjoining empty lot where a horse frolicked in the spring, heady with freedom. There must have been a tree or two, because there was shade. Bushes along the fence provided little hiding places where a child could play at being invisible. Altogether, it afforded me much pleasure.

In the fall I was enrolled at Jefferson Avenue School, directly across the street, where I was shortly promoted to second grade. The year was notable for just two incidents.

School had scarcely begun when I committed a crime; I became a thief. Once a week we were each given a handful of colored pegs to play with at our desks. They were an inch long and about the diameter of a matchstick. I was ecstatic about the color. Never had I wanted anything so bad as I wanted a few of those pegs for my very own. One day when they were gathered up, I held out six of them, one in each color. Having got home with them tightly clenched in my fist, the next thing was to find a hiding place. I stuffed them way to the back of one of Mama's sewing-machine drawers, which were a jumble of sewing odds and ends.

Once a week or so, I would look and see whether they were still there; and for a moment I could hold them in my hand, enjoying those wonderful colors. Even this momentary pleasure was soon eroded by anxiety. The fear of being found out lived with me night and day. I became obsessed with the need to get those pegs back in the box at school where they belonged. It took me months to get up my courage to risk the transfer. When at last I brought myself to it, an awful load of guilt fell into that box along with the stolen treasure.

At home I lived in terror of the hired girl who now did the housework, since Mama had to be in the store when Papa was out. She was abusive and dishonest. Neither Anna nor I could play with anything that she could not find some way to damage. Paperdolls, she threw onto the hot kitchen stove to curl up and scorch. When Mama was away she emptied our piggy banks. She went through Mama's drawers and tried on her clothes. When she found Mama's wedding dress, she put it on and strutted around in it. She told us that if we told on her she would drown the cat. We believed her fully capable of it. Mama knew nothing of this until we were safely installed in our next residence on Highland Street. The first thing I did after the movers had left was to run to her and cry uncontrollably. Then the story came out.

Early in that year I was deemed literate enough to attend catechism classes. We used a child's version, of course, but it made few concessions to children's minds in either vocabulary or doctrine. I deeply resented giving up my Saturday afternoons to matters that interested me not at all, and Friday afternoons too. That was when I had to study the lesson and submit to being drilled by Mama until I was letter perfect. This had one desirable consequence. After I had mastered such words as "omnipotence" and "predestination," long words held no terror for me.

More fundamentally, I objected to the whole idea of ready-made answers that precluded further questioning. There was nothing I could do about it, so I learned the answers, produced them on demand and was considered a model child. At least, when the class was over, there was the pleasure of the walk home and of Mama's bread hot from the oven. Walking, preferably alone, was a very great pleasure. The world was full of wonders: beautiful houses, beautiful gardens, natural beauties in season. Sunlight through the early blossoms of flowering quince; and later, apple blossoms. In the fall, the dry rustle of maple leaves underfoot and the pungent streamers of smoke from bonfires in the street. The light touch of snowflakes on my face or the strong thrust of March winds at my back. Rain puddles on the sidewalks were windows into fresher, cleaner worlds than this.

By the time I was grown I knew my quarter of the town by heart: from Lyon Street on the north to Hall Street, which divided the cemetery; and from Division Street east to the city limits, marked by the streetcar barns, dark and cavernous inside. The most pleasant walks were on "the Hill," Cherry and Fulton and Fountain Streets, where there were fine houses with *portes cochères* and shining plate-glass windows, surrounded by well-tended lawns and old elm and maple trees. A few of the houses were pretentious, but as I remember it, there was very little of the ostentatious architecture that characterized residence neighborhoods in so many American cities in the late Nineteenth Century.

In the fall of 1903 we moved again. Papa had got a new job with his old firm, this time as a traveling salesman for the wholesale end of the business. He sold yard goods and notions to small stores in the northwest quadrant of the Lower Peninsula. Travel was by slow, local trains, north on the Grand Rapids and Indiana line, with side trips west.

This job, Papa loved. He was a born salesman and he throve on the independence. All his customers became his friends. Although he was seldom away for more than a week, he wrote to Mama regularly, invariably signing his letters with an amusing combination of formality and feeling, "Your husband and lover, C. Broene."

Now that Papa had a steady job that he liked, he bought a house. It was on East Street, now Eastern Avenue, at the corner of Sigsbee. The neighbors in our block were a mixed lot, but in general the neighborhood was divided by Wealthy Street into two quite distinct communities. To the south, Dutch working men lived in small, cottage-type houses with flourishing flower gardens. Dutch was spoken at the church they attended, where Sunday services were held morning, afternoon, and evening. One family, apparently in accord with Old Country custom, walked to church strung out in a line; father first, mother next, and the children bringing up the rear, as befitted their station. To the north, the families were of relatively old American stock, affluent on the whole. The fathers were doctors and lawyers and owners of businesses. The children took music and swimming lessons and went to dancing school on Saturday afternoons while I suffered through catechism. I longed to be one of them. I played with the daughters of the two doctors who were among our nearest neighbors, but I was not one of their set.

This move was particularly painful for me because I was unable to do the third-grade arithmetic at Henry Avenue School. This was a new experience and quite upsetting. About Thanksgiving time Mama persuaded my teacher to put me back in second grade until I could catch up. I was chagrined but recovered quickly when I found that I could once again do my lessons easily. Unfortunately, I got stuck there for some time. A little before Christmas, Anna and I came down with whooping cough, followed almost at once by measles and, in the spring, by chickenpox, which kept us out of school a good half of the year.

Whooping cough was a misery and it hung on for many weeks. In our house, as in most of the older houses, the master bedroom was on the first floor next to the sitting room, where it could get a little heat from the stove. Our bed was now set up in the parlor, where Papa and Mama could seize us up quickly when we got a whooping spell in the night. These attacks were utterly exhausting. Lying limp on the bed after one of them, it seemed to me that I must be dying, and I felt too weak and tired to care very much.

Mama was worried, and when Mama was worried she would try any remedy she might hear of, no matter how unlikely. One morning at breakfast she presented me with a generous spoonful of ground and toasted eggshell! How shall I describe the experience? As fast as I could get there, I spit out what I could into the ash-pit of the kitchen stove. Tongue and cheeks remained lined with bits and pieces unwilling to be dislodged. After such a debacle, Mama did not pursue the issue.

Measles followed on the heels of the whooping cough. The worst of that was the boredom. Mama, fearing for my eyes, kept the room dark the whole time, so that I was unable to do anything to amuse myself when I began to feel better.

The house was, of course, under strict quarantine during both of these illnesses. Since we had no telephone, we were completely isolated. I suppose Grandpa went out for groceries. It was a long winter.

Anna got the chicken-pox first, along with her friend, Helen Williams, across the street. Neither of them was really sick. They played together outdoors, enjoying the unscheduled vacation. Then I got it and was as sick as I have ever been in my life.

As it happened, there was an epidemic of small-pox in the city at the time. Ambulances passed the house day and night on their way to the contagious hospital, that stood ominously next to Oakhill Cemetery. We called the place the pest house. People were dying all around us. The severity of my symptoms raised the painful question of whether this was indeed chicken-pox or its dreaded counterpart. Mama was in a state of near panic. Nothing could have induced her to call a doctor and risk my being taken away.

Aunt Kate, as usual, came in to help, but no one else was admitted to the house. I got well in due course, having had little treatment beyond cooling applications of witch-hazel to my forehead when the headache was severe.

I was nearly well when Grandpa developed flu symptoms and Mama called Dr. Hulst to come and see him. Since I still had a few pocks on my face and arms, I was given strict orders to stay out of the room when the doctor came. Curiosity overcame me. The doctor took one look at me and left to call the city health officer, who shortly arrived and said my disease was merely chicken-pox. Dr. Hulst disagreed, and for a moment the situation was tense. I think I must have been too nearly recovered for an accurate diagnosis. The officer may have figured that, whatever I had had, I was no longer infectious. All I know is that nobody else got sick.

When at last it was all over, Mama decided to fumigate me and the house in one easy step. She set a dish of burning sulphur in the middle of the floor in the room I had been in and made me walk around it. I made the best time in and out of that room that I have ever made anywhere.

The churches had been asked to forego Sunday services for the duration of the epidemic, but the Dutch church in our neighborhood was unwilling to comply. Since life and death were entirely in God's hands, they saw no reason why they should not hold services as usual. Dr. Ruffe's house, across from us on the other corner of Sigsbee Street, sat on a very large lot in a grove of native oaks. Hoping that fresh air might somewhat reduce the danger, he offered his front yard for services, and the offer was accepted. So, among the trees, under the open sky, our Dutch neighbors met to praise the Lord in the midst of death. This demonstration of faith was in its way heroic, but all I felt was embarrassment. I had realized for the first time that my people were "different," not entirely American, therefore not quite acceptable.

During the next two years, when I was nine and ten, Mama was ill most of the time. In the first of those years, after many painful months of refusing help, she underwent a serious major operation. Then, the week before Christmas, not quite a year later, she took to bed with a malady diagnosed only as "inflammation of the lungs." She was still in bed in late May.

Mama was afraid of doctors, not without reason in those days. She never consulted one until she could no longer stand on her feet. Before the operation she tried, with ever-increasing difficulty, to perform her usual tasks. She grew edgy and scolded a good deal. Everything was too much for her. One day when she was combing my hair, which was badly snarled, and I was impatient, she burst out with, "Oh, I wish, I wish—" She did not finish it. I knew then that she was at the end of her rope, and my fear of losing her flared up full force.

The day came when she had to give up. Papa took her by special appointment on a Sunday afternoon for a medical examination. My alarm increased when my parents returned in a hack, the horse-drawn taxicab of the period. Mama sank into a chair and told me to run over and get Aunt Kate, a request that I took literally, running the whole half mile. We were having a January thaw, which meant that the unpaved streets were a morass and the gutters were streaming. Our ankle-high rubbers were insufficient protection unless we stepped carefully. On this occasion I plunged in and out, heedless of wet feet. Mama was waiting for help.

When I got home I learned that she was to go to the hospital next day for an exploratory operation. It was the only way the doctors could find out what was wrong. (It turned out to be adhesions, attributed to the typhoid fever six years before.) That night was probably the worst night of my life. Mama was going away, probably to die. The fear was almost unendurable.

The operation was successful but recovery was slow. In my memory this illness and the next have run together into one long nightmare.

I do not recall how we managed during the first one. During the second, an elderly Cockney woman, a relative of a neighbor, came in and took charge. Since Mama required almost all of her attention, Anna and I got little and we felt orphaned. Meals were dreadful. Mama had to have beef broth every day, so every day the nutritive juices were slowly simmered out of the meat and we got the fiber that was left. Nothing had any taste. When Papa was home he complained, to no avail.

Her accent offered a little comic relief. We were much amused by her account of some incident in which a man "'itched 'is 'oss to an 'itching post." There was little else to smile about.

Up to this time my difficulties with my parents—or should I say, their difficulties with me?— had been minor. So long as we were little we were governed with a light hand—Sundays excepted. Sundays were a trial from the beginning. In the morning there was a scramble to get breakfast and start the roast for dinner and get four people off to church on time. In church I had to sit still on a hard pew for an hour and a half through a service I could not understand. This was followed by an hour of Sunday school. One of my diversions was studying the women's hats, which were marvels of ingenious decoration. I must have admired them, for I once remarked, as Papa told it, that someday I was going to have a hat with flowers and feathers and a ribbon around and a rag in the back— a little fanciful but based on observation.

Sunday afternoons lasted an eternity. Play was forbidden and the only reading allowed was books from the Sunday-school library. They were either about excruciatingly pious children or sinners who got their come-uppance. I don't remember any of them, but I do remember a story written to the same formula that Mama used to read to me whenever she considered that I was in need of edification. It was about a boy, a little boy as I remember it, who got diphtheria and died because he had been disobedient. The title was, "Be Sure Your Sin Will Find You Out."

Even my mother's friends were considerably less strict than she was. One Sunday afternoon when we were visiting her best friend, Lizzie Oltman, I was playing jacks with her daughter Rhea when Mama came upon us, stopped the game, and gave me a lecture on Sabbath day behavior. Aunt Lizzie remonstrated, "Oh, Cena, they are only children."

These matters, however, I could take in my stride. My differences with my family went much deeper. My parents lived in two worlds: the everyday one where reason ruled, or was supposed to, and the spiritual world where truth was immutable and questions were out of bounds. My mind was unable to admit the distinction. It was characteristic of me that when I lost my belief in Santa Claus my next thought was, "Nobody has ever seen God either."

For several years after this, I vacillated between unbelief and repentance. On my believing days I was resolved to become a missionary to Turkey. I had fastened on Turkey because I had heard reports of the squalor that the poor lived in over there. As a member of a spic-and-span Dutch household I could imagine nothing more penitential than spending my days in a dirty slum.

I could be frank with Mama up to a point. Kate Rosbach, one of three spinster sisters who belonged to our church, had gone out to our mission at Gallup, New Mexico, to help convert the Navajos. Once a year, she came home for a vacation with some Indian boy in tow who had accepted Jesus. This was always an occasion for reminding the Sunday School children to be generous with their pennies so that other unfortunate heathen children might hear about Jesus and be saved from damnation. Hell fire seemed to me a high price to pay for ignorance. I said to Mama, "It isn't fair." She replied that such matters were not for us to judge, and I retorted, "You wouldn't do it."

Our minister was eloquent on the subject of human depravity. Our hearts were black with sin; we were worms of the dust in God's sight. I rejected any such description of myself. My heart was not black and I was no worm either, and I said so to Mama. Such talk bewildered her; she had never heard anybody talk like that.

I could not talk to Papa at all. Children were not supposed to have opinions. It was their duty to accept the truth as their elders taught it to them. Any questions indicated a dangerous willfulness that could not be allowed.

Both of my parents were instinctively gentle with children and would have been deeply grieved if they had known what misery the conflict caused in me, but where righteousness was at stake, instinct had to take second place. They were bringing me up the way they had been brought up, the only way they knew, and it just wasn't working. One day when Mama in desperation exclaimed, "Can't you ever do anything because I tell you to!" I replied, "No, Mama; it has to be me." That is still the only explanation I can offer.

I knew it was useless to resist openly, but I could not always conceal my reluctance or refrain from "talking back." At the age of ten or thereabouts, I became more assertive, sometimes provoking serious confrontations. The most distressing thing of all, to me, was that Mama took every small childish lapse so seriously. Any naughtiness was a manifestation of sinful human nature that must be held in check. This was utterly frustrating when I was trying to be good.

What ultimately saved the day for me was that Mama gradually came to realize that I had my reasons, however incomprehensible they might seem to her. I think I was in my first year in high school when I asked her for advice one day and was astounded to hear her say, "I can't tell you that; you are different from me." The joy! The relief! She had accepted me as I was. From that day our relationship took a new turn. We continued to have our differences; but Mama was now my ally, doing everything in her power, which was considerable, to shield me from criticism and allow me to develop in my own way.

My sister experienced no such difficulties. Although she was, as a woman, as resolutely herself as I ever was, as a child she gave my parents no cause for concern. She asked no worrisome questions; no wind of doctrine ruffled her. She simply never troubled her mind about matters beyond her scope. Her childhood was happy. To this day she has never understood what I was disturbed about.

Disturbed I was, nevertheless. For several years, I must have been a difficult and unpleasant child, moody and taciturn. Mama, always sensitive to my moods, was worried. She often said, "You never smile; why don't you smile?" and I could only say, "I don't feel like it." How could I tell her that I felt unable to please her and that this was more than I could bear?

There was little of interest to occupy me. My one escape was reading. I was on my way to becoming bookish by default. The things that had always given me the greatest joy were sensuous: light, color, movement, the wind in the trees and, later, when my eyes had become more sophisticated, form. I sometimes wonder what turn my life might have taken if I had been encouraged to develop artistically.

Interest in the arts was awakened the year I was in second grade by a week-long exhibit of photographs at school. I think they must have been what we called Stoddard's views. A man of that name had gone around the world photographing everything of note. He was much in demand for lectures with lantern slides. His photographs had also been reproduced in portfolios. I discovered a year or two later that my mother had a number of these, which I was allowed to look at on rainy days. Anyway, the pictures at school were of this nature: foreign cities with their art and their architecture. Every day I rushed home for lunch and rushed back to have as much time as possible for these new-found wonders. They came as a revelation, intensifying my desire to know all there was to know about the wonderful world I lived in.

My social life was another source of distress. Other children were not unkind to me, but I simply didn't fit into any kown category, and so they left me out of their activities. The playground was where I felt my isolation. If I wanted to join in group games I had to invite myself. A favorite game was "Crack the Whip." We joined hands in a long line and ran forward until the leader, with a sudden jerk, switched the whole line around like a lashing whip. The girl in the end position was almost invariably thrown to her knees. My knees were well scraped. It was better than being left out.

My clothes were no help. My parents were perpetually in debt for Mama's illnesses. It took them five years to pay off the doctor and the nurse and the grocer for the first one. They had scarcely celebrated their freedom when new debts were incurred for Mama's operation. As a result, the budget was always tight. Mama, who held the purse strings, was even-handed in meeting individual needs. We got new coats by turns, and my coat sleeves sometimes grew embarrassingly short before my turn came round. In the winter Anna and I each had one Sunday dress and one everyday dress, the latter being the Sunday dress of the year before. When the hem was let down, the old crease tended to show. In the summer, color was the telltale. Our gingham dresses were not sunproof, so the let-down hem was always a darker shade. Mama said I shouldn't mind such trifles; God looked at the heart. That was all very well, but what my schoolmates looked at was of more immediate concern to me.

The feelings engendered by this sort of thing led to an incident, trifling in itself, that haunted me for ten years! Valora Quinlan was one of the "in" group towards whom I felt an irrational spite. She had done nothing to offend me; I simply could not see why she was any more acceptable than I. She was a Catholic; and in this distinctly WASPish community, Catholicism was looked on somewhat askance as unfamiliar and therefore dubious.

One day Valora was asked to monitor the room while our teacher left for a few minutes, and I seized the opportunity to vent my feelings. I passed a note to a girl whom I ordinarily ignored, with the not-very-clever message, "Valora thinks she is smart." Minnie, the recipient, who had no reason to like me, at once passed the note to Valora, who read it without expression and laid it aside. I was so mortified that I could not speak to her. Since we had little contact anyway, this might have escaped notice if Fate had not decreed that we should meet face to face fifty times a year. Every Sunday morning when we walked to church, we met Valora and her father coming from Mass. I looked the other way, and every time I did so my embarrassment grew deeper. This went on until we found ourselves on the same college campus. If this foolish impasse was not to last forever, something would have to be done, and it was my move. But how was I to approach someone whose existence I had steadfastly ignored for years? While I hesitated, Valora wiped the slate clean with one gracious gesture, asking me to serve on a committee of which she was chairman. Although such kindness and tact were more than I deserved, I accepted the invitation with alacrity.

To get back to my childhood, that year had its bright side. Lucile Ruffe, the pretty daughter of Dr. Ruffe who had offered his yard for the church services, left a note on my desk, soon after school opened, that read, "Will you be my friend?" I would, indeed. She was the most intelligent and the most interesting friend that I had until well into my adulthood. She later studied medicine and became a pediatrician in a day when few women, most of them unattractive with nothing to lose, had the courage to invade male territory.

We always played at Lucile's house because there was so much more we could do there. There was a big house, a big barn, a big yard, and a playhouse as big as our kitchen. We had the run of the place in the afternoon without supervision. I don't recall ever seeing the maid after lunch. Mrs. Ruffe kept to her room—a large, bright room, as I remember it, that extended across the front of the house. We visited her there once.

Most of our activities were unremarkable. Sometimes we bumped ourselves down the back stairs on our fannies or explored the farther reaches of the barn. Once, Lucile's father came home early and gave us each twenty-five cents, a large sum, to weed the garden. Often Ruth Patterson came over. When that happened, I was supposed to leave because Ruth's mother was divorced. Mrs. Patterson was, moreover, a professional singer, rather handsome in a full-blown and somewhat flamboyant way, most unbecoming in a middle-aged woman and a mother. I liked Ruth, and unless we were outdoors and I was afraid of being seen, I stayed.

Lucile had lots of books. Often we just sat and read, each engrossed in her own story. One of our favorites was *The Wonderful Wizard of Oz*. There we got the idea of making ourselves up like witches to scare Lucile's younger brother and my sister. We would dress up in weird clothing, and appear screaming, our hair standing up in wired braids or hanging over our faces. Another pastime was to play doctor and nurse with Glenn and Anna for patients. How they survived our ministrations remains a mystery. We concocted medicines in the kitchen: salt, soda, mustard, vinegar—anything, so long as it tasted bad. This game did not go on very long because our patients rebelled.

Dr. Ruffe's office was in a wing of the house, and it, too, was open and empty of people in the afternoon, giving Lucile access to her father's medical books. It was she who first gave me information about the Unmentionable. I had long been curious but knew nothing except what I could gather from hints and whispers and Old Testament stories and *Mother's Magazine,* and from observing my aunts when they were "in a family way." Unfortunately, I comprehended the new information very imperfectly. I was little more enlightened than I had been before, but now my curiosity was thoroughly aroused. Mama, as always, knew when I had something on my mind and drew it out of me. I used a word that nearly blew her over. Lucile must have had other sources besides medical books. I was made to promise that that word would never pass my lips again, and that I would never, never listen to any more such talk. Even grownups did not speak of such a shameful subject. If Mama had got a shock, so had I. I had evidently got onto something perfectly dreadful, and *my parents did it*. All parents did it. The waves *that* stirred up were many years subsiding.

After this, Mama forbade me to play with Lucile, and I dared not even speak to her. I continued to plead, promised to be good, and at length Mama relented. It was too late. The incident had made us self-conscious and embarrassed, and we were unable to get back to the old footing. Time would have taken care of that, I am sure, but the Ruffes moved a short time later. When we met again in high school, we spoke when we met; that was all. My first friend, my first loss. It still hurts.

School was one place where I could count on being on top. What stands out in my mind about lessons is continual drill in spelling and arithmetic, and much writing. We had spelldowns regularly, and similar exercises in the multiplication table. At one time we had to write reviews of the geography lesson every day, which was a bore until I invented a Papa and a Mama and a little girl like myself who were traveling in the European countries we were studying. In Switzerland they were all astonished to find that a baby had been deposited with them during the night. No problem. They went on without delay, the baby as pleased as any of them by all the fine sights, especially the fancy clockworks in the Strasbourg cathedral.

I remember music periods with special pleasure. We learned to read music from a large chart hung on a rack at the front of the room. When I began to take piano lessons at the age of ten, I knew most of the scales. Singing was an outlet for much pent-up energy and enthusiasm, an activity that I could join in with gusto if not always on pitch.

When all is said, a school is as good as its teachers, and mine knew their business. A number of them were outstanding. Teaching was then almost the only profession open to women of education and culture, and male prejudice against women who were "too smart" left many of them unwed. Generations of school children benefited from their plight.

Discipline problems were not serious. We all whispered and passed notes, of course. When we got out of hand we were ordered to sit quietly with our hands folded on our desks for a few minutes. Occasionally we were put through a few minutes of exercise to work off excess energy. There were always two or three boys who relieved their boredom by throwing spitballs or dipping some girl's braid in an inkwell. That was about it. I recall no real intransigence or even impertinence. Civility was taught early at home.

Life at home was by no means all trouble. Papa's exuberance was irrepressible. Mama's natural gaiety occasionally broke through in spite of herself, to the delight of everyone present. When she was well, there was much coming and going of friends and relatives. Holidays were made much of. There were outings, often impromptu, and pleasant vacations. I shall get around to such things in due course. Nevertheless, these were trying years and might have been disastrous. I could with-

36

stand the attempt to recast me in an alien mold; I could not escape being warped by the struggle. Inevitably I became self-conscious, timid about revealing myself to a critical world, and prepared to withdraw into my shell at the first sign of disapproval. It was my good fortune that I was never troubled by self-doubt. I understood, blindly but with unwavering certainty, that holding out was a matter of self-preservation. If I could not be myself I was nothing.

One of the high spots of those years was my tenth-birthday party, although the prelude was inauspicious. Mama had promised to write the invitations on a certain afternoon, and I was to deliver them after school. Mama would be out, but Grandpa would be home. When I arrived, breathless from running all the way, the door was locked— something that had never happened before. Grandpa had stepped out for a minute, probably for tobacco. I couldn't wait. Mama's bedroom window was sometimes left unlocked so I decided to try it and was horrified when the whole sash fell out. Now my only thought was to get those invitations and get away before Grandpa came back. That done and my party assured I was prepared to face the music.

The party was a great success. Marietta Lambert, a pleasant child from my Sunday School class, played a tune on the organ; somebody said, "Let's dance," and in a moment we were all dancing. What I did with my feet I wouldn't know, but I thought I was dancing, and it was sheer joy. Mama couldn't bring herself to spoil the fun. With some qualms of conscience, no doubt, she waited until the party was over to remind me that dancing was sinful and this must never happen again! When she let her instincts guide her she invariably did the right thing.

It was during these years that I began to realize how indispensable Grandpa was to all of us, and especially to Mama. He carried our drinking water from a neighbor's well. He split the wood for the kitchen stove and stacked it in the woodshed. In the winter he brought in coal and wood for the fires and carried out the ashes. In the spring he took down the storm shed outside the back door and put up screens, reversing the process in the fall. He prepared the fresh vegetables for our dinner at noon. He mowed the grass. He shoveled snow. He was a functioning member of the family and he was happy. Sometimes Mama worried about his working too hard. She would say, "Why don't you leave that for Neil?" His reply was always, "Neil! Oh pshaw!" to Papa's great amusement.

There were days when Grandpa read for hours. A hanging bookshelf in his room held a Bible commentary in three thick volumes and a small collection of sermons by eminent clergymen, which he never tired of reading. I can see him now, in his favorite chair, an old platform-rocker with back and seat of stretched-on ingrain carpeting in a tapestry design, the cat purring contentedly on his shoulder or stretched out upon his chest, reading until they both fell asleep.

Fall was the best time, when I would come home from school on a beautiful afternoon to the heavenly smell of hot peaches or pickling spices. Mama would be at the stove with a skimming ladle and clean towels and hot jars, and Grandpa would be peeling fruit from a bushel basket. As the preserving season approached, Mama would tell the grocer to reserve so many bushels of this or that when the price came down to so much. This meant the peak of the season, the fruit at its best.

There was much physical labor connected with everyday living that has since been taken over by machinery, but for women with an adequate income and not too many children it was not unduly burdensome. There is much satisfaction in a reasonable amount of physical activity. Child-raising was a respected occupation. I think many women felt privileged. Their work was varied, they were free to plan their own time, and they had more time for children and friends than women do today. They would have been horrified if they could have foreseen a time when mothers were expected to double as bread-winners. How, they would have asked, could our values have become so distorted?

It must also be said that many services were available that have since been made obsolete by the automobile. Milk was delivered daily. The laundry man, the butter-and-egg man, and in summer the ice man made regular rounds. The tinker (who mended pots and pans), the scissors-grinder with his bell, the rag man with his rickety wagon and skinny horse appeared at more or less regular intervals. On summer mornings hucksters drove through residence neighborhoods with fresh-picked fruit and vegetables, and again in the afternoon, at which time they offered their perishable wares for pennies. A popcorn man and a waffle man popped or toasted in carts that radiated light and warmth and waves of happiness in chill autumn twilights. All stores of any size made deliveries. School districts were small and children walked to school. The family car has not been an unmixed blessing. Ask any mother of small children how much time she spends doing errands.

At twilight on winter Sundays, Papa and Mama enjoyed sitting around the stove with Grandpa and singing Dutch psalms. These were sung very slowly, each note drawn out with great solemnity, so that even the happy ones sounded like dirges. Their voices were filled with nostalgia. As the light faded and only their faces could be seen in the glow from the fire, I felt very close to them and yet somehow cut off. The darkness induced a feeling of intimacy, but their thoughts were far away. At such moments I loved them all very much.

New Year's day was Grandpa's birthday. It began with church in the morning, and throughout the day friends and relatives came to call. After a good dinner, Grandpa would get out his Dutch skates and go skating. He could have done this almost any day all winter but it was a once-a-year ritual. Grandpa considered amusement a waste of time and he felt no need of it. On this one day he was able to relax and celebrate with a clear conscience. On this day he was full of gratitude towards family and friends who had made his old age happy and towards God who had granted him health and peace. In the evening there was always a party for him. His children came, and Levinus and Mathilda, and a host of Van Heulens. New Year's day was the best day of the year.

The last months of Grandpa's life were sad. Old Man Van Heulen had died rather suddenly. Neither Mama nor Papa could bear to tell Grandpa, but someone had to, and Papa finally brought himself to do it. Grandpa just walked over to a window and looked out for a long time with his back to us. It was a heavy moment for all of us. For him it was the end of the world.

One night in May, 1906, Grandpa had a cerebral hemorrhage, and the next night he died. This was my first brush with death, and I was bereft. Mama got me excused from school and sent me to Aunt Lizzie's for the day so that I would not be at home when the undertaker came for Grandpa. Aunt Lizzie was busy, and the children were at school. There was nothing to do but read, and no reading that interested me that day. I settled for the fairy tales of the Brothers Grimm. All day I read, drowning my grief in imagined horrors. One world seemed no more unreal than the other.

Before the funeral, I was taken into the parlor, much against my will, to see Grandpa for the last time. It is good that I did; he looked natural and peaceful, and I lost my fear of the unknown. At the cemetery I was simply numb until I heard the words, "Ashes to ashes. . . ." Then, with Papa's arm around me, I cried as I had never cried before. That was good too. I had seen Grandpa through to the end, and I had taken a step toward an understanding of the human condition.

This marked the end of another stage in my life. The next fall I entered the fifth grade at the new Sigsbee Street School. I was really a big girl now, and I began to look around me with new eyes and to take an interest in more things outside my immediate family.

4

FAMILY CIRCLE

Few days passed when we did not see one or more of my parents' relatives. They were an intimate part of my life from the earliest days, and some of them were important formative influences. I think the parts they played can be best shown by giving them a chapter to themselves.

BART AND PAULINE

Uncle Bart, sadly, played no active part in my life because he fell into my father's bad graces through no fault of his own. I think it was a year or so before Grandpa died that relations were broken off completely. This was very hard on my mother, who loved him dearly, and his shadow was always there.

Aunt Pauline was the cause of the trouble. In the early years of her marriage to Bart, relations were cordial. When Kate was in trouble, Pauline went out of her way to help. My parents were married in her home. I have no reason to think that there was anything strange about her in the beginning. During the Nineties, however, two of her children died: Ben, in 1892, when he was eight years old; and Katherine, in 1897, when she was five. Ben died of diphtheria; Katherine was run over by a streetcar, owing to the negligence of a neighbor who had taken her shopping. It is my belief that Pauline's mind became unhinged.

She first offended my father when my mother had typhoid fever and everyone but Father had given up hope of her life, by asking if she might have my sister. He was outraged. That she should have thought he might be willing to give up his child was bad enough. That she should have asked while my mother still had breath in her was unconscionable.

I was first conscious of something amiss when we lived on Highland Street just around the block from Bart's house on Green Street. Something was going on that nobody talked about. All I know for certain is that Grandpa came home from Pauline's one day in tears. She had told him that we did not really want him and were keeping him only for his money. This was ridiculous on the face of it; the money Grandpa had was nothing to excite greed. Father was furious. He told Bart that if Pauline did not retract her accusation and apologize, Bart was not to enter our house again. He never did, except for his father's and his sister's funerals. Father had, of course, asked the impossible; and Bart, being a gentleman, could not defend himself.

Mother accepted the situation with fatalism. It must have occurred to her that she could see her brother any time she wished at Mathilda's, but she would have considered that disloyal. A wife sided with her husband.

The situation impressed upon me when I was very young the dark side of all orthodoxies. They are inherently divisive, since two absolutes can no more occupy the same place at the same time than two physical objects. My father's standards of right and wrong were as fixed as his religious beliefs. No one who offended his code ever got a second chance. So my mother lost a brother as surely as if he had died. I thought much about this.

Too late, after Mother died and Anna and I were grown up, there was a truce of sorts. It was told to me that when the two men met, as they were bound to do occasionally, they behaved amiably with no reference to past hostilities. Father by then was having his own difficulties with his exceedingly neurotic second wife. She was agreeable when she felt secure; but she was full of ailments, afraid to meet people, easily offended, and cruelly sharp when she felt injured. One by one Father's friends fell away. This may have given him some insight into Bart's predicament. However that may have been, Bart's behavior at this point was more than generous. I think I missed much by not knowing him.

LOUISE

Aunt Louise was a nursemaid; that is to say, a servant. When I visited her I had to use the back door. But those back doors opened upon broad avenues of social sophistication. Typically, her employers lived in large houses in the best neighborhoods, kept two or more servants, owned the first automobiles, made annual trips to Europe, sometimes semi-annual trips to New York, sent their daughters to private schools and later to finishing schools or women's colleges in the East. I learned how they lived, what they wore, where they shopped, which were the right schools; and I read their *St. Nicholas* and *Vogue* magazines one month late. Some of these people were the Best Society, and entertained visiting celebrities, like Alice Roosevelt, who stunned the élite of Grand Rapids by lighting a cigarette at an afternoon reception.

The care of small children was the one thing that Louise knew something about when her home was broken up by my mother's marriage and she was obliged to look for work. A position as nursemaid also took care of her need for a place to live. Here, even her diffidence was an asset. She was, of course, absolutely honest and reliable, her manners and her speech were irreproachable, and she asked little.

41

for prayer meeting, and the usual Thursday afternoons. The rest of the time she was on call, if need be, at any hour. For this she received a room over the kitchen, sometimes shared with the cook; her meals, sometimes better, sometimes worse; and three dollars a week. In later years, it may have been five. Out of this she saved, over a lifetime of labor, five hundred dollars.

The years I remember best are those she spent in the family of Dr. Richard Smith, a surgeon. Besides Beatrice, whom my aunt cared for, there was an older child, Dorothy, about my age. Sometimes when their parents were away in the summer both children were left in Louise's care, and I would be invited to come and play with Dorothy. We got on very well together. However, when her parents returned, it was the back door for me again. I think this was the germ of my determination to go to college. I intended to be as good as anybody.

Certain events became rituals. Every summer, just before school opened, I was invited to see the new dresses that Mrs. Smith had bought for Dorothy in New York. She must have had as many new dresses in a year as I had in five. After Christmas I was invited to see Dorothy's presents. There were more than I could take in. I don't suppose it ever occurred to Louise that I might see cause for discontent. She held Old World ideas of class, reinforced by hierarchical religious beliefs. One's place in life was divinely appointed. There was a chasm between Dorothy and me that admitted no comparisons. Mother was not so sure. She frequently reminded me that I should not "get ideas," meaning ideas of entitlements above my station. She saw no inconsistency in also reminding me that there was always room at the top and that I was expected to be a lady.

I saw Louise in a gay mood just once. She and Mama took Anna and me to the beach at Grand Haven one day. There was no one else within shouting distance. In a rare mood of levity, after sitting in the sand a while, the two women took off their shoes and stockings, hiked up their long skirts, and splashed about in the water, giggling like schoolgirls. I had never seen adults behave so frivolously. I felt that I should die if anyone I knew should come by and see them. Undoubtedly, they would have been even more embarrassed than I. Decorum was everything.

After I was grown, I pitied my aunt and tried to be kind, but I was unable to return her love and always felt guilty.

LEVINUS AND MATHILDA

My mother's cousin, whom we called by his middle name, Levinus, and his wife, Mathilda, exerted a greater influence on me than anyone else outside my immediate family. They provided me with a close-up view of an alternative way of life with a marked absence of stress. At our house, life required eternal vigilance lest we fall into sin and error. When we went to see Levinus and Mathilda, I could check all that at the door. They were good quite simply because goodness was in itself a good. There was nothing to worry about.

I must have been very young when I first remember visiting them on Goodrich Street. It was their parlor that made the biggest impression on me. It bore no resemblance to the stiffly formal rooms I was accustomed to. There was a so-called square piano of pleasing proportions. In front of it lay a leopard-skin rug, head and all, with open mouth showing sharp teeth, that both fascinated and frightened me. I liked to put the tips of my fingers into those fearsome jaws, feel the shiver run up my spine, and then quickly withdraw them. This had all the excitement of a challenge to fate. In one corner, there stood a tall glass cabinet filled with miscellaneous small *objets d'art,* silver and porcelain. On a wall, hung two small wooden boxes with glass fronts, containing tiny rooms with furnishings and people, all carved out of wood. These things entranced me through the years.

Mathilda made no concession to fashion in either furnishings or dress. Her walls were plain in a period when wallpaper, like everything else, was a labyrinth of design. Her dining-room furniture, so-called Mission, was of dark wood, straight lined and substantial, when the fashion was highly varnished golden oak, replete with spindles. Her rooms were not overcrowded. One could move about freely.

She made her own dresses, all from the same pattern, in a variety of materials for all seasons. The bodice, low necked and short sleeved, was gathered into a wide waistband above a gathered, ankle-length skirt. It was simple, attractive, and becoming.

Mathilda seldom entertained, but there was always afternoon tea for anyone who cared to drop in, and someone always did. There were candied ginger and tea cakes, or perhaps European honey cake, delicious thinly sliced and spread with butter. Whether there was one visitor or half a dozen, the occasion was always festive, Mathilda presiding, with her gift for making people feel at ease. This routine was invariable, even in times of trouble, of which she and Levinus had their share.

She had been orphaned young and had been brought up by an aunt, Marie Boone, a tiny, friendly woman whom we all called Tante Fie (Fee). They lived in Middelburg, and Mathilda was sent to a school in Rotterdam to finish her education.

Levinus grew up, I presume, in Wissenkerke or some similar village. I believe he also had studied to be a teacher, but whether he ever taught I don't know. He came to the United States as a young man, already engaged to marry Mathilda, and set himself up in business making and selling picture frames. When he was sufficiently well established, he and Mathilda were married by proxy, and Mathilda then came over with her aunt. This must have been in the middle Eighties. My mother said that Mathilda was only sixteen.

They had one child, Marinus, called Rientje, whose mind never developed beyond infancy. He lived for fourteen years, a huge baby with a very large head, who could only cry and gurgle. He amused himself with a rattle and appeared to be contented, but there was no indication of intelligence. Mathilda's finest trait was her devotion to those she loved. She tended her poor child, as she was to tend Levinus in the end, happily and with infinite patience. Tante Fie, of course, was indispensable. Between them, the two women managed to get everything done without any fuss and to present smiling faces to guests.

Financially, all seems to have gone well until there was a nation-wide depression, I believe in 1903. Then there were no more customers for picture frames, and Levinus lost his business. I remember his talking with Father about various possibilities of making a living. In the end, he took the examination for the postal service and became a mail carrier, a humble occupation for a man of his capabilities. He was assigned to a branch office on Hall Street and eventually bought a lot and built a house on Madison Avenue in the block south of the Catholic cemetery. This was across the street from the Jim Van Heulens, who were intimate friends; and it was within Levinus' mail route.

My parents bought a house in 1913 that was, for practical purposes, right next door. The house between us, which had been a farmhouse, sat so far back on its lot that we were separated only by a sunny expanse of grass. For the next six years we were almost like one family. Even our cat felt as much at home at one house as at the other.

Levinus, in his quiet way, was a fine friend. He must have had some intimation of my questionings when he gave me a collection of Emerson's essays as an eighth-grade graduation gift. I could make nothing of it at the time, but I kept on trying. Emerson's name was spoken almost with reverence; he must have had something worthwhile to say. So I struggled with him off and on until, some three or four years later, I read with understanding for the first time, "He who would be a man must be a non-conformist." Those few words were worth the trouble. I had been vindicated by none less than the Sage of Concord.

When I was graduated from high school, Levinus wished me happiness. By that time, I had long waited impatiently for something, anything, to happen besides school and church and family gatherings. I replied, "I don't ask for happiness; I want experience." I shall never forget his startled and dismayed look when he said, "Child, you don't know what you are saying." I was afraid he was right, but I still wanted it all, the whole human lot. I was hungry for life. I could not wait for it to begin.

KATE

My feelings toward Kate were ambivalent. When she was relaxed she was affable and hearty; no one could help liking her. But she was volatile, blowing hot and cold unpredictably, so I was afraid of her too. My impressions of her are rather vague, since she moved to Colorado when I was ten or twelve years old, and I saw her only once after that. During the years that I knew her, Kate was under dreadful pressure. Lafe's first wife had died in childbirth, leaving a daughter, Lottie, who was believed to be mentally retarded. It seems much more likely that she was a victim of cerebral palsy. She had passed her life between her bed and a chair and had been taught nothing. It was impossible to know how much she understood because, when she tried to talk, she could get out nothing but meaningless, throaty sounds.

In such a situation, it is no wonder that Kate found things too much for her at times and erupted in a torrent of words. At such times, she invariably lapsed into Dutch, of which Lafe understood not one word. When the sparks flew in his direction, it struck him as funny that all that energy was missing its mark. He would laugh, Kate would come down to earth, and they would take up where they had left off—no feelings hurt, no harm done.

They had two daughters: Grace, who was just two weeks younger than Anna, and Ruth, who must have been eight or ten years younger.

Kate was happiest when taking charge in an emergency. Mother depended on her almost entirely for medical advice. She was our family pediatrician, relying heavily on castor oil and arnica salve.

THE BROENES

The influence of my father's family was collective except for Grandpa and, to some extent, Uncle Johannes. Grandpa Broene was so good in the fullest sense of the word, so radiantly happy in his trust in God, that to know him was a revelation. It was a thing of the spirit, beyond and apart from any creed, and it shone like a ray of light on everyone whose path crossed his. This was especially remarkable since he had been hunchbacked from the age of seventeen when he had gone back to work too soon after a nearly fatal attack of typhoid fever. He served the Crosby Street Church in Grand Rapids until 1905, and he and Grandma lived in the parsonage next door.

The housework was done by Katie, a spare and prickly spinster, who ruled the roost. Nobody wanted to offend Katie. She wore severe black dresses, like Grandma, and stiffly starched aprons. Her duties included the preparation of morning coffee and afternoon tea, as well as three hearty meals a day, for Grandpa and Grandma, and Gerrit and

Dick, who were still at home, and for numerous callers and any of the family who might be there. I don't think I ever saw her sitting down.

The highlight of a visit to Grandma's was Katie's cookies, crisp and brown with points around the edge. I used to nibble at the points slowly, to prolong the satisfaction, and when they were gone I still had a big round cookie left. I was not often welcome in the kitchen, but occasionally Katie would let me grind the coffee in one of those little wooden boxes that you hold in your lap while you turn the handle.

Grandma's sitting room had two outstanding attractions. The first was the big bay window filled with plants, including many that have since gone out of fashion: sorrel with its starry blossoms, many varieties of begonia, asparagus fern. The crowning ornament was the canary in its gilded wire cage, which was blanketed every night when the lamps were lit. I felt sorry for it because it had to go to bed so early. The other attraction was the large-domed lamp that hung from the ceiling. It could be let down for the daily chores of replenishing the oil, trimming the wick, and cleaning the chimney. The shade must have been ornate; what I remember is the fringe of dazzling prisms. All this glory was suspended above the center table, which was covered with a heavy chenille cloth. The table was a repository for pipes and tobacco, and for knick-knacks like seashells and a glass paper-weight in which you could produce a snowstorm.

Parlors were formal rooms, reserved for important callers and special occasions. Grandma's was furnished with the customary sofa and stiff straight-backed chairs upholstered in black horsehair. There was also a lamp table that held the big family Bible and photograph albums. On the walls hung enlarged family photographs, in which everyone looked stiff and sober; also my grandparents' marriage certificate, framed, with their photographs inserted in oval spaces at the top.

I never really knew my grandmother, since she could neither speak nor understand English. She did not need it in her tight little circle. Nor did I ever feel entirely comfortable with her. When I was very little I avoided her because she liked to hold me on her lap, and she had no lap. She had lived a very energetic life, and when she was no longer able to she became very fat. She was as slippery as her horsehair sofa. Much more important, as I grew up, was her puritanical view of what was proper in a woman. There seems to have been, in women like her, a continuous undercurrent of concern about sex. In their dress and in their deportment they repudiated it. Grandma did not hesitate to tell Mother when she thought my skirts were too short. This would have meant, perhaps, an inch or two above my shoe tops. I kept my distance.

It was not until I read my grandfather's account of their early married life that I realized what a strong and capable and generous woman she had been. Grandpa could never have done what he did without her. They were complementary in every way, and their happiness in one another was complete.

On Thanksgiving, for many years, the whole family usually got together at Grandma's house. On such occasions Grandpa took the opportunity, when he was saying grace, to tell the Lord everything that had happened to each member since the last time and to thank Him for each and every blessing. With a holiday dinner waiting, these prayers seemed endless. I could not resist sneaking a look now and then at the bounty that stood ready if Grandpa ever got through.

In spite of the good food, I anticipated these holidays with dread. All my cousins were much younger than I, and until I was grown up, I had little patience with small children. There was nothing whatever for me to do. It would have been disrespectful for me to bury myself in a book at a family gathering. After dinner the air was soon thick with cigar smoke. I often went home sick.

Visits to the aunts and uncles were usually family gatherings so I never had the same feeling of intimacy with them that I had with my mother's family. I learned to appreciate them after I was grown up. They had a strong sense of family solidarity, and when there was trouble they were always there to help. They were good, kind people.

Although Uncle Johannes was seldom home, we knew him best. He loved children. When he was teaching in the East he often sent us postcards and always remembered us at Christmas. When he was home on vacations he took us to John Ball Park to see the animals in the zoo, or up the river in a rowboat. His dominant characteristics were gentleness and integrity. People loved and trusted him. He was the only one of Father's brothers who went to college. His undergraduate work was done at Valparaiso University and his graduate work, in philosophy and psychology, at Clark, where G. Stanley Hall was making history by introducing the new psychological concepts of Sigmund Freud and others. I think this must have been around 1910 or 1912.

When he was in his eighties and I in my sixties we lived near each other again in California. and easily took up where we had left off. It was nostalgic for both of us. He was the last of his generation.

5

VOICES

The middle years of childhood are years of waiting and wondering. The mind is on tiptoe, listening, watching, sniffing the air for meanings, making voyages of discovery within itself and in the world it must one day cope with alone.

Fortunately, at this point my mother's health improved. For nine of the remaining ten years of her life she was reasonably well, and her naturally happy disposition reasserted itself. I learned, little by little, to avoid conflict; and although I continued to chafe under restrictions that seemed to me unnecessary, life was on the whole peaceful and there were compensations. Since my father continued to be away much of the time, Mother turned more and more to Anna and me for companionship, and we enjoyed many things together. On Friday evenings my parents went out with friends or we had company at our house. Saturdays and Sundays were family days.

At some time early in this period, Anna and I were informed that our parents would no longer be "Papa" and "Mama" but "Father" and "Mother." I was aware of the significance of this. Our babyhood was over and our relationship would now be somewhat more formal. For a while I resented this, but the new terminology soon became familiar, and I even began to like it. It gave our relationship a certain dignity.

The new order may be dated from my first day at school in the fall after Grandpa died. I rushed home full of excitement to tell Mother about the new girl with golden hair. Her name was Marguerite Ellis and we were to be "best friends" for four years.

What brought us together was a common need for more color in our lives. I had never had enough to do that was pure fun, or enough physical activity. I longed to swim, to skate, to dance, to ride a bicycle. But dancing was sinful, swimming and bicycling were dangerous in Mother's eyes, and all of these things were expensive one way or another. Basically the trouble was that in Mother's mind play had low priority. One of the fundamental tenets of puritanism was that anything was wrong that attached a person too strongly to "the things of this world." Mother had never had time for play. By *her* mother's standards she was lenient, and fortunately she was far from consistent. Nevertheless, such ideas had weight when she was trying to balance the budget. Recreation was not a necessity.

Neighborhood children my age were mostly boys. I was welcome to join them in their baseball games in the Kooiman's back yard or the empty lot behind our house, but that was not to be. Mother did not intend that I should grow up a tomboy.

There was one game that brought us all together, boys and girls. On summer evenings we played hide-and-seek as long as the light lasted. The goal was always Dr. Rozema's front steps, but we hid in all of the adjoining back yards. The pleasures were manifold: to run hard and to rest, to be one of the group, to stay up later than usual, and to be out in the mysterious night when darkness fell. After such evenings I went to bed happy.

Marguerite's life was much more circumscribed than mine. She and her mother had come up from New Orleans after her father died, and her mother was working as a practical nurse. During most of the years that I knew them, their only home was a rented room in a private house. They attended the Church of Christ's Disciples, and they must have had a few acquaintances, but they appeared to have no close friends. Marguerite was alone much of the time.

Enter King Arthur and his knights and ladies. We must have read some of the tales in school. Miss Flaherty may have supplemented them with readings from *The Idylls of the King*. However it came about, Marguerite and I acquired our own copies and memorized whole passages: "Elaine the fair, Elaine the lovable. . . ." and "All day the din of battle roared. . . ." From there we got into the Pre-Raphaelite painters. I can't imagine how we happened to stumble upon them. Those languid damsels, so remote from anything in this world, were the stuff of our preadolescent dreams.

Reading was not only an escape but an indispensable guide to an understanding of how people conducted their lives. For years I was absorbed in *Little Women* and the whole series of March-family books. Concord was as real to me as my own back yard. In Jo I found a kindred spirit who had learned to accommodate herself happily to her small world. These were books to grow on.

Other books read avidly at one time or another during this period included *Heidi, The Swiss Family Robinson, Little Lord Fauntleroy, Sarah Crewe, Rebecca of Sunnybrook Farm, Pilgrim's Progress* (read as adventure in a strange landscape). There were also several series of books for girls; most importantly, "The Little Colonel" and "The Five Little Peppers" books. Mother saw to it that I had an allotment of edifying tales about orphaned or handicapped children who redeemed their families through sheer patience and goodness. Sunday school library books were still the prescribed reading for Sunday afternoons.

My favorite occupation, when not engaged in reading, was designing and making clothes for a small doll and for my paperdolls. Small bisque dolls with jointed limbs, eyes that opened and shut, and "real" hair, were available for twenty-five cents. They were about six inches long, I should say, requiring little material and not many stitches. The tiny details, on the other hand, required a certain degree of expertise. At a time when dresses were made at home or by a dressmaker, there was never a lack of fabrics or of ribbons and laces. On the back of the attic door hung a large flowered-chintz bag that held scraps of everything we had worn for years back. In addition, there were books of samples that Father discarded each season. These went to Mother for quilts, but not all were suitable for the purpose; the rest were mine.

Dresses for paperdolls were painted with watercolors after drawing an outline around the doll and penciling the details in lightly. A large part of the pleasure was the endless experimenting with color. This was a major interest for years. My earliest ambition, when I began to think about such things, was to study clothing design at the Chicago Art Institute. This notion was firmly put down. Art of any sort was not real work, and there was no money in it. There also hung in the air an unspoken fear of the whole dissolute sphere in which art and artists had their being. As a matter of fact, such a course would have got me nowhere at the time. American fashion simply didn't count. Anyway, women did not think in terms of careers. Marriage was a woman's career and no other mattered.

During all of these four years I took music lessons from piano teachers and practiced on the family organ. This was not a promising way to acquire a technique, but the lessons were by no means wasted. I loved to play and I became familiar with a considerable amount of good music.

My first teacher was a neighbor whose name I have forgotten. All we knew about her credentials was that she had taught Irene Hunt, and Irene could pound out almost any tune on request with vigor and enthusiasm. I think the woman was a pretty good teacher, for beginners, at any rate. I got as far with her as simple "pieces," like MacDowell's "To a Wild Rose," and then she got pregnant. Mrs. Hunt came over to convey the news to Mother, who found it hard to believe. How could a seemingly respectable woman be so indelicate, so insensitive, as to continue teaching an innocent child when she was in *that* condition. My lessons stopped abruptly. I was bitterly disappointed, and my mother's attitude was beyond my comprehension.

The next fall Mother decided that if I was to have more piano lessons I should have the best. She took me with her to the Sacred Heart Academy of Music, where we talked with Sister Mary Thomas. If I had been religiously inclined I might have been powerfully swayed by my admiration for this woman. She had a strong and beautiful face, and she was all kindness and courtesy and concern for our needs. When it turned out that we could not afford the tuition, she arranged for a promising senior student, Esther Hirschberg, to give me lessons at home.

At the end of the season I took part in the academy's annual student recital, and the occasion stands out as the most devastating social experience of my life. I was to play the bass part in a four-hand piece to be played simultaneously on four pianos by eight of the less accomplished young musicians. It would be a humble performance, but nevertheless it was a public appearance, and I was to have a new dress.

My mother could see no good reason to engage a high-priced dressmaker for children's clothes. The woman who made mine was a competent seamstress but unblessed with any sense of style. I was unhappy about my school dresses and was beset with misgivings when we took her a design and material for so special an occasion. When I went for a fitting I knew my worst fears had been realized. The woman had been inspired to add her personal touch in the way of tight-fitting French sleeves set in close-fitting armholes like those of a riding habit, and a high collar, fashionable at the time, wired up to points under my ears. These embellishments accentuated my thinness and, what was worse, were altogether inappropriate for a child. There was nothing to do but wear the dress; I had no other. I went on stage looking ridiculous and I knew it.

The next year, Mother decided again to change teachers. Esther was replaced by Miss Emma Schneider, who taught at home, so that I got to play on a piano at least once a week. The most valuable aspect of lessons under these unpropitious circumstances was an increased appreciation of music—getting the "feel" of Bach and Mozart, Schubert and Chopin, through my fingers. I liked Miss Schneider, except that I wished she were a little more rigorous. She would say, "That will do," when I knew it wouldn't. I am not sure whether she knew that I did not have a piano. For most young ladies, in any case, piano playing was merely a social grace. Perhaps there was good sense in not pushing them so hard that they took no pleasure in it.

We did many things together as a family. What impresses me about them today is their extreme simplicity. My parents and, I think, most of their friends, were happy in their lives, and they needed only a little relaxation. Excitement was not in the picture and it was not missed.

I don't know whether it is possible today to convey the mood of that time. The nation was bursting with vitality. During its difficult first century it had proved that democracy could work. It had preserved the union and secured its borders. We still believed our natural resources to be inexhaustible. Mass production, still in its infancy, was believed to herald a new era of abundance for all. If this country was not an earthly paradise, it was the next thing to it. The day was near when no one would have to work more than half time. The most worrisome question was whether people would know what to do with so much leisure! That is one worry we don't have today.

When my parents' friends came in for the evening, they often played a card game called "Flinch." Ordinary playing cards were taboo, I suppose because they were associated not only with gambling but with fortune-telling and other occult hocus-pocus. In Flinch there were no face cards or symbols, only straightforward numbers. This was the only significant difference.

One evening when we were entertaining some people from the church, a neighbor came in and asked if we would lend him a pack of cards. Mother regretted that we didn't have any. Whereupon I, always willing to be helpful, piped up with, "Oh, yes, we do. There is a pack in Father's collar box." Given my father's convivial nature, it is highly improbable that he should not have spent some of the thousands of evenings in small-town hotel rooms in friendly card games. This did not change his belief in their baneful effect on daughters. I stowed away such inconsistencies to ruminate upon.

Father's preferred way of letting down was tending the lawn. He was not interested in gardening, just grass. Since he never got the last weed, he was never without occupation while summer lasted. For the rest, he wanted people around him, preferably outdoors in good weather. On Saturdays he would often say, "Let's have supper at Reed's Lake tonight"—or North Park. At other times such excursions would be planned ahead with friends or relatives.

North Park was simply a picnic place, an open space and a cleared grove with no provision for recreation except a few swings. There were two things that claimed my attention for a little while. I could gaze at the gypsy encampment among the trees across the river: horses grazing and covered wagons and women in gay dresses preparing a meal over a camp fire, with children under foot. They came regularly every summer. Or I could stand on the fenced wooden walk at the edge of the river, where the moving water made the walk appear to be moving, and pretend I was on a boat.

Reed's Lake was the place; it had everything! The fun began with the streetcar ride. If you were lucky you got one of the cars that were put on to take care of summer crowds. These were open on all sides except for the glass shield at the front. The seats extended the full width of the car, and you boarded by way of a running board, on which the conductor perched precariously while he collected fares. There was a wonderful breeze when the car was in motion.

At Reed's Lake, the end of the line, the passengers were deposited between the ball park and the pavilion. The latter was a round structure with a semi-open vaudeville theater in the center. On the surrounding veranda soft drinks and ice cream were for sale, and crackerjack in boxes that had prizes in them. The prize was always a disappointment, but there was always a breathless moment when a child might hope that *this* time it might amount to something.

There were the usual entertainment features, of which the one that most interested me was the merry-go-round. That was the joy of joys. To ride high on a beautiful, galloping horse, holding on for my life, round and round to loud brassy music—what more could life hold!

Sometimes we took picnic lunches or suppers to eat in the woodsy picnic grounds. More often we ate them aboard the little steamer that chugged around the lake all day and evening. One fare was good for as long as one wished to stay. There were picnic tables on the upper deck. For children, the pleasure lay in the freedom to roam about the boat: to stand in the stern and watch the little boats bobbing in our wake, or up front pretending to steer, or going below to watch the noisy engines from a safe distance.

In the daytime we could get off at Manhattan Beach on the far shore. This was a grandiose name for another cleared grove with more picnic tables and a swimming beach. Bathing suits for women and girls were a decorous black or navy blue, with middy tops and full, awkward bloomers under full, knee-length skirts—surely one of the most ridiculous sports garments ever devised. The bloomers were still required gym uniform when I was in college.

Sometimes on holidays we went on all-day picnics with other couples and their children. On such occasions we could choose among a number of lakes at no great distance from the city. As automobiles became more common, and tires more dependable, we could go considerable distances, though there was always a chance that a tire might blow out. Such rides were hot and dusty at best. The men fished, and played baseball on improvised diamonds. Sometimes the women fished too, but often they liked to just sit and talk or take little walks along the shore. Women of my mother's generation seldom engaged in sports. A game of croquet was about their limit. When they went out in a rowboat the men did the rowing.

I was happy exploring, skipping stones and watching the rings spread out over the water, collecting pretty pebbles, discovering new wildflowers, or disjointing "snake grass" to make necklaces and bracelets.

The main feature, of course, was the swimming and bathing after lunch, in which everyone joined.

The simplest of our pleasures was taking the Taylor Street car to the end of the line with Mother on summer evenings. For thirty cents, round trip, the three of us could get out of the hot house for a couple of hours. Towards the end of the line, out near North Park and on to the fairgrounds, there would be no one else on the car; and the motorman would get up full speed, blowing our hair and fanning our faces.

The most exciting event was the circus parade. (The shows were prohibited.) School was always closed for a day when the circus came to town. Mother would take us downtown early so we could find a good place to see the gaudily bedecked elephants and the caged lions and the snake woman in her glass car and the blaring calliope. Afterward there might be an ice-cream treat at the soda fountain at Peck's drug store. That, to my joy, was still on its corner when I was last home in 1959—the dark, polished woodwork, the convoluted-wire ice-cream-parlor chairs—everything just as it should be.

I always looked forward to family vacations eagerly, not least because rules were relaxed. My parents were decidedly less vigilant when we took off for Lake Michigan or one of the smaller lakes.

The best vacations by far were those we spent at Highland Park on Lake Michigan, just over the dunes from Grand Haven. To call it a summer resort would probably be misleading today. All the resorts in the dune country were remote. There were no paved roads through the heavy sand to the beach, no concessions, no crowds.

At Highland Park the dunes were real hills. Some cottages sat a hundred steps or more up from the beach. At the back they opened onto the pleasant woods that held the dunes in place on the far side. On the lake side there was only clean white sand with scarcely a trace of growth of any kind; and where it was not walked upon, the sand was wind-riffled into beautiful wavy patterns. There was one small hotel, set into the hillside at mid-level—a typical, rambling, white-painted frame structure, with wide veranda facing the lake.

One small streetcar ran along the beach, well back from the water, beside a row of poplars that had been planted to hold the sand. It made the round trip from Grand Haven and back once an hour. For a moment there would be a great clatter, and then all would be quiet again till the next trip.

The big pier was, I think, maybe half a mile away to the north, but it may have been a mile or even considerably farther. Distance meant nothing to us. This was one of the principal attractions. There were always people fishing off it. The outgoing and incoming ships could be seen close up. It was fun to wave to the lifeguards across the channel, who had little to do in good weather and responded cheerfully. The size of the lighthouse, seen from its base, never failed to be amazing.

The pier also offered real thrills, owing to the state it was in. Many of the heavy wooden flooring planks were missing, leaving gaps with jagged rocks below—thrown in, I presume, to hold the structure in place. Even when the water was relatively quiet, it broke over those rocks in full sound and fury, with dizzying effect. If planks were missing on both sides of the one you wanted to cross, the thing to do was to fix your eyes on the far end and go for it. The planks must have been about a foot wide, affording safe enough footing if you were not distracted by the commotion beneath or seized by sudden fear. Even so, I don't know how my mother could have let me do this. At home she was all too careful about my taking any chances.

For a few summers we shared a cottage with Casey and Della Haan (Hahn) and their son Harold during these vacations at Lake Michigan. Casey was Father's best friend. He was a quiet man with a gentle good humor that was a foil for Father's vitality and assertiveness. We all loved Aunt Della. Harold, whose age was between mine and Anna's, was not averse to spending a little time with girls at the beach. It was pleasant for all of us.

In the morning we children combed the beach for the iridescent beetles that littered the moist sand where the water had washed up during the night. They were dead and smelly but so beautiful! We kept them in old spool boxes until the next morning brought a fresh supply. We walked barefoot along the shore for the pleasure of feeling the water and wet sand running between our toes. Sometimes we set out to reach the point of land visible to the south but we never made it; it continually receded as we advanced. At a certain hour every afternoon, we climbed the highest dune to get the first glimpse of the Chicago or Milwaukee boat on the horizon. Another hour might pass before it was visible below.

Father and Casey fished. The women got their household tasks out of the way with dispatch and then sat and talked on the shady porch, or read, or napped after lunch until it was time to join the rest of us for the afternoon bathing. The water was always cold, chilling unless you kept moving, but invigorating once you got used to it. The shore sloped out gently a very long way. One day when the water was quiet, I decided to see for myself how far out I could go. I was beyond calling distance when I suddenly realized that I was becoming buoyant and was unable to turn around. Every time a wave slapped me it raised me off my feet. I was terrified but succeeded in backing in slowly. The incident was not reported.

Supper, by common agreement, was usually the day's catch of fish with fried potatoes and fruit or berries. After supper we all went down to the beach again and collected driftwood, of which there was plenty, for a fire—old washed timbers that stirred thoughts of shipwrecks. The men built a great fire that lasted all evening without attention. There might be three or four other fires as far as one could see. We sat around it on big square beams while the sun set and the afterglow painted the wet sand and the stars came out. As it grew later the wind came up and the fire died down, and all at once the night seemed dark and threatening. It was time to go in and fall asleep with the pines murmuring outside the window and the whip-poor-wills crying in the woods.

All of this was heaven. More than anything else, I think, it was the exhilaration of limitless space. As far as I could see or imagine, there were no boundaries—only sand and water and sky to the world's end.

School in the fall was looked forward to as eagerly as vacation in the spring, but it soon became humdrum. I can think of nothing especially significant between King Arthur in the fifth grade and Shakespeare in the eighth.

In the eighth grade I began to pick up interest. Miss Eleanor Rawlinson, my teacher, was, I should think, in her middle thirties. I greatly admired her looks. She was tall, with a good figure and good carriage, beautiful fair skin, and handsome, clean-cut features. She was moody, however. There were days when she seemed to positively dislike children and to have no care for their feelings. On such days we were all subdued. The day before Christmas we put our pennies and nickels together to buy her a plant, which was set on her desk during the noon recess. In the afternoon we made sure to get back early, expecting oh's and ah's and a pleased thank you. She gave no sign that she even saw our gift.

In spite of this unhappy characteristic, she was an excellent and ingenious teacher, and sometimes kind. She knew how to make things clear and how to arouse enthusiasm. She read to us from the English romantic poets: "The splendor falls on castle walls" and "Music that gentlier on the spirit lies than tired eyelids upon tired eyes." I was so enthralled by songs from Tennyson's *The Princess* that I read the whole poem without understanding a word of it. Looking at the poem recently after nearly eighty years, I found it still unreadable. It is fifty pages of romantic nonsense designed to put down young women so misguided as to aspire to higher education. A woman should not "lose the childlike in the larger mind. . . . If she has failed in sweet humility she has failed in all." Five editions of the poem appeared within six years between 1847 and 1853. There must have been many worried fathers. By 1910, women had won that round and were seeking the right to vote.

The greatest pleasure was acting *Julius Caesar*. Every afternoon we chose parts and emerged from the cloak room, book in hand, reading our lines with all the oratorical flourishes at our command. If there had been rafters they would have rung. Is there a better way to teach a play!

Shakespeare, I learned at this time, was the greatest writer in the English language. If this was true and if *Julius Caesar* was a fair example, then I must have more of him. The school library had an edition of Shakespeare in which each play was in a separate volume. One day I selected two volumes with titles that appealed to me (I wish I knew what they were) and read them inside my geography book during study periods. I could make nothing of either, and I took my failure very hard. I had thought I was quite smart, and now I knew that I was totally lacking in understanding. The greatest writer in the English language must remain a closed book to me. The feeling passed. There were enough books I *could* understand to make life wonderful and exciting.

Miss Christine Keck, the principal, was also a first-rate teacher. At regular intervals she took our class for an hour and gave us samples of the kind of lessons we might expect in high school. One day it was a simple algebraic equation; solving it was like playing a game. Sometimes it was a song in a foreign language. She taught us the first stanzas of *"Die Wacht am Rhein"* and the *"Marseillaise"* and *"Adeste fideles."* The last inspired me to elect Latin, which is, in my opinion, the most useful subject I ever took besides the three R's.

Whose idea it was I don't know, but somebody decided that I did not need much of what was going on in the classroom and saw that I had something else to do whenever possible. The school had acquired a hand printing press and a font of type, and Leroy Austin and I were delegated to set type for something or other for hours at a time. This was fun and a fine introduction to the fascinating subject of typography.

My reading had now reached a critical stage. I came home from the library one day with a couple of novels, which my mother at once forbade me to read. They were "too old" for me. "But I have read all the children's books," I protested. Something would have to be done. It was decided that Mother would choose adult books for me and would read them to me, which she proceeded to do, skipping the parts that were too old. The result of this, naturally, was that I read the skipped parts with close attention when Mother was out, or on Saturday mornings when I was supposed to be dusting and Mother was in the kitchen with her hands in pastry or bread dough.

The first book we read together in this way was *Ben Hur*. If I know my mother, she chose it because Jesus appeared in it. That made it safe, like the Bible, edifying in effect, whatever there might be in it of sin. It was not quite that simple. A play made from the book appeared at Powers theater that season, and the *Grand Rapids Press* offered free tickets to a hundred school children who should send in the best essays on some aspect of the story. I won one of the tickets with a paean to Iras, the Serpent of the Nile. She was the first *femme fatale* I had encountered, and I was in the state of mind of Miniver Cheevy.

> Miniver loved the Medici,
>   Albeit he had never seen one;
> He would have sinned incessantly
>   Could he have been one.[2]

It could be argued that my parents' fears for me were not unfounded. I was bedazzled, certainly, by a vision of beauty and glitter and frank sensuality. What settled the matter for me was the woman's mettle. Iras was a person in her own right; not, like Esther, merely some man's shadow. She knew what she wanted and she dared to play for high stakes. In defeat she remained proud. I was all for her.

The next book was *David Copperfield*. Here my attention was centered on little Em'ly. Society's judgment of the sinner had not changed significantly since Goldsmith had penned his verses on the subject some hundred and fifty years before.

> When lovely woman stoops to folly
> And finds too late that men betray
> What charm can soothe her melancholy?
> What art can wash her tears away?

Mother's sympathy for injured innocence was overflowing. Plainly she understood the state of mind in which a woman might heedlessly throw her life away. Even so, expiation was supposed to be lifelong. Such love was bliss but it was also sin. When it was over, "Get thee to a nunnery!" Mother's reading program was not having the desired effect. I was beginning to find the subject of carnal love extraordinarily interesting.

*   *   *

I received my grade-school diploma in June, 1910. William Howard Taft occupied the White House. Great Britain ruled the seas. Germany, late comer to empire, had decided to change that, but for the moment the great powers were at peace. The United States had made clear its intention of tolerating no competition in the Western Hemisphere. The unruly countries to the south of us were a nuisance, but we could handle that. And the Panama Canal was abuilding.

When Father and his brothers or his friends got together and talked politics, they extolled the virtues of the Republican party, lamented the passing of Teddy Roosevelt and his Big Stick, gave grudging admiration to William Jennings Bryan (who ran for the presidency and lost as regularly as the sun rose and set), or voiced their disgruntlement with our senator, William Alden Smith, or their low opinion of City Hall.

A few technological experiments were subjects of animated debate, none more so than the flying machines that the Wright brothers had been tinkering with for so many years. It was not impossible that something might come of it. Glenn Curtis had actually flown from Albany to New York in less than three hours! Few, however, would have put much money on such far-out ventures. The Twentieth Century was still in embryo.

My parents' wedding picture. December 6, 1894.
Still in love twenty-two years later.

Frances and Anna, 1899.

Grandpa Beneker and Frances, 1896.

Grandpa Broene at 70.

Grandma Broene with Frances and Anna, 1903.

Levinus Beneker
and Mathilda,
about 1894. A
marked absence
of stress.

Mathilda as I
knew her.

6

ASCENT TO SUMMER

Now I was a young woman, no longer a child, although I could not have said when I became conscious of the change. My mind was reaching out impatiently for new experiences and new ideas. My relationship with my parents had changed, for the better on the whole, but not without creating new anxieties.

As I have said earlier, my mother had by this time come to realize that this strange child of hers, so dear to her but so difficult, so eager to please but so intransigent, marched to some music of her own that was not to be gainsaid. She decided that she could trust me, and we began to be open with each other. Her mind began reaching out too and she grew along with me. She was at this time between forty-six and fifty.

She told me tales about her own youth: how she had once accepted a young man's invitation to go to the theater and had scarcely known what was going on, on the stage, so absorbed was she in her guilt; how a neighbor had once given her a headache remedy before a party—apparently a narcotic—and how, for once in her life, she had felt uninhibited and gay, and afterwards ashamed. Our conversations forged a close bond between us.

In those days before telephones were universal there was much impromptu visiting. The house always had to be shipshape by noon, in case someone should drop in. Often on a summer afternoon Mother would ask, "Whom shall we call on today?" It was taken for granted that we would go with her. Sometimes these calls were mildly pleasant, sometimes boring, but always the walks with Mother were a pleasure. She was good company.

On winter evenings we read aloud together. Often it was Dickens that we read, and he remains an old friend, none the worse for time. We also attended readings by one of Dickens' sons at the Fountain Street Baptist Church. I enjoyed those evenings. Dickens "reads" well, and the audience was appreciative.

That part of my life was good, with one exception. Mother now got down to business about making a lady out of me. This was no light matter. A lady doesn't slouch. She doesn't cross her legs. She doesn't sit on the floor. She doesn't complain about wearing a corset. She puts her gloves on before she leaves the house. She does not stare boldly at boys. And she *never* gives a boy reason to believe that his attentions might be welcome unless he has made the first move. Being a lady was a full-time occupation. The name of my grandmother was often invoked.

What all this seemed to me to add up to was, if it comes naturally don't do it. If this was adulthood, what was the use of growing up? Fortunately, it was not really that bad in my time. The stiff manners of my mother's day had already undergone considerable modification. A book of etiquette that Mother had bought before her marriage was good for a laugh on nearly every page.

For moments of decision Mother had two guidelines that served all situations: What will people think? and Never mind what people think. One had only to decide which one was applicable, and everything supposedly became clear. Mother herself was never in doubt.

My father and I, regrettably, were never able to come to an agreement. My mother used to say to me, "You are just like your father," and I had no idea what she meant. Neither one of us could give an inch. As he saw it, he would have failed in his duty as a parent if he should be unable to bend the twig in the direction the Lord would have it grow; and I would never be able to please him without surrendering my fundamental integrity. He was never unkind. It was his displeasure that I could not bear. I did my best to appear to conform; there was nothing to be gained by pursuing a collision course. But this gave rise to a new dilemma. So long as I wore the mask of an obedient daughter, I could have no life of my own; and, having put it on, I could not remove it later without disastrous consequences. Neither alternative would bear looking at. I had, moreover, a painful sense of loss when I thought of how much we were both missing. The daughter he loved so much was a creature of his imagination that bore little resemblance to me. I must be forever a stranger to him.

I spent the first semester in high school in the doldrums. The new Central High building was not quite finished, and the old one on Ransom Avenue could no longer accommodate all of the students at one time. Freshmen attended classes in the afternoon; all others, in the morning. There was little opportunity to get acquainted with classmates and no time for after-school activities.

Mornings I had to do my homework at the dining-room table under Mother's watchful eyes. This was my first experience with homework, and it was not at all to my liking. So far, learning had been almost effortless, and I was impatient. Soon I learned that by paying close attention in class and cramming for exams I could keep up my grades without bothering overmuch with daily assignments. The fact is, I was not, then or ever, a student. Books were a magic carpet that carried me anywhere I wished to go in time or space. Studying was something else. I was interested in many things but had no wish to pursue any one of them beyond what I needed for my own purposes or my own pleasure. In that respect I am unchanged today.

In February the new building on Fountain Street was ready, and a new phase of life began. The building itself was a source of pleasure. It was made of soft red brick, well designed in the tradition of campus architecture. It sat well back from the street on a nicely landscaped plot in a spacious residence neighborhood, on a street overarched by old elm trees. Inside, it was new and clean and bright, and it stayed that way the whole time I knew it.

The front doors opened onto a landing between the first and ground floors with a wide central stairway leading up to the first floor. At the top of the stairs stood a larger-than-life plaster cast of the Victory of Samothrace. That majestic, soaring figure was the first sight that met my eyes every morning. It seems to me impossible that anyone should look at it without a quickened heartbeat and new courage. In the same position, on the floor above, stood the handsome Discobolus, poised for the throw. This would have been much if there had been nothing else, but it was only the beginning.

The whole first-floor corridor was hung with large reproductions of European paintings. The one I remember most clearly was a Corot that hung outside Miss Hopkins' classroom. It showed a farm scene in the background, through a grove of those wispy young trees that are Corot's hallmark. It must have been the novelty that appealed to me, the scene half revealed and half hidden. However that may be, it brightened my days.

It would be interesting to know where the idea—and the money—for all this abundance came from. I imagine that our principal, Jesse B. Davis, had more than a little to do with it. All I know about him is that he was a graduate of Colgate. Under his administration the school was oriented towards the liberal arts, although there were vocational courses for those who wanted them. When he was criticized for catering to the élite, as happened occasionally, he replied that young people who were not going to college should have the opportunity in high school to learn at least a little about the culture they had inherited.

As the second largest city in the state, and also as a pleasant place to live, Grand Rapids drew well-educated and experienced teachers. I remember three with special affection.

Miss Myra Hopkins taught ancient and European history. She had traveled much, and her standards and biases were upperclass. Her only complaint about Greece, where she seems to have spent most of her summers, was that it was impossible, anywhere in the country, to get butter with one's breakfast egg. She lost no opportunity to tell us that we owed it to our country to have as many children as possible, lest the numerous progeny of the uneducated take over the Ship of State. Such notions aside, she represented the best of Western culture. One of her first assignments in Greek history was to memorize the prayer of Socrates in the "Phaedrus" that begins, "Beloved Pan and all ye other gods who haunt this place, pray give me beauty of the inward soul." It was my first intimation that the "heathen" might aspire to goodness, that they might even have something to say to us about it.

History with her was far more than book learning. She had sheaves of notebooks filled with clippings and photographs, which she passed around during class. The chalk trays held large, matted photographs, related to the events we were studying. Framed pictures hung on the walls. She knew the art and the architecture, and when she got through with us we knew them too. We learned to identify the great cathedrals of France and England and to recognize the masters of painting. I owe to her the perception of art as the reflection of, and key to, an entire culture.

Miss Mildred Hinsdale, who taught English and American history, was the daughter of a history professor in Ann Arbor whose scholarship was a legend at the university for a generation after his death. She herself was a highly intelligent woman, with no sympathy for carelessness or negligence. She could be sharp, though never cruel, with those who failed to meet her standards. Her reprimands were usually touched with a mischievous humor that made the culprit laugh with the rest of us. She put us on our good behavior by calling us "Mr." and "Miss," which no other teacher did. We respected her.

Her teaching methods were more conventional than those of Miss Hopkins; she stressed politics and the development of law. She required us to memorize the dates of all the English kings, for which I thank her. I no longer remember them exactly beyond Edward I but I can still place them in their proper centuries, which is a great help in remembering the course of events. I wish I knew the French kings as well.

She lived all her life with two sisters, one of whom, Miss Mary, held a Ph.D. Miss Mildred had an almost devout admiration for her sister's learning, undoubtedly well founded. Still, Miss Mary lived so exclusively in a world of her own that it was difficult to imagine her as being in any way effective in this one. She seemed always to be available when Miss Mildred needed a substitute, and I have always wondered whether she dreaded those times as much as we did. I can see her sitting behind her desk, muttering inaudibly, as if she were present only in the flesh while her spirit roamed elsewhere, a kind of ghost in reverse.

I think of all three sisters as the victims of a highly intellectual upbringing in a period when intelligence in a woman was looked upon by most men, and more than a few women, as a kind of deformity, a lamentable departure from the norm. We know little about how such women felt about their lives, since they lived behind a mask of reticence and self-sufficiency; but it seems certain that they must have felt bitter at times, for they were virtually exiles from society. They fitted in nowhere.

The other teacher for whom I had a fondness was Miss Anna Jones, the head Latin teacher, who also taught Greek. In appearance she was the typical old-maid schoolteacher; little, colorless, with graying hair pulled back tight into the usual bun. The impression she made would have been mousey except for her brisk manner and quick mind. She lived with a sister, who, I believe, kept house for her. It was reported that they had adopted an infant boy who was being taught Latin as a native language!

Miss Jones put up with no nonsense. We were there to learn Latin and she was going to see that we did. She puts me in mind of the colloquial use of "learn" for "teach." Miss Jones *learned* us thoroughly.

One year she took a long leave of absence. I imagine she was going through some middle-age crisis not uncommon in lonely women who saw old age coming on. In those days we called it a nervous breakdown. Miss Anna Workman, an amiable young English teacher, took over our class. Shortly before Miss Jones was due to return, we came to a particularly difficult passage in Caesar having to do with crossing a river. Both the class and Miss Workman were out of their depth, and we feared that Miss Jones would expect us to translate the passage for her.

The first thing she said when she got back was, "Have you crossed the river?"

We all shouted, "Yes."

"Good," she said, "we will go on from there."

I liked Latin for its precision. It had all the qualities that built the empire and made its armies invincible. I valued it for what it taught me about my own language. It seems to me no accident that the English language has fallen on evil days since Latin died a second death, in the schools.

I had always been good in arithmetic, and I did well in algebra and rather enjoyed it, but geometry I hated. I could see no use in it. Why should I have to prove that two triangles were equal when it could be seen by inspection? I don't know that anyone ever asked for an explanation. Certainly I never did. Teachers represented authority. It would have taken more courage than I had to question the value of a subject. After geometry I wanted nothing more to do with mathematics.

English was sometimes interesting, but on the whole I found it tedious. I intensely disliked writing themes. The subjects were always inane. We spent weeks on reading that I could have done in a few days. Nevertheless, I was learning more than I realized. Grammar, which had been incomprehensible to me, suddenly became clear during my first year. Perhaps my mind had not been ready for it earlier, but I think some credit must go to Miss Workman's teaching. The course that I most dreaded, in anticipation, was probably the most valuable. An entire semester of the junior year was spent in analyzing the arguments of Edmund Burke's speech "On Conciliation with the American Colonies." An understanding of what constitutes sound reasoning is surely central to anything that may properly be called education.

My outside reading was haphazard. We had a complete set of George Eliot, and the Jim Van Heulens had a complete set of Dickens. I read both with great interest. There was a time when I felt almost as much at home in Dickens' London as I did in my home town. For the most part, I was dependent on the public library; and since most of the books were in the stacks and I didn't know what to ask for, I picked at random from the reading-room shelves.

I read historical romances, like Helen Hunt Jackson's *Ramona* (the Spanish in California); folksy authors of the day: Kate Douglas Wiggins and Booth Tarkington; autobiographies of immigrants: Mary Antin and Jacob Riis; backwoods tales: *The Little Shepherd of Kingdom Come* and *The Girl of the Limberlost;* the social critics: Frank Norris and the American Winston Churchill. In spite of the randomness, they added up to a fairly broad view of the American scene.

Mother had given up trying to censor my reading, but now Father took a turn at it. He subscribed to the *Saturday Evening Post* year in and year out, and I read it as assiduously as he did. When he noticed this, he began looking through it for unsuitable material and telling me that I was not to read this and that. I promised with a clear conscience. The catch was that the *Post* came on Thursday and Father did not get to it until Saturday, by which time I had already read it. I cannot imagine what there may have been in that respectable magazine to corrupt me.

One of the most important features of my high school experience was an increased knowledge of music and drama. There were classes in music appreciation, and we had an enthusiastic high school orchestra that frequently played at assemblies. A full-time teacher of public speaking directed the drama group. I wished I might belong to it, but I dared not even raise the question with my parents. I did see the plays, however, and I still remember how thrilled I was with *Twelfth Night.*

I also managed to see a little professional Shakespeare. The Robert Mantell repertory company came to Powers Opera House every year for several weeks, and Mother let me go. Shakespeare and the Bible were so often mentioned together that the playwright had achieved a kind of sanctity by association. The company seems not to have been first rate, but I was not hard to please.

Father loved Bach's vocal music, and often at Christmas and

Easter time we went to the Congregational Church opposite Fulton Street Park to hear their Bach chorus. Opera music was available through a company that came to the high school every winter for a series of concerts. Mother and Anna and I had season tickets, and I became familiar with some of the more popular operas: *El Trovatore, Carmen, Aïda.* The high point of the whole four years was a concert at the high school by the Chicago Symphony Orchestra. I was in heaven. I had heard a few phonograph records but nothing like this.

All of these things, however, were subsidiary to my concern with my social life. I had become stiff and shy, all the spontaneity trained out of me. Although I had much of my father's capacity for enjoyment, it was all shut up inside me. Never one to accept trouble passively, I decided that I would have to learn to be more outgoing.

It was hard for me even to greet people in passing. This was one place where I could begin. A cheerful "Good morning" and a smile to go with it should not be too difficult. To my surprise, this small gesture began to bear fruit in a very short time. I took public speaking because I was mortally afraid of it and determined to conquer the fear. At assembly one morning I had to give a speech with my knees shaking visibly, and it was agony; but if anyone noticed my terror I did not hear of it. By one such small step at a time I reached my goal.

Marguerite and I were growing apart as we both began to make new friends. Our friendship continued into adulthood, but it was no longer close. This was disillusioning. If friendship could cool, what could one trust? There are many kinds of growing pains.

My first new friend was Irene Nuechterlein. She was petite and pert with a mass of red hair and a piquant freckle or two, and she had style. What was special about Irene was a talent for bringing out the best in people and making them feel good about themselves. Everybody liked her. So I was pleased when she showed an interest in me. We spent a lot of time together, including many nights at her house, talking into the small hours. I learned much from Irene.

She was one of a handful of girls who were invited to join a club at the end of the second year. The next fall she put my name up and I was invited. It was one of the two most desirable clubs, so I was launched, if not as a bright star, at least as a member of some standing in my class.

These clubs were sponsored by the school to replace the fraternities and sororities that had been banned. Each club was required to have some serious purpose (which was not taken too seriously), and the purpose of my club was to keep abreast of current events. Breezy news magazines were as yet unknown. I believe we used the *Literary Digest.* It was drearily written, and in any case our interest was minimal. Public policy and the shenanigans of politics were not our concern, and we were just as happy to have it so. What was important about a club was simply to belong, to wear the pin, to be bracketed with the right crowd. Of such small vanities the joys and sorrows of adolescence are made. For a girl like me, longing for acceptance, the boost it gave to my confidence was inestimable.

My junior year was the best. Besides the club membership it brought me another new friend. Doris Grissinger was the daughter of a widow who taught country school near Owosso. She sent her daughter to Grand Rapids for her last two years of high school, and from the first day Doris' popularity was unrivaled. It was my good luck that she lived just a block from our house. I had the advantage of walking to school with her and of seeing her after school without advance planning. Among her graces were large blue eyes and lovely blond hair, but it was her singularly happy spirit that seemed to shed a light around her and make her irresistible. She was engaged to marry a prospective farmer, which she did immediately upon graduation; and they prospered, selling beans to the federal government during World War I.

That year also saw the beginning of a few other friendships, and one that was unhappily aborted.

Lorraine Newman was the intelligent and attractive daughter of a Jewish tailor. We became friendly in a class that we both attended, and when she asked me if I would go home with her after school some day, I was eager to accept but said that I would have to ask my mother. Mother said no emphatically. There were very few Jews in the city. There had been only two girls whom I knew to be Jewish during the whole time I was in grade school, and there were only two in my high school class. No prejudice was evident. I knew that my mother liked her one or two Jewish acquaintances. So I was unprepared for this refusal. It shocked me, and it put me in a position where I must disobey my mother or hurt my friend. I obeyed and was ashamed. I was also pained and puzzled by Mother's attitude. How was I to reconcile it with the goodness and kindness that I knew to be the mainspring of her character? Clearly, religious differences were at the bottom of it. She saw it as her first duty to protect her daughter from heretical influences. Even so, to hurt another's self-esteem——It was more than I knew how to deal with.

Today I can understand that a person is no more responsible for prejudices learned in the cradle than for any other beliefs acquired in infancy. These are the rocks on which our personal worlds are built, and it is more than most people can do to question any part of them. At the time, such philosophizing was beyond me. The incident was a painful lesson in the complexities of human nature.

There were as yet no boys in my life, which was by no means unusual. A few couples "went steady," and the affluent crowd had private parties and dated among themselves. Many of the girls went out with boys once in a while. But dating was no big deal. Naturally, the girls enjoyed male attention, but sexual involvement was a game not worth the candle, and everyone knew it. Moreover, we were not subject to a barrage of sexual stimuli from every quarter as young people are today. It was not a major concern. The whole climate was different from what it has become since.

What was unfortunate in my case was excessive timidity. I had no brothers and I had had little contact with boys. They were an unknown quantity, and it was because of them that so many restraints were laid upon me. When I found myself alone with one, I froze. What do you say to a boy? It was an inauspicious beginning.

My clothes were still a handicap. I had rebelled against my "Dutchy" dressmaker and begun to make my own dresses, and my failures and successes were about equally divided. I had persuaded my mother to give me a clothes allowance, and when it was gone it was gone, so I had to live with the results. Gradually I learned, and began to feel more at ease. In my senior year I had my first ready-made suit, with a bloused jacket and peplum, flattering to my matchstick figure. For class day Mother let me have a dress made by Irene's dressmaker, and it was charming: a flower-sprigged pink crepe with net yoke gathered at the neck into narrow beaded edging. This was happiness.

In my memories of my senior year, however, troubles predominate. It began with the election for the class advisory board. I was nominated along with Gatha Scott, one of the most popular girls in the class, and I lost by one vote. Against Gatha that was a very good showing, and I should have congratulated myself. Instead, I went home and cried bitterly. Later I was nominated for class historian and won. It afforded me no pleasure. It was inevitable, given my fear of rejection, that I should seek to avoid competition.

The greater part of the year passed uneventfully, but towards spring a thunderbolt struck. Doris' mother was leaving her job and she said she would see that I got it if I wanted it. Where had she ever got such an idea! Father had promised that I should go to college in the fall. If I were to put it off I might never get there. I knew absolutely that I would not be able to handle the situation; I had neither the confidence nor the energy. Father would undoubtedly expect me to save money to help with college expenses, and how could anybody save money out of a country school teacher's pay! The worst of it was that I was sure he would expect me to take the job, and so he did. He said it was time I learned the value of money. No excuses would do. I must apply.

So, one cold drizzly morning I took the train to Owosso to see Mrs. Grissinger and apply for the job. She lived in a rented room in a boarding house, that I would probably inherit—a dismaying prospect in itself. I don't think I have ever again felt so depressed. The interview was perfunctory. The job was mine if I could pass a three-day examination to be held in Grand Rapids sometime later. I was told what subjects I would be examined in, including agriculture. Mrs. Grissinger lent me a textbook, and I boned up on such matters as Bordeaux mixture.

The examinations were held in late May or early June, shortly before school closed, and I was excused to take them. I was half sick for fear of passing, yet it never occurred to me that I might fail deliberately. I did my best, as was my habit, ruing the day that I was born.

Fate was with me. The examinations were held in the *Press* building, in a room directly above the printing presses. The weather was intensely hot, and in the afternoon when the noisy presses started rolling, with vibrations that shook the mind as well as the building, the situation became almost intolerable. On the third afternoon, during the arithmetic test, which I should have passed with ease, my mind suddenly deserted me. The questions no longer had any meaning; the numbers swam around in a vacuum. There was a question about the volume of a silo; that is, of a cylinder. I knew the rule but I could not summon it up. I was finished.

Some weeks elapsed before I got a letter informing me of the results. Even with the help of 100 or near it in agriculture, I had failed dismally. The relief was so great that even the announcement of the opening of a junior college in the fall, which would postpone my enrollment in the university for another year, was only a minor disappointment.

Graduation was observed as usual with an admonitory speech. It was like Mr. Davis to have invited Rabbi Wise of New York, then a national celebrity, to give the address. I was astonished by his learning. Father was out of town but Mother was there with Aunt Kate, who was visiting from Colorado. Grandpa Broene was there, too, and he was distressed, less because the speaker was a Jew than because, in deference to him, the name of Jesus was omitted from the prayer that followed. To him, such a concession, even as a courtesy, was a betrayal.

There was a brief, happy sequel, a club houseparty at Port Sheldon on Lake Michigan. There were only three cottages besides ours, and only one of them was occupied so we had the place almost entirely to ourselves. This was a stretch of shore that was nearly inaccessible, since it lay across an unbridged river. We took a train to Holland, where we transferred to a small north-and-south line and were let off at a flag stop. There a farmer picked us up and drove us to the river beside his farm. Then we had to row across, one small boatload at a time, and before the farmer left us we had to learn to tie the boat up with a special knot so it would not pull loose in a storm.

It was a carefree week, tinged with nostalgia, since we would all be going our separate ways at the end of it. We did the aimless things that one does at the beach: loafed, swam, ate ravenously, lingered at twilight till the stars came out. One night some of us slept out. If there is a more uncomfortable bed than compressed sand with all the lumps in the wrong places I do not know what it is, but what is comfort compared to a night under the stars where they can be seen in all their glory!

One day four of us set out to walk the ten miles along the beach to Grand Haven. I have a hilarious snapshot of us, taken from the rear, that shows us in suit skirts, jackets over the arm. This was for the sake of respectability when we returned on the train. We had just started but we were already barefoot. This was the only time in my life that I have been seriously sunburned. The side of my face that had been towards the water was the color of boiled lobster; the other side was normal. The effect was rather startling. This led to another one-time experience. The following Sunday, Mother ordered me to stay home from church.

All that summer I felt vaguely apprehensive. The future that had beckoned so brightly when it was distant now loomed like a menacing cloud. The days of my dependence were nearly over. I took refuge in reading, but here, too, the future lay in waiting. I read *The Mill on the Floss*, and it affected me profoundly. Maggie was someone I could understand. In many ways I was like her. As I read, I *was* Maggie; and for the first time I understood, imaginatively, the dangers within our own natures. The obscure forces that brought disaster upon Maggie existed in all of us, existed in me. I was glad that I still had a few years of school ahead of me before I had to face the world alone.

* * *

This was the summer that World War I broke out in Europe. There had been mounting tension since June when an Austrian archduke was assassinated in Serbia. The incident had set a torch to old national enmities and foiled ambitions. Germany, which had long waited for an opportunity to expand its borders, took advantage of the situation to goad France and Russia into war. During the last few days of July the whole world waited tensely as events built up to a climax. By the middle of August, Europe was at war from the Ural Mountains to the Bay of Biscay; and England had come in on the side of France. By December the Balkans and the Middle East were also embroiled. This was war on an unprecedented scale.

It was most unsettling, especially since we had hoped, and tried to believe, that war among the great powers was obsolete. Was there not a Peace Court at the Hague? In this country we tried to shrug off our fears. War in Europe was not our concern. Still, from that day, the war was never out of mind.

7

HALLS OF LEARNING

I no longer remember when the decision was made that I should go to college, only that during my last year at high school the question was no longer whether, but where. I had set my heart on going to the university in Ann Arbor, but universities were alarmingly big, and Michigan was one of the biggest with a student population of around five thousand! Universities had a reputation for free thinking, and Mother had no more liking for thoughts flying around uncensored than Samuel Johnson had for birds flying around uncooked. Why shouldn't I go to one of the several small colleges in the state sponsored by the various Protestant sects? Olivet, for instance, where two of my friends were going? She didn't mention Hope College, the Dutch Reformed one; Father would have countered with Calvin, and we would have been back to square one. I tried to explain that my idea of education was not the kind of teachers and facilities that a small denominational college could afford; neither did I view favorably the idea of spending four years in a small town with no cultural advantages whatsoever. Next she proposed the agricultural college at Lansing, where girls could study home economics. That was not my idea either. I guess I just wore her down. The university it was.

I was disappointed about having to spend the first year at junior college, but I would have been ungrateful if I had objected. The teaching was probably better than I would have had as a freshman at the university, since it was the most experienced high school teachers who took on the college students. That year was not much different from those that preceded it except that we were a very small group and took no part in high school activities. There were about a dozen of us, equally divided between men and women. The men, with one or two exceptions, were a dull lot; and except for one couple neither sex showed any interest in the other. It was pretty flat.

I took English, German, European history, and biology (divided into zoology and botany) and enjoyed them all, except botany, which was mostly classification. Lab work was new to me and I found it interesting, but I was clumsy. Nothing ever seemed to go quite right. The first thing required of us was to draw an amoeba. The swarming life in a drop of water fascinated and alarmed me: worms and paramecia and the Lord knows what else, but no amoeba. I finally gave up hope and drew my idea of one. Miss Ellis observed drily that she had never seen one like it, but she did not press me. We had to collect earthworms before the ground froze and store them in tin cans for future use. When the time came, my can was empty. I didn't know whether to think the worms had slithered away in the night or simply evaporated. When I had observed everything inside a frog except the male organs, every frog I dissected turned out to be female. One day when I fished one out of the tank I left the cover off, and within minutes the lab was a madhouse of leaping frogs. Science was not for me.

In English we were given a list of about two hundred books from which to choose a certain number to read. My friend Jeannette Kiekintveld and I vied with each other to read the greatest number, and we both came close to reading the full list, greatly increasing our knowledge of literature, including foreign works.

During my high school years, my unbelief had become a torment. When I was eighteen I would be expected to join the church, and the propect of disappointing my father's expectations terrified me.

My senior year had come and gone without the feared crisis but now the minister who had served our church ever since I could remember accepted a call from another congregation, and before he left he made an all-out effort to bring as many young people as possible into the fold. My father put no pressure on me. Once I was grown he showed an unexpected reticence about inquiring into my personal affairs. My mother told me, however, that one of his brothers was needling him about why I did not "come forward." A showdown was imminent, and I felt hysterical. On the other hand, continued submission to my parents' rules of conduct was becoming more and more frustrating. I asked my mother, if I joined the church, would she and my father let me make my own decisions about right and wrong. She replied, "That seems fair."

So one cold winter night I set out for the minister's house to tell the assembled elders that I wanted to join the church. I wished the earth would swallow me up, but I arrived safely at the minister's door, and when I left I was a member in good standing of the Lagrave Avenue Christian Reformed Church.

I took communion once, having sat through the reading of the long communion service with its warning to communicants that if they partook of the blood and body of the Lord with sin in their hearts they were "eating and drinking damnation unto themselves." I knew then that what I had done was very wrong, and also very foolish. If I were to recant at this point, as I ought to do, my father would feel irreparably disgraced. It was unthinkable. I had merely exchanged one source of anxiety for another. During my college years it was possible to let the matter ride. I attended church during vacations and no questions were asked. This was, however, an uneasy truce. Sooner or later I would have to face the consequences of my action.

My friendship with Jeannette was the high spot of the year. Both her parents had died young, and she and a younger sister and brother had been raised by their maternal grandmother, who apparently was hard pressed to support three grandchildren. In order to go to high school, Jeannette had lived with and kept house for one of the teachers and her mother. She belonged to my club but I had not known her well until this year. Now we spent most of our free time together. When spring came we used to go to the library after school, or find some other excuse for going downtown, which lay in the opposite direction from home, and walk and talk until dinnertime. '

This was the beginning of a lifelong friendship that was almost sisterly. We had much in common and also fundamental differences. Jeannette knew what she wanted, which was enough money so she would never have to worry about it again.

She succeeded. When she died in 1951 she was advertising manager for Bloomingdale's in New York, maintaining a modern apartment in the fashionable East Fifties and sending her son to an exclusive private school. She sympathized with my search for work that was meaningful but considered it quixotic. A person could do nothing without money so why not settle down and do what it took to make it?

She must have kept her end in view from an early age. Her looks were unremarkable, and in the beginning her clothes were few and old and undistinguished; yet she saw to it that everywhere she went, people knew who she was. In college she wore folding eyeglasses on a long, black string, such as a dowager in the movies might wear; and when she put them on, slowly and deliberately, she might have been going to sign state papers. Later, when she smoked, she flourished a long cigarette-holder with a nonchalant air that seemed to lift her above the battle. When she had got what she wanted she dropped her mannerisms. They were pure publicity.

Towards the end of the school year, preparations for leaving home generated a good deal of excitement. I had been accepted by the university and admitted to Helen Newberry Residence, one of the first two women's dormitories, which both opened that year. Meta Prange and Ada Fitch, two classmates, were to live there too. We had received welcoming letters and a list of furnishings to bring. That summer we planned and shopped, and fretted because the time passed so slowly; and then one day everything was ready and I was on my way. At the last minute I was briefly overcome by the parting with my mother, but hope was running high and left little room for other feelings.

At last my years of waiting were over. I was actually in college and *my life was my own*. I loved my family, I loved them dearly in spite of our differences, but over-riding every other feeling was the exhilaration of being a free agent. I had not yet given thought to what responsibilities this might entail nor did I have the faintest notion what I was going to do with my freedom.

The dormitory was all I had hoped for and more. On first sight it was not prepossessing. The exterior had no style; it was merely a stuccoed box with porches on both of the long sides. The girls' rooms, most of them singles, were long and narrow, rather disconcerting at first. But the parlors were those of a comfortable home, nicely furnished, with enough good antiques to give them character. The dining room was light and cheerful, with two walls of glass doors opening onto the porches. There were nine tables, each seating eight to ten persons, and we sat down to meals and were nicely served.

First on the order of business was selecting courses. I had received a note saying that Professor So-and-so was to be my adviser, but I never looked him up. I saw no reason why I should consult a stranger about what I should take. This was foolish, but I was reacting against twenty years of being told what to do. No major was required at the time. Michigan was still under the spell of President Eliot of Harvard, who theorized that a student left to his own devices would find his way to what he needed. As a result I chose, each semester, what appealed to me at the moment.

My interest was always, first and foremost, in people: the heights and depths of their aspirations and their follies, the complexity of their motives, their infinite adaptability—none of this on a theoretical level. I dismissed metaphysics, rather too easily, as inevitably misguided; it was the old fable of the blind men judging the shape of an elephant by the part they happened to get hold of. I avoided English courses because I figured that I had a lifetime in which to explore my own language. I had no talent for science. That left foreign languages and history. To a certain extent my interests *were* taking me in the right direction. The trouble was that I had no end in view and that I was too much influenced by unimportant and irrelevant considerations. My abandonment of French after only three semesters is a good example.

I liked French; it was rational and lucid. I felt a sympathy for the French ways of seeing, and I enjoyed the wit. The first year I had the good fortune to have Philip Bursley for my instructor. Ada and Meta and I sat in the front row, Ada in the middle. She could never let an opportunity pass for creating a bit of excitement. She took to nudging Meta and me when we were called upon to recite, and we were both easily thrown off by that kind of thing. Meta invariably giggled. All three of us were learning easily and not bothering to really study.

After about a month of this we were called to Bursley's office and given a good scolding. He said we were disrupting the class and we were not learning French. If we were not going to learn it one way he would see to it that we learned it another way. We were each given a different book to read, without vocabulary, to be returned in one week with a written comment in French. What I understood of my first book was easily imparted in one or two sentences, but by the end of the semester I was reading French fiction with little difficulty. That summer I read Victor Hugo's *Quatre Vingt Treize*, which I found in the public library at home.

The result was that in the following year, under another teacher, I found the pace intolerably slow and ceased to pay attention in class or out. I should not have been surprised when I was transferred to a class for slow learners. An appeal to Mr. Bursley got me shifted back in fairly short order, but I dropped out at the end of the semester, unwilling to get down to business and learn grammar and composition.

I had better luck with German. In the middle of my second year Mr. Eggert, my instructor, told me I was wasting my time and suggested that I apply for permission to skip the next semester's work and go directly into a reading course, which I did, and permission was granted. The next semester, with Professor Hildner, I read two plays by Goethe and got on all right; so the next year I elected two more advanced courses with Professor Boucke, whom we all called Herr Boucke. One was *Faust* and the other was a comprehensive coverage of Goethe's other works.

The first week in the latter course was discouraging. The assignment was the essay on Gothic architecture. I tried reading it without a dictionary and could make nothing of it. I read it with a dictionary; still, no success. Perhaps it had been a mistake to try to get on so fast. I told Herr Boucke that I was afraid I was not ready for his course. He patted my shoulder reassuringly and said, "Child, if it was in English you would not understand it. Don't worry." I stayed.

These two courses were probably the most valuable I took; less for the subject matter, though that was important, than for the experience of being taught by a real scholar who was much more than a scholar. He brought everything he knew to bear on the subject in hand; and he seemed to know everything in the fields of literature and philosophy, however exotic. He would turn the subject around, exposing one facet after another to the light, until the whole was luminous.

He was a grandfatherly little man, in late middle age, stout, with the knobbiest bald head I have ever seen. Low in the back, ear to ear, was a single row of red ringlets. His face was cherubic, with friendly blue eyes and a small red moustache. In winter he came bundled up to his eyes in a heavy wool scarf and would not permit a window to be opened even a crack.

This wise and kind man, along with several others, was forced out of the university towards the end of World War I because of his German birth. I was told that he went back to Germany heartbroken.

According to a later report, he was teaching at Heidelberg.

The history courses that I found the most interesting were those given by William Lytle Schurz. His field was Latin America and the age of discovery, including the trade with the Orient and the history of the major Oriental countries. He was young and good looking and unabashedly romantic, which was all to the good because the tale was all of derring-do. Schurz later distinguished himself in the United States foreign service.

The buildings on campus were heterogeneous and by no means beautiful; but old University Hall with its beautiful bronze doors and vine-covered wings, and the old library with its round reading room had charm; and the great old elms that lined all the main walks were a pleasure in all seasons and transformed the scene from spring through fall with patterns of dappled shade. Classrooms on upper floors were in the treetops, and sometimes in April when the trees leafed out in lacy webs against a blue sky, it was difficult to keep one's mind on the business in hand.

Ex-president Angell still occupied the president's house, adjoining the library, and he could often be seen reading near one of the windows. He liked to take walks around campus, greeting the students he passed as if he knew them all. He was a beautiful old man: wise and good and seemingly serene. His presence was like a benediction.

Social life centered around the dormitory, and my memories of it are warm. This is owing in large part to Mrs. Erie Leighton Gates, the director that first year, who must have been the world's best housemother. She had a natural courtesy to which we instinctively responded with our best behavior.

Helen Newberry was not too big. There were about seventy of us and it was run as much as possible like a home. Meals were excellent; we had our own dietician and a first-rate cook. At breakfast and lunch we came and went at our convenience, but we all went in to dinner together, and we were required to be on time and to be neatly dressed.

Tea at four on weekdays was a ritual. It was usually served in the small back parlor, but in fine weather the tea-cart was sometimes rolled out onto the south porch. Friends took to coming in at that hour. It was nice and relaxed. When I was in Ann Arbor in later years I often stopped by at tea time to have a chat with my old friend Lillian Brazell.

An account of life at Helen Newberry would be incomplete without mention of Lillian. For eighteen years that I know of, and I don't know how many more, she presided at the telephone switchboard, distributed the mail, answered the doorbell, took messages, and was a friend to all.

Lillian was painfully deformed. Both her back and her chest

protruded in a sharp angle as if she had been compressed. This was the result of an accident her mother had had before she was born. She had a sharp mind and a ready Irish wit and the unflagging good spirits of those who have known the depths of suffering and survived. The only word to describe her is gay. Where Lillian was, there was laughter.

She had hoped to attend the university, but she did not have the necessary high school credentials, and she had been denied the alternative of taking entrance examinations; so she worked at the dorm and brightened the lives of five or six generations of college girls.

Saturday afternoons in the fall, when the football team played at home, always had a holiday air. The stadium was small, and the games were attended mainly by students and their guests. Admission to all sports events was a fee of five dollars at the time of registration. Seats were not reserved. A group of us from the house used to go early and get front seats on the center line. The streets between the campus and the athletic field were jammed with students, which added to the excitement. At street corners vendors sold hot chestnuts. For big games there was a proliferation of big yellow 'mums. The weather could usually be counted on to be fair and crisp and not too cold. In the evening there were parties all over town. It was fun.

There were five of us in the house from Grand Rapids who were fairly congenial, and at first we stayed together. We went on picnics up the river or on the island or in the arboretum and sometimes went out together for a snack in the afternoon. It didn't take much to deplete my dollar-a-month allowance. Still, it went quite a long way in those days. Movies were a dime and so were ice cream sundaes. Banana splits were somewhat more extravagant at fifteen cents. Sometimes we had tea with little tea sandwiches at Foster's gift shop, or with chocolate fudge cake at a tearoom around the corner on Thayer Street.

Before long our circle of friends widened. One of my first new ones, who was to be a friend for life, was Gertrude Gunn from Detroit. She had been orphaned when she was very young and had been brought up by her maternal grandfather, a physician, and a maiden aunt. At first she didn't interest me, every move she made was deliberate and proper, but it was soon evident that her staid demeanor overlaid a wonderful zest for living and that she had a brand of humor all her own. Of all the people I have known, she had the greatest tolerance of human foibles; and she derived endless amusement from them.

I did not see a great deal of Jeannette. She was waiting table three times a day at a large boardinghouse and had little leisure. We dropped in on each other rather frequently for a brief chat, and she sometimes came to see me when she wanted to get something off her mind. It was an old-shoe relationship. We both took comfort in knowing that the other was there.

For the first time in my life I was able to get out in the country as often as I pleased. Anna Miller, of East Orange, New Jersey, was my favorite walking companion. In good weather, and sometimes not so good, we used to buy a bag of peanuts or, in the fall, a couple of Northern Spy apples, and head for the country, usually about three o'clock, and walk and loiter until dinnertime. Along the river, upstream from State Street on both sides, and down stream on the far side, there were open patches of woods where, in spring, violets and wild phlox could be had for the picking; and in fall, goldenrod and asters.

The arboretum was full of delights, and on weekdays it was almost deserted. Where the ground falls away near the Geddes Avenue entrance, the hollow was a river of soft, tall grass, riffled by every passing breeze. In spring when the candles of new growth appeared on the Scotch pine trees, they might be alive with cedar waxwings. In late spring a large planting of sweetbriar roses, the eglantine of English poetry, perfumed the air with its fragrant foliage even when it was not in blossom. In a small area of natural woods towards the hospital, a pair of scarlet tanagers returned every year. One Easter Sunday when I went out to the arboretum and met up with a homesick boy from Maine, we had a migration of bluebirds all to ourselves. They were everywhere, in the trees, in the air. I have never since seen anything like it.

Those afternoons were life-saving. I needed freedom from pressure more than anything else in the world, and this was daily refreshment. In fine weather my studies got skimped but they could wait. I was not studying for a profession; I was sampling the wonders of the world, stuffing them in like a ruminant, to be digested later.

One thing I regretted was that I could not afford to attend musical events. The university brought fine musicians to Ann Arbor all through the winter season, and during May Festival week there were concerts every afternoon and evening. Any student could obtain free admission to the latter by joining the university chorus, but I failed the audition. Members of the chorus enjoyed not only the concerts but a whole year of rehearsals.

A downtown theater brought good plays to town. Even though seats in the gallery were cheap I could not afford to go often, but I managed it a few times. When Forbes-Robertson, a celebrated English actor, came in *Hamlet*, I went to see him. I found him cold and unappealing but Ophelia was lovely and moving. When she came on in the mad scene, strewing flowers, "Here's fennel for you, and columbine," I was entranced.

I also saw Sarah Bernhardt on her last American tour, when she had but one leg and performed seated. Even so, critics are said to have acclaimed her as hypnotic, incandescent, a miracle worker. I regret that my only memory of that evening is the sadness that came over me. Madame Sarah had been so beautiful, so vital, for so long that she had seemed ageless; but in the end, time had not spared her. A new and poignant realization of the meaning of mortality seems to have over-ridden all other impressions.

In spring, canoeing was a favorite pastime. Seasoned canoeists sometimes portaged around the dam for all-day trips, but most were contented to stay below the dam and pass a leisurely afternoon or evening on the water and along the bank. Some winters were cold enough for skating on the river. There was some bob-sledding, but it was not popular after a girl was seriously injured.

Dancing was the all-season favorite social activity. In my day that meant fox-trots and waltzes, smooth and graceful, to light, catchy tunes with sentimental lyrics. After dinner at the dorm we moved back the tables and danced for about an hour to a victrola that had to be cranked about every five minutes. On Saturday evenings there were mixers at the gym and at the parish houses of several churches. Occasionally dances were held at the dorm. There were always girls who were kind enough to get me a date, and at first I accepted their offers gratefully, but the situation was too painful. Sometimes the boy was as frightened as I was, and we would both sit tongue-tied and paralyzed. Before long I avoided parties. It was no fun to sit in my room with music and laughter floating up from below, but it was less distressing than feeling inadequate in company.

A chance remark by Olivia Demmon marked a turnabout in this unfortunate state of affairs. Demmy was a freshman from Grand Rapids, a high-spirited girl, who had a brother in the forestry depart-ment. She appeared to have the whole department to draw on for dates, and she became an unofficial matchmaker. She also knew a number of young men from the West Side of Grand Rapids, including Alex McColl, an architecture student, whom she thought I should meet. She arranged a date and, as was usual with me, it was a flop. "The trouble with you," Demmy said to me, "is that you never let yourself go for one minute." It was true. That had been the goal of all my training and it had succeeded all too well. Surely there could be no harm in loosening up a bit. I began to practice on the girls in the house, and slowly I learned to be more spontaneous and found that it made life a lot easier.

Most of the girls at the university at that time came from families with comfortable incomes; and usually, I think, one or both of their parents were college graduates. Although many of them would work for a while, they were not under pressure to earn a living. Most of them anticipated no career except marriage. College was their preparation for life as the wives of educated men, and it was a not-unworthy objective. These were the women who would later staff, and often direct, the many volunteer agencies without which this country could hardly function. They were the women who were to raise the status of art in a society where there still remained much of the frontiersman's disdain of anything not immediately useful. They were also women who would know how to help their children develop their abilities.

One of the advantages of the University of Michigan was that it drew students from all around the country, which was not true of many state universities. At Helen Newberry we had the honor of having the first two Oriental women to come to Michigan on a Barbour scholarship. They were both Japanese.

Mutsu Kikuchi was very pretty and very popular with Japanese men, of whom there were quite a large number. She was also very proud. Girls who lived on her floor said that she used to sit in her room, all dressed and ready, while she kept her callers waiting. Her manner was formal and reserved. I don't think anyone knew her well. Sad to say, Mutsu died before school reopened in the fall, reportedly of tuberculosis.

Kameyo Sadakata was as different as night from day. She was not pretty and she never had a date, so far as I know. She studied all the time, and she had much trouble with the English language and was afraid to speak it. How much she understood, it was impossible to tell. Although conversing with her was extremely difficult, she endeared herself to everyone by her gentleness and sweetness. In spite of her difficulty with the language she persisted through medical school; and by 1927 or '28 she had achieved a sufficient reputation in Japan as a pediatrician to be sent back to Ann Arbor by her government for further study.

During my first year, so full of novelty, there was no room in my mind for anything but excitement and pleasure, but in my junior year I began to feel a vague discontent. All the new impressions were stirring up my mind. Questions were popping like a string of Japanese firecrackers, and I had no one to talk with. I do not recall ever hearing any serious discussions among the girls except on the subject of men. Serious interests were not a social asset. If a woman was intellectually inclined she did well to keep it dark. I would have liked to talk with one or two of my teachers who appeared to be sympathetic, but I was too timid. I did not, however, lose much time fretting but looked around for something interesting to get involved in.

The first thing I did was to try out for the junior-girls' play. This was a tradition, like the men's opera; but unlike the opera we played to small houses, all female. It would have been scandalous to permit men to see women in pants! The play was a musical with a large cast; there must have been several dozen of us. It was time consuming, we rehearsed every afternoon for weeks, but it was fun, and it generated much good feelings and a sense of class unity.

That year I also went to work on the *Michigan Daily*. It was staffed almost entirely by men but, as on all newspapers, women were employed to report activities that men were not interested in. It was not the reporting that interested me; I had had an idea. Here was an opportunity to meet men in a situation where I had no need to worry about the impression I was making. I would beard the lion in his den!

I went to the office every afternoon to pick up my assignments, and again later to write up my copy. This was a slack time and there were always several people, mostly men, sitting around, talking. Before I knew it I was behaving without self-consciousness.

In my senior year I became much more involved. The war had intervened. Most of the junior and senior men had already left, and there were not enough younger ones with experience to fill the editorial positions. Since the editor had to be up most of the night, there was a different editor for each night of the week. I became one of them. There were three or four of us who were women. At first the men resented our presence and some of them tried to dissuade us, saying that the linotype man was seldom sober and that his language was unfit for women's ears. We were not deterred. Besides, they needed us.

We edited the stories, calculated space, wrote headlines, read proof, and soothed the linotype man when he sputtered about too many corrections. (His bark was worse than his bite, and his language when ladies were present was impeccable.) By the end of the year I had lost my shyness. Going to work on the *Daily* was the smartest thing I ever did.

The entry of the United States into the war was, of course, the most momentous event of those years. There had been indications for many months that it was inescapable, but anticipation did little to dull the blow. Nobody really believes in disaster until it is upon him.

I remember being wakened early that April morning in 1917 by a newsboy beneath my window, shouting, "Extry, extry! U.S. declares war," or something of the sort. I ran to the window, although obviously there would be nothing to see but the boy and his papers. Then I remember sitting on the edge of my bed for a long time, trying to take in the meaning of this incredible news.

Overnight the campus was a different place. In a matter of weeks the scarcity of men was noticeable. More left by every train. Those that remained appeared to be constantly drilling. The drill ground was a large open space between the chemistry building and Waterman gym. When girls passed by on the adjoining walk, the drill sergeants amused themselves by directing their men to march straight at the girls, which they were obliged to do with poker faces. No more whistles! There was nothing for the girls to do but run for it.

In May there was a mass meeting in Hill auditorium the night before one hundred and fifty men were to leave for the army. I wrote my sister that it was very impressive, but all I remember about it is that there was singing by a student named Thomas E. Dewey, who was to be governor of New York and to run for president of the United States against Harry Truman in 1948.

The girls had been knitting all along for soldiers overseas, but now they were asked to redouble their efforts. We took our knitting everywhere we went, even to lectures. We were also asked to contribute old linen for bandages; it is lint-free. The Red Cross held first-aid classes; I remember being the victim one evening. Alice Lloyd, class of 1916, later dean of women, who had signed up for nurses' training, was encouraging the women in the graduating class to do the same. Suddenly everyone was serious.

My personal life had also been turned upsidedown. My mother was seriously ill during the whole of my junior year and she died in early June. It was the most devastating blow of my life. We had just begun to appreciate each other as individuals. On a summer evening the year before, when we were talking together on the front porch, she had said to me, "If I could bring you up over again I would do it so differently." I thought I heard regret in her voice and I wanted to dispel it, so I embraced her and kissed her lightly and said in a joking voice, "Don't you like the result?" That put an end to confidences. I wish I had let her talk. I wish I might have kept her a few years longer.

Until after the funeral I seemed to be living inside a bubble, removed from the meaningless comings and goings of people around me. As soon as I could get away I went back to Ann Arbor to take make-up exams. I could have waited till fall, but I wanted to get them out of the way, and I wanted to get out of that empty house.

That summer was a misery. Aunt Louise had given up her job and come to live with us, expecting to take Mother's place. Her melancholy was oppressive. She resented any sign of returning normalcy in Anna and me. I was not yet sufficiently mature to understand her awful loneliness. My mother's inexhaustible love and patience had been all that made her life bearable, and she could see nothing ahead but desolation. In the end, life was kinder to her than might have been expected. She spent most of her later years with Mathilda, and they got along together surprisingly well. She had a home at last.

After I went back to Ann Arbor in the fall, Father closed the house, and he and Anna went to live with Uncle Johannes and his first wife, Margaret Kleinhuizen. Aunt Louise went back to work for another ten or twelve years.

The next winter I went through a new stage of grief. I had periods of depression alternating with periods of hysterical excitement, not unlike intoxication. At such times everything seemed hilariously funny, and I would disturb the peace of quiet hours. Miss Wells could not understand it. I was out of favor for a long time and regained it only when I was invited to join Phi Beta Kappa in the spring.

I must have made a nuisance of myself in other ways, too, because my friend Mabel Wilson brought me up short one day, telling me that I must stop burdening other people with my troubles if I wanted to have any friends left. I took her advice and pulled myself together. Work saved the day. A heavy schedule and my night job at the *Daily* left little time for giving way to feelings.

*   *   *

So far I have said little about my sister. In the beginning I saw her as a competitor. I had to give up my cradle to her. Whatever I played with she wanted, and Mama would say, "Let her have it; she is only a baby." For a couple of years when I was perhaps eleven or twelve, I took out my unhappiness on her, bossing her around and being mean generally, until she stood up to me one day and refused to be bullied. Later we were on good terms but our temperaments were very different. We did few things together except as a family. Mother's death brought us together. As big sister I was the person she naturally turned to for comfort, and I began to take a protective interest in her. Eventually we became good friends, respecting each other's differences.

She had a rough time the year Mother was ill. A housekeeper came in mornings, but since Father was home only on weekends Anna had to be at home every afternoon and evening. It must have been agonizing for her to see Mother failing day by day. I had begged Father to let me stay home that year, but he would not hear of it. I had set out to get a college education, and I must get my diploma without delay.

The next year, when Anna was staying with Uncle Johannes, she again had no social life. They were living in the east end of town near the city water reservoir, which was then far out, and too far from transportation for a young woman to go out alone in the evening. Her two best friends were in college in Lansing. The school year had scarcely begun when she wrote to me:

> Sunday afternoons are extremely dull. They all sleep most of the afternoon. I seldom go out because most affairs come in the evening. I never see anyone. I almost wish I wasn't in junior college this year. I'm busy all the time and still don't accomplish anything. . . . I don't get a chance to practice more than about four hours a week. . . . Honestly, if you knew how stupid things are around here you wouldn't blame me for longing for Nov. 8. [*She was planning to visit me on my birthday*.] Write often. It is the only fun I get.

Those two years changed Anna permanently. She had been vivacious and carefree. Now she became serious and thoughtful; and although she retained her happy disposition, the child who had bubbled over with gaiety was gone forever.

*　*　*

Until my senior year I had put off thinking about where I was headed. Graduation had seemed remote, and then suddenly it was very near, and I became anxious. If I didn't have a job when June came, there would be nothing to do but go home to Grand Rapids, and what then? Teaching in a grade school, since I did not have a teacher's certificate. Living with Father and being told when to wear my rubbers. A replay of my childhood. To Father I would always be his little girl to be cared for and guided.

I saw one small ray of hope. I had taken the beginning course in economics to see what it was all about, and I had done well in it. There was a slight chance that it might lead to something. And it sounded impressive: corporations, foreign trade, money and credit. I loaded up on economics. I had no interest in it whatsoever.

When spring came I was one of three girls in Professor Dowrie's course in banking. Mabel Curley, a graduate student, and I were doing well, and he showed considerable interest in us. One day he asked, "How would you girls like to work for the Guaranty Trust Company in New York?" New York! How would I like to fly?

Mabel's mother was a widow who went everywhere Mabel went. They planned to take an apartment in New York, and they asked me if I would like to share it—another hurdle cleared! I could take my time about finding a place to live. The only difficulty was telling Father that I was going so far away. He took it very hard.

> You have perhaps been wondering why I did not write but, my dear girl, it has been such a time for me to think that all our looking forward to being together again has been for naught. You don't know how it made me feel, because I surmised from your letter that it would be for a long time, and I feel that it should be so, because if you succeed you must stick and I want you to succeed, but nevertheless it will leave such an empty place.

He went on to say that Mr. Dosker, a brother-in-law of the Steketee brothers and a member of the firm, "says for you to go to the Fifth Ave. Presbyterian church and take an active part in Sunday School and church work, so as to come in contact with the best people and to improve your Christian character." Then Father turned to his own plans.

> And now I want to make a confession. . . . I want to join the Y [*YMCA*] and go to France, because I feel that I might be of some good there, and it is too big a thing not to have had some part in it. But what must I do with Anna?. . . I can only do it because I feel it's my duty and I shall try to make her see it in that light.

This, in the same letter in which he lamented that we could not be together in Grand Rapids. Evidently his feelings were in turmoil.

The YMCA turned him down on account of his German ancestry. I think it was better so. Father was only forty-eight, healthy and fit, and would have been good in some ways with the men behind the lines. He was, however, so utterly unable to admit any views but his own that I am afraid he would have run into difficulties sooner or later and perhaps returned disillusioned. And I am not at all sure that he could have borne seeing the consequences of war close up. Emotionally he was as vulnerable as a child.

He came to Ann Arbor for the graduation exercises, which cheered me a little, but we were both rueful, thinking of Mother, who should have been there too. The ceremonies were clouded by the absence of nearly all the men in the class. They were represented by stars in a large flag, and that flag dominated all our thoughts. My school days ended on a minor chord.

My job was to begin the first of August. Meanwhile I returned to Grand Rapids with Father, who had recently reopened the house. I used the time to make two pastel-colored linen dresses, which were useless in New York. We did not talk about the future.

8

FIRST VOYAGE

New York was a tremendous experience. I grew in ways that I might never have grown if I had remained in a familiar environment. As things turned out, I was overwhelmed. In six months I was back home again, but the young woman who returned was not the young woman who had left such a short time before.

I arrived in the city on a hot summer morning after an overnight train ride. Mabel and her mother met me at the station and took me to breakfast and then to the apartment they were renting from friends who were in Europe for the summer. It was on West 55th Street, just off Fifth Avenue. Although I did not know it, this was living in style. All I could see was how small it was. There were a large living room and bedroom, a small kitchen, and a foyer where we ate breakfasts and dinners at a folding table. There was also a maid's room, which fell to me, just wide enough to permit a person to get in and out of bed. I was appalled that people of means should live in such small quarters.

The daily life of the city was another shock: the hordes of workers pouring into the business districts in the morning and jostling each other for standing room in the outbound cars at night; the absence of green growing things; the scant ration of sky. How could people live like this! Riding to work on the El through the garment district, I could see, through the windows, large numbers of men at work, cutting army uniforms from high stacks of khaki cloth—all day, every day, the same rough cloth, the same motions. In the evening, a stone's throw from the trains, people leaned out of their windows to get a breath of air, seemingly oblivious to the noise. Sometimes when the lights were lit, they revealed the cramped little rooms where whole families lived and children grew up. No privacy, no space.

If anyone had asked me what I expected of work at the bank I could not have answered. I had never given it a thought. My mind had been set on New York; the work was incidental until I got there. The actuality was dismaying. The Guaranty Trust was one of the largest banks in the country. It occupied the whole of a skyscraper in the Wall Street district, with basements and sub-basements. It was a monster, and I had indentured myself to it for $15.00 a week, not even enough to live on decently.

My first assignment was mildly interesting. I worked independently, trying to trace the owners of long-unused accounts. It was a kind of sleuthing, yielding a certain satisfaction when I was successful. Another advantage was that it took me all over the bank. I was never able to stand being confined to a desk. I was willing to wait and see what would happen next.

That I survived those early weeks as well as I did was largely owing to the Curleys. So long as I lived with them, I enjoyed advantages unknown to most city-dwellers. One of these was a private car. Mabel had bought a swanky, bright green Hudson, and she was still excited about her new toy. Every evening, unless we had something else to do, we took it out and explored the city. I could have ridden the subways for a lifetime and known less about the city than I did within a few weeks of my arrival. Harlem on a Saturday night could have been a setting for a musical comedy. Young dandies stood about on the street corners watching the girls, who paraded by in costumes that shouted for a stage—castoffs, probably, from wealthy mistresses; colorful silks and velvets, formal and informal.

We sensed no danger. I do not know whether it existed. Race relations were quiet on the surface. The people appeared to be too much absorbed in their own Saturday night business to pay any attention to us. We did, however, get a scare in a foreign community one evening. It was still light, and the street was filled with children at play. We could barely move ahead. Thanks to our crawling pace, there was no damage beyond a bruised knee when a boy darted out in front of us—purposely, I think—and was knocked down. Immediately we were surrounded by a mob of infuriated parents, screaming and threatening. Until a policeman showed up, my heart was in my mouth. Having ascertained that the boy was uninjured, he told Mabel to start the car and keep going. The crowd gave way reluctantly as we crept ahead, thankful to get out with our skins intact. We did no more slumming.

On weekends we explored the countryside around, up the river or along the sound into Connecticut. There were as yet no road signs, no numbered roads. Mabel's guidebook read like old land titles: left at the cemetery, straight ahead for three miles, right at the schoolhouse. We got lost just once, on the Sawmill River Parkway. It was late, there was no one about, and nothing to do but keep going. After cruising without direction for an hour or more, we found ourselves back in the same spot. The second time around, by pure chance, we came out at a point that we recognized. We were fortunate that we had not run out of gas.

I think it was the first of October when I left the Curleys for a rented room on West 85th Street. It was a few doors from Amsterdam Avenue, in a neighborhood of not-too-well-off families, many of whom let rooms to students at the Juilliard School of Music. Mildred Royce, one of the women at the bank, lived there with her mother in a family-size apartment and took roomers. Someone slept in every room in the place except the kitchen. Mildred occupied the couch in the living room. A voice student from Maine had a small room that opened off this one. Mrs. Royce slept on a cot in the dining room. Only Elizabeth Hughes and I had rooms of our own.

Elizabeth was the niece of Charles Evans Hughes, justice of the U.S. Supreme Court, who had run unsuccessfully for President two years before. She was a graduate of Barnard College and, I believe, of the Juilliard school. She earned her living by playing the piano at social functions, and she must have made a pretty good living because she was always booked up. Yet she lived no better than I. There were as yet not enough women living away from home to create a demand for studio apartments. Few would have been able to afford them, and to live alone would probably have been considered scandalous. The situation was not peculiar to New York or even to big cities.

My room was small and gloomy, with one window opening on an airshaft that carried sounds from all over the house. On Sunday mornings a voice student on a lower floor practiced scales at an early hour. Then another woman, in a room opposite mine, would lean out of her window and mimic the first one in a deliberately unpleasant, twangy voice. I woke up regularly to this duet on the only day of the week when I might have slept a little longer.

Mrs. Royce was little, old, and worn—about sixty, I should say. I paid her five or six dollars a week, I think, for my room and breakfasts. I am sure she did as well as she could by me, but it was not very much. The *pièce de résistance* every morning was a boiled egg of the lowest quality on the market, with a slightly fishy taste not entirely concealed by a generous dose of salt.

My weekly $15.00, little enough, had been reduced by a "voluntary" withholding of two or three dollars to purchase a Liberty Bond. Carfare to work and back cost sixty cents a week. Silk stockings, which lasted a week, with luck, took another dollar. The bank furnished a substantial mid-day meal, so I ate all I could and allowed myself thirty-five cents for dinner. After work, partly to avoid the rush-hour crowds, partly to save a nickel, and partly to stretch my legs, I usually walked the three miles uptown to 38th or 39th Street to a YWCA cafeteria where the food was good and cheap. Recreation that cost anything more than a little wear and tear on shoe leather was out. With a Thanksgiving bonus I bought a marked-down winter coat. I had never been so poor.

All this was, of course, only one side of the coin. The city itself was all the excitement I needed for the time being. I never tired of exploring it in what little time I had. Riverside Park was two short blocks west of where I lived. Central Park was three long blocks east;

and the Metropolitan Museum, on the other side of the park, just one mile. There I made my first acquaintance with original paintings and ancient artifacts. The attractions were inexhaustible. I always stopped for tea in the pleasant tearoom before I left and lingered a while to forget I was a working girl and savor the moment.

On Saturday afteroons I liked to further my acquaintance with Fifth and Madison Avenues, from Altman's at 35th Street to the small shops on 57th Street, and the cross streets between, where all the wealth of the world was on display. A cat may look at a king.

I also discovered the public library. Reading was of lesser importance that year so filled with novelty, but I remember the thrill of carrying the card of a great library.

The walk to dinner took me through the financial district, up Broadway to Madison Square, and then up Fifth Avenue. In Union Square a navy training ship had been installed, and there was always a wash on the line. The unexpected domesticity of undergarments floating over a public square never failed to amuse me.

In New York, as nowhere else except Washington, there were reminders of the war at every turn. It was, of course, only the pageantry that we saw and it was strangely thrilling, a heightening of awareness of life and death. For all their dash and color, these uniforms, these flags, these brass bands were reminders that, overseas, men were dying in cold and mud in the trenches. That knowledge pervaded everything; and yet, of all things, it seemed least real.

The unexpected happened regularly: a Brazilian band, resplendent in scarlet uniforms, blowing its way up Riverside Drive; or a contingent of handsome Australians, all spit and polish, with Sam Browne belts, marching along Fifth Avenue to "God Save the King."

All the songs were war songs now. Many were sentimental: "There's a long, long trail awinding," and "Keep the home fires burning." Others, like "Tipperary" and "Over There," were spirited marching songs:

> Over there, over there,
> Send the word, send the word over there,
> That the Yanks are coming, The Yanks are coming,
> The drums rum-tumming ev'rywhere.
>
> . . . .
>
> We'll be over, we're coming over,
> And we won't come back till it's over over there.[3]

The words by themselves would make no heart beat faster; but set to music, with the roll of drums and the confident voices of the brasses, and sung by men committed to do or die, the song became a promise of victory.

The all-time favorite of the men in camp was an early hit of Irving Berlin's.

> Oh, how I hate to get up in the morning,
> Oh, how I love to remain in bed,
> For the hardest blow of all
> Is to hear the bugler call,
> "You've got to get up, You've got to get up,
> You've got to get up in the morning."
>
> Some day I'm going to murder the bugler.
> Some day they're going to find him dead.
> I'll amputate his reveille
> And step upon it heavily,
> And spend the rest of my life in bed.[4]

An alternate version of the last lines, presumably improvised in camp, carried the vindictiveness a step farther:

> And then I'll get that other pup,
> The guy that gets the bugler up.

It was the humor of those who whistle in the dark.

There were canteens all over town where soldiers and sailors might spend an evening or a holiday with carefully selected young women in a supervised setting. Mildred Royce introduced me at the Soldiers' and Sailors' Club in the Murray Hill section of Madison Avenue. The house belonged to a branch of the Roosevelt family; and an elderly Mrs. Roosevelt, beautiful and dignified, was always present to keep an eye on things. The furniture, except for a large buffet and a few chairs, had been removed from three rooms that opened into each other with wide doors. There, every evening, a teacher gave dancing lessons for half an hour, and then there was dancing for the rest of the evening. Each of the young women gave one evening a week.

The men were, for the most part, a bunch of homesick boys, many of them from farms and small towns in Iowa, Nebraska, Tennessee. Some were soldiers stationed at Camp Upton in Yaphank, Long Island. Some were sailors on shore leave or on duty in New York. Many came regularly, and each of the girls had a following. One of my friends was a petty officer in the navy medical corps, who was extraordinarily moody. Sometimes all he wanted was to sit and talk, and at such times he would mutter about not being fit company for a decent girl. I have no idea what he felt guilty about. Other times he was good company.

I remember a few others: an amusing sergeant from the South who showed the same politeness and handed out the same line to every girl in turn; a British sailor who could dance like no one else. Waltzing with him, one felt as light as air. Another British sailor seemed a child; I could not refrain from asking him how he came to be in the navy. The sense of his answer was that the navy caught them young; no one in his right mind would sign up if he was old enough to know what he was doing. He may have been sixteen at the outside. He looked more like fourteen to me.

One of the sailors' favorite occupations was to show the girls how to make the regulation knot in their ties. First the tie must be put around the girl's neck. Then she must stand in front of her teacher, facing the same way, for, as everybody knows, a person gets all mixed up when he tries to reverse the procedure. This necessitates putting both arms around the pupil, and it takes a little time, since the knot is intricate. Then the tie is given a slight, final pull, and all the work comes undone and has to be repeated. All very pleasant.

One day in October I woke up feeling very sick. I called the bank to say that I would not be in, and then went to see a doctor across the street. I told him I was afraid I was getting the flu and asked him to give me something that would see me through if I was unable to come in again. He gave me a prescription for a nasal spray and some pills, and that was the extent of my medical attention. I was one of the first persons in New York to come down with the virulent type of influenza that killed thousands of people that year.

For a week I downed my unappetizing breakfast somehow, spent the day in bed, and dragged myself out to a short-order restaurant on the corner for my only other meal. More often than not I could eat nothing when I got there. I don't know what kept me going. At night I would fall into a feverish sleep and wake up with my heart pounding wildly. After a week I felt enough better to try to go to work, but by the time I got to the bank I was so sick that I had to turn around and go home again.

By this time I could not stand my gloomy room any longer. I had a physical hunger for the sun. So every day I spent my mornings in Riverside Park with the old men and the vagrants, soaking up sunshine. It may have helped. At any rate, I got well, though for many weeks I felt weak and depressed.

By the time I was on my feet again, the flu was all over town and all over the country. Letters from Ann Arbor told me that the gym had been made into an emergency hospital. One of my *Michigan Daily* friends of the year before had died. I was glad I had not known the extent of the danger while I was sick and alone.

All this time I had heard nothing from my father. He had got my old and new addresses mixed up. So I was worried about him too. My longing for my mother returned full force. I was desolate.

I decided that I must do something about meeting people and got in touch with the local Michigan Alumnae Association. The women I met were all much older than I, but I learned that they sponsored a lounge and meeting place for service men, and I signed up as a Sunday evening hostess.

It was not an officers' club, but the first evening I was there an ensign from Detroit came in to see if he could locate a friend. The chaperone called me over to see if I could help, and we discovered that we had mutual friends. It was the beginning of a friendship that made the remainder of my time in New York much more enjoyable. He asked if he might see me home, to which I agreed. On the way to the El station he suggested that we have something to eat first, so we took a train downtown to Greenwich Village to a restaurant on the ground floor of an old brick house. It was very nice, filled with couples or small parties, eating and drinking quietly. The drinks were evidently alcoholic, and when the waiter asked what he might bring me I didn't know what to answer. When I said, "Milk, please," he stood transfixed, as much at a loss as I had been the moment before.

My escort said, "The lady would like a glass of milk." He was greatly amused.

After that we dated quite regularly on weekends, usually going to the movies. We corresponded for several months after we had both gone back to Michigan, and I saw him once more. When I realized that he was getting serious, I backed away. He was a thoroughly nice person but he had no spark. At thirty or so he was already a junior executive in a large manufacturing company. Business was all he knew or was interested in. It had been pleasant to find at long last that I was able to interest a man. It had given me confidence and had aroused a flirtatious instinct that I did not know I possessed. It had not occurred to me that I might be playing with serious feelings. It is unfortunate that some things can be learned only at the expense of another person.

My father's letters, when they came, only added to my distress. He was so very lonely, and I knew how much he missed me. I must have written to him about my dislike of working at the bank, for he wrote:

> I trust we will be able to find something for you here next year, as we have only a few short years to live and why live apart? I do not like our housekeeper at all. The rooms are not kept clean and my laundry is never ready. . . . I am like a wanderer in my own house—too many strange women.

Besides the housekeeper, he had taken in a roomer to be company for Anna when he was away.

On the 11th of November the armistice was signed. Probably only a few people living today remember that a false report of an armistice had been celebrated a few days earlier. That was when the big excitement occurred. The news came about four in the afternoon, and all places of business closed immediately. When I emerged into the street there was no question of which way I should go. I was caught up into the crowd and carried along on the tide, north, up Broadway. It was a stampede of shouting, mindless humanity giving expression to two years of pent-up anxiety. For several blocks I walked with the knees of the man behind me locked in mine. This was not intentional, merely unavoidable. At Union Square the crowd had thinned out enough so I could worm my way out. The excitement lasted into the night, by which time I was home and thought it best to stay there.

The crowd had been good-natured, but the pitch of excitement was frightening. Any slight incident that displeased it could have transformed it into a mob. I think my principal emotion was uneasiness. Yet it moved me more than any other public demonstration that I can remember. When I look at an old photograph of the scene in a yellowed clipping from the *New York Times* I get a lump in my throat.

A few days later I was offered a promotion at the bank. The supervisor of the mailing department was a Belgian woman who had been stranded in the United States during the war and had heard nothing from her family during all that time. Immediately after the armistice she began making plans to go home, and she asked me if I would like to be trained to take her place. The thought scared me stiff. To spend my days seeing that a machine got fed! I declined, and the woman could not understand it. Neither could the woman in the personnel office who talked with me later. "Where *would* you like to work?" she asked. Grasping for some answer that would make sense to her, I said, "The new-business department." Why that came out instead of something else I don't know. So to new business I went, as a file clerk. At least, it was a card file and I could sit down. With a little cap on my index finger I riffled tissue-thin files, got out the desired accounts and put back others. Before me stretched days and years of meaningless paper work. I shared a big desk with a pathetic, middle-aged woman who was supporting her mother as well as herself on her small salary. She had given up hope of ever getting any more from life than this, and she used to say to me, "Get out while you can." Her advice echoed my own thoughts. I handed in my resignation as of January 15th.

I was back where I started, with one big difference: I knew a lot more about the world.

Mother with Anna, 1912. She grew along with me.

Grand Rapids Central High Seniors, 1914. Doris Grissinger far right.

Frances, 1916.

Afternoon tea at Helen Newbury Residence, 1916.

Out for a walk. The island, Ann Arbor, in spring flood, 1916.

My father at fifty. Emotionally as vulnerable as a child.

9

OFF AGAIN, ON AGAIN

Home was not what it had been. The roomer was an elementary school teacher and would be with us till June. She was silly, giggly, and gauche. I disliked her heartily. Father had forgotten about my having a career and would have been happy to have me stay home and keep house for him, but it was no life for a young woman. Before long I would be off again, but for the moment I needed a respite. As a stopgap I signed up to teach fifth grade for the rest of the school year at Sigsbee Street School where I had been a pupil less than ten years earlier.

The children were a pleasure. I don't remember what I was supposed to teach or whether anybody learned anything, but I think the children liked me because they could have run all over me, and they refrained. I was too lacking in confidence to have good discipline, and the children knew it. Children always know it. There was a continual light flutter and buzz of extracurricular activity, but they never got completely out of hand.

The girls were wearing their hair long and loose that year, held in place by a circular comb. Minnie, one of the slow ones, invariably took out her comb when she was called on, gave her head a shake and let her hair fall over her face. Just as invariably it brought the house down. I saw no harm in letting them laugh for a minute or two, but I would not have been happy if the principal had walked in at such a moment.

Billy was a sad child. When he waved his hand it was always to stand up and recount some fantastic exploit, obviously imaginary. He was unable to sit still for more than a few minutes and would slip quietly every little while into and out of one of the two or three vacant seats in the room. It was so obviously a physical need that I paid no attention to it, and no one else did either until one day I noticed that two of the other boys were trying the same thing. I ordered them back to their seats, saying, "Billy may do that; nobody else." It never happened again.

The most interesting child, to me, was a boy who had recently been adopted by a physician. He was a little insecure, drawing attention to himself during recitations by playing with things on his desk. When I looked at him he would grin good naturedly, and I would say,

"I think you had better put that on my desk until class is over." One day he spoke up before I could say anything. "You can't have this knife; it is tied to my pants"! I had to laugh too.

The life of a teacher was what I had known it would be. Many of the teachers were in their late twenties, frantic with the growing realization that life was passing them by. The pay was too small to afford much recreational activity or vacations where they might meet people. Teaching was definitely a life to be avoided.

In the spring, on a visit to Ann Arbor, I saw a notice of a course to be given by the American Red Cross in Chicago the following summer. College graduates were wanted for work with war veterans and their families. I enrolled promptly.

It was a fine summer. We had classes three half-days a week and case work all day the other three days, that took us into black or foreign neighborhoods all over the city. The Red Cross had undertaken to help war veterans and their families in every way possible, so our cases were greatly diversified. Some clients needed only a little help in signing papers or getting to a doctor. Others were parents or widows of servicemen, who had been left with little or no support. Sometimes the men themselves had difficulties: war-related injuries or mental disturbances. I found it most interesting.

We were sent out singly with a city map, a guide to the streetcar lines and, for protection, a Red Cross button two inches or more in diameter. We were told, "No one will harm a representative of the Red Cross." Most of the streets were safe in the daytime but there were areas where no sane person, most certainly no young woman, would venture alone at night. I was afraid just once.

Chicago was paralyzed for several days that summer by race riots. The trouble had begun when a young black man went swimming at a public beach and was assaulted by a small group of whites. I don't remember any details, except that public transportation came to a standstill; but there was violence and the tension was palpable. No one ventured out at night, or even in the daytime, unless he had to. The streets were dead.

A few days after the trouble ended I was sent to a middle-class black neighborhood near the University of Chicago. A man let me into the apartment and showed me into an inner room, where I met the woman I had come to see. While we talked, I became conscious that the outer room was filling up with men, black men. The tensions of the past week had been unnerving, and fear seized me. I knew it was irrational. No one who planned to harm me would have assembled so large a company. Besides, these were respectable people. Most likely they had come to discuss the riots and what they should now do. But fear is fear, however unfounded. The sense of relief when I found myself outside and away was almost overwhelming.

I think this incident gave me a better insight than I could have got in any other way into the latent fears that some minority groups must live with all their lives, surfacing when they feel threatened and sometimes erupting into violence. The worst of these sad incidents is that they can undo the patient work of decades to overcome the prejudice that gives rise to them.

I made one new friend, Grace Butler from Iowa, whom I saw mostly on weekends, since she was living at a settlement house where she earned her room and board by playing with neighborhood children. We helped each other through the lonely winter that followed by pouring out our frustrations in long letters.

Back in Grand Rapids in the fall I applied to the local Red Cross Home Service office for temporary work, and the secretary was glad to have my help until my own assignment should come through. It gave me a little more experience, which was good, but I only made house calls and turned in reports. Often I didn't know how a case was disposed of.

That same fall I confessed my unbelief to the new minister of our church, whose somewhat stern manner belied an understanding and compassionate nature. To my surprise, he was not greatly disturbed.

He said, "We all go through that. You grew up in a God-fearing family. Your parents dedicated you to the Lord in baptism. You will come back to the church." He believed that absolutely and apparently was willing to let time take care of the matter.

From that time I received a letter every two years inquiring whether I wouldn't like to have my letter of confirmation sent to a church in the city where I was living. I always replied that I preferred to leave it where it was. It was twelve years before any action was taken. On an occasion when I was home for a time a young deacon came to see me. He was the son of one of my mother's best friends, scarcely older than I was. I told him the truth about the situation, and he said he would take care of it. A short time later I received my letter of confirmation in the mail. I am sure the church fathers must have been as relieved as I was.

The first of the year, 1920, I accepted an assignment to Cadillac, Michigan, a lumber-mill town about one hundred miles north of Grand Rapids, under contract for one year. It was a town of about ten thousand, if I remember correctly, of whom ninety percent must have been mill hands.

For a month or so I had no time to think about my situation, for the flu that had hit most of the country the year before broke out in this remote town soon after I arrived. Most of the victims were poor.

Besides doing my own work I was on call to help the one public-health nurse in any way I could. During the day I visited homes where whole families were sick and helpless. Evenings I made pneumonia jackets and delivered them to pathetic shacks, sometimes far out in the country, often getting home after midnight. My landlady was not happy about my exposing myself. She warned me, "If you get sick don't expect me to come near you."

When the emergency had passed, the exigencies of life in a small town soon thrust themselves upon me. Some of the work was routine —help with insurance papers, for example—but some of it was urgent, concerned with real misery, and it was frustrating to try to get anything done about it because my board was apathetic. They conformed to the general bourgeois view that people who needed help were more likely than not, not worth helping.

When I did accomplish something, the consequences were not always what I had anticipated. I arranged for a fourteen-year-old girl to have her tonsils removed. She had been sickly and stunted, and now she began to grow and became quite pretty. I was happy about it until I learned that her parents had put her to work at a stag hotel. I was afraid I might have helped her from the frying pan into the fire.

Not all of my cases were properly Red Cross cases. Some were referred to me by one or another local authority, and since there was no one else to attend to them, I did what I could.

My worst case was a couple far gone with syphilis. The man, who was frightfully deformed and could hardly walk, sat on the street and begged. The wife lived at home with an infant and a toddler in a shack, where a double bed dominated the only room. On it the baby, with some inflammatory skin disease, lay and cried continually. The place stank of urine.

My board was uninterested. Help was wasted on such riffraff. I persisted. After some time the case came to the attention of the law. There was talk of removing the children.

One day when I was alone in the office, the door swung open, and there was the woman. She was a sight to scare anybody in any situation. Her mouth was twisted to one side and her speech was almost unintelligible. Now she strode towards me furiously and stood over my desk. She had heard that her children might be taken away, and if this was my doing she would kill me. She stood between me and the door. All I could do was to try to reassure her. I said I had not heard about it, and this was true. After a bit she calmed down and walked out. I felt shaken. The poor woman was not a fit guardian for her children, but her anguish was real. They were all she had in the world.

Another family, with many children, was ineligible for aid because the husband, who was unable to hold a job, had no physical disability. Leaving their house one day, I reflected that they would all be better off if he were out of the picture. That night he was killed by lightning. I felt uncomfortably like a witch!

I lived in a rented room, not too comfortable, and ate at a boardinghouse with a dozen or so teachers. There were about seventy teachers in town, all but three of whom were women. Local young people were almost non-existent. I remember only one. The chance of ever having a date was zero.

Main Street was two blocks long. Cultural facilities consisted of one movie house with weekly changes of program, a small public library in which I could find nothing to read, and four Protestant churches. I was told that if I wished to have any status I should attend either the Presbyterian or the Congregational, preferably the former. Social lines were finely drawn. I was invited once to Sunday dinner by a member of my board. Once I went bob-sledding and once attended a high school basket-ball game. That was the extent of my social life. Grace was in a similar situation in a small Nebraska town, and we comforted each other in long letters that cemented our friendship.

By the time spring came I had fallen into a depression. I felt so tired all the time that it was difficult to get through my day's work. The new life bursting out all around me was almost more than I could bear. Sometimes the scent of a locust tree in blossom filled the air in the evening and brought me close to tears. Another six or eight months looked like an eternity. The upshot was that I broke my contract and left on the first of July, having advised headquarters that I would be ready for another job the first of August.

When I left, I spent a few days with Grace in Shawano, Wisconsin, to which she had been transferred, and then went on to Highland Park, our old family vacation ground, to be with my father for a couple of weeks. He had sold the house, now that Anna was away at college, and had spent the past winter in a hotel room, and he was very lonely. This seemed the least I could do for him. Our rented cottage was not very satisfactory. The roof leaked, and one night when it rained I slept under an open umbrella. On the whole, however, it was a good time. Father was happy in my company and his affection helped raise my spirits.

Before we left I had received notice of my new assignment in a town of a few hundred people in the Illinois corn belt.

There were two or three stores; a courthouse in the usual shady, green square; a few short streets lined with old houses, where chickens roamed in the back yards; and then the tall corn, planted right up to the roadsides. Mile after mile it stretched in all directions—all there was to see in the whole flat land.

I was given a room in the courthouse, and I had to depend on the county officers to take me to the still smaller towns in the county where most of my cases were. They were an easy-going lot; it would have been difficult to be anything else in the intense heat, which seemed to penetrate your bones and become part of you. Good corn weather! Every afternoon we all knocked off for half an hour to enjoy the temporary refreshment of a big watermelon. The situation would have been tolerable for a few months if one of the men had not become infatuated with me.

I feel foolish saying this, but that is what happened. The first week he spent half his time hanging out in my office, which could not fail to attract attention. I was moved upstairs to an empty courtroom and he followed, sitting on a table and chatting inconsequentially while I tried to get some work done. He was attractive but he was married, and in a small town that was an invitation to disaster. The reaction in the courthouse was amused tolerance, but the whole town would soon be talking. There was no way out but to leave. I informed Chicago that I would be able to clean up the work in two months instead of the scheduled three, and I added that I would not be in need of another assignment. I was through with small towns.

So what next? In Detroit I had friends. I bought a ticket to Detroit.

* * *

The first thing I did in Detroit was to notify my friends that I was there. Jeannette was writing advertising for the J. L. Hudson Company, the leading department store, and she invited me to come and see her at her office. There she introduced me to the manager, and in a few minutes I was a copywriter too!

Everything about the work was new and interesting to me. Much of my time was spent with buyers, discussing the merchandise they wished to advertise. They were highly competent people who had reached the top through years of hard work. I learned much from them that was useful about laces and leatherwork, furs and fabrics, and the fine points of garment making.

From the start, copywriting paid twice as much as most other occupations open to women. The people in the department were congenial. Advertising was a new field for women, and those who entered it were usually clever and somewhat venturesome. I made more good and lasting friends during my years in advertising than at any other time.

The social scene in which I found myself, however, was profoundly disturbing. At home and in the small towns where I had spent the past two years, life had gone on in the old patterns. Here in the city the Jazz Age was in full swing. Born of postwar disillusionment and aggravated by the lawlessness attendant on Prohibition, it was an approximately ten-year binge that came to an end only when the 1929 stock-market crash undermined its financial base. It was a time of reckless living and disdain of consequences, of wild spending and get-rich-quick schemes and political corruption.

Women, already on the march, took advantage of the loosened manners to assert themselves in ways that had been impossible a short time earlier. They smoked and drank in public. They shortened their skirts and bobbed their hair. The vanguard was claiming the same sexual freedom that society had always tacitly accorded to unmarried men. The line between "nice girls" and girls not so nice was fading.

Most of these things touched my life and that of the people I knew only on the fringes. Only the very rich could afford to destroy themselves with the abandon of Scott Fitzgerald's characters; but their attitude, as Lloyd Morris has said, expressed the national frame of mind.[5] Cynicism was in the air we breathed and the books we read, notably Fitzgerald and Hemingway. Drinking had become almost universal. No sooner had liquor been outlawed than drinking became the thing to do.

Frances Handibo and Vera Brown, who had been college class-mates, were working for the *Detroit News,* and I sometimes lunched with them in the *News* lunchroom. There I met several newsmen, and one of them invited me to go with him to the home of a young couple who kept open house for friends on Saturday evenings. I went expecting an evening of congenial company and good conversation. It was, as I learned later, typical of the time. Hard liquor was served through-out the evening, and Prohibition liquor produced no mellow glow; it could only stupify, with the promise of a savage hangover the next day. There was no merriment, no wit, just desultory conversation that grew inane as the hours passed. Was this pleasure? It was the begin-ning of a short course in sophistication. My head reeled.

Fortunately I found a friend, a man some ten or twelve years older than I, who shepherded me through the first bewildered months. I could talk with him about anything. We talked of men and women and love, of aspiration and disillusionment and compromise, of what men live for and what they live by. All of my dissatisfactions surfaced, my inability to find a niche I fitted. His advice to me was, never be resigned. I did not need the advice, resignation was not in my nature, but I needed the reassurance.

I was no longer uneasy with men, and from now on I had my share of attention. A few years earlier an unmarried woman of twenty-five would have been labeled an old maid and dismissed as of little further interest. That was one thing that had changed for the better after the war. As more and more women achieved success in business or a profession, refusing to be shelved, the old stereotype gradually faded away. There was life after twenty-five.

But now I had other difficulties. I had no interest in a career. I had no outstanding talent that demanded expression, no interest so strong that I desired to devote my life to it. My early training had discouraged assertiveness and initiative, without which no one can be happy or successful in a competitive situation. Moreover, I needed affection; I wanted a family. I doubt that anything I might have undertaken would have held my interest for long unless my emotions had first been satisfied. Single life had its compensations, but working only for my own bread and butter was savorless. Without a purpose I was restless. Every situation would sooner or later become a dead end from which the only escape was to take a new direction.

In Detroit I was happy for a while. In those days when theatrical companies went on the road, good plays were to be seen in any sizeable city. Detroit had its own symphony orchestra and there were recitals by such musicians as Rachmaninoff and Chaliapin. The Denishawn dancers and Pavlova and her company came to the city every year. In winter I took evening classes in drawing with some of the staff artists. In summer there were staff picnics on Belle Isle, pretty much like family affairs but pleasant enough. I often spent weekends with Anna in Ann Arbor. If this was all rather tame, it was a vast improvement on what a small town had to offer. Sinclair Lewis' *Main Street*, published that year, was right on target. Millions of Americans recognized in Zenith their own home towns.

During the first winter I shared a one-bedroom apartment with three other women. An Ann Arbor acquaintance who left to get married had invited me to take her place. The apartment was grossly overcrowded, and I had little in common with the other women, but I had it all to myself on weekends, and it had the virtue of being cheap. My share of the rent was $25.00 a month. It would do until I could find something better.

In the spring, Getty Gunn asked me if I would like to live with her family and I accepted gratefully. The family consisted of her Aunt Jessie Ellis, who had brought her up, and of Aunt Julia, the widow of Jessie's brother. We all worked and went our separate ways but ate dinner together at night. They were pleasant and interesting people, and the arrangement was enjoyable in many ways. Living in a spacious house was a luxury. Still, it was not my house or my family. A grown women wants a place of her own.

By the summer of 1922 everything had changed in Getty's family. Aunt Julia had left, Aunt Jessie was dying slowly and miserably from pernicious anemia, and I had moved into a boarding house. It was first rate and served excellent meals, and it was in a nice old neighborhood near the library. Still, all I had was a single furnished room. One of the greatest disadvantages of being single was the inadequacy of living arrangements available. It took more money than most women had to furnish an apartment. As a result a woman might live her whole life essentially homeless.

* * *

My father had married again, a woman whom he had met through me in Cadillac. Magdalen looked something like my mother and she was essentially kind and affectionate; but she was also neurasthenic and afraid of strangers and grew more so as the years passed. For her it was a happy marriage—Father was gentle with her—but for him it was twenty years of misery. Fortunately she felt comfortable with me; I was always welcome at home for as long as I cared to stay. When I lived not too far away I went home for vacations and Christmas. On such occasions Father planned my entire stay: whom I should see, what we would do. If I had remained at home it would always have been like that; and I could not have lived that way. For a few days or a few weeks, I didn't mind if it made him happy.

* * *

In the spring of 1921 Jeannette went to New York, which drew bright young people like a magnet. Her place was taken by Eve Kittelson from Wisconsin, who was to be another of my best friends. At the time I didn't know what to make of her. She was intuitive rather than rational, and her head was often in the clouds. Only after she gave me a copy of *East of the Sun and West of the Moon*, a collection of Norwegian fairy tales, did I understand that she was merely a Norwegian of the type that has a strong strain of Peer Gynt in the blood.

In New York at a later date, a stranger approached her one day and asked how to find Christopher Street. Eve was on it and didn't know it. She replied sweetly,"I'm sorry, I almost never know where I am"! It was typical. She longed to be another Virginia Woolf, but what she wrote always turned out to be more suitable for the *Ladies' Home Journal*. This distressed her, but her common touch—if that is what it was—stood her in good stead. She made more money than any of us except Jeannette, writing copy for Sears' and Ward's catalogues.

After the first year my work palled. The whole purpose was simply to sell more and more of everything in good times and in bad. Even during a recession sales quotas were raised, and they were posted high on a wall of the employees' cafeteria; the pressure was unremitting. Buyers became short tempered and hard to please, and the tension was felt all down the line. Even in a good year, after the novelty wore off, living with and thinking about nothing but merchandise six days a week was stifling. There had to be more to life than this.

But now my comfortable salary was a strong deterrent to change. When I talked with a prospective employer in some other line, the invariable question was, "How much are you making?" and the invariable response to my answer was, "I can't pay you anything like that; don't quarrel with your bread and butter." Since I was not a lily of the field, I had to bide my time.

I was also tired of Detroit. It was not much of a city, it had grown too fast and was sprawling and ugly. Miles of trees were being destroyed to widen the streets for the rapidly increasing automobile traffic. Above all, it lacked verve. It seemed to lay a heavy hand on the life within it, reducing it to an even flatness like the glacial plain on which the city stood. I had been there not quite two years when I decided I had had enough. About the first of August I quit my job and went to New York again.

By chance I secured an interview with Sarah Burchall, who headed the advertising department of Condé Nast publications: *Vogue, Vanity Fair* and *House and Garden*. When I phoned she thought I was a woman she had talked with before. Since I was there, she looked at my samples and liked them and hired me on the spot. I had found a job in just three days, and a job that was the envy of everyone who knew anything about publishing. To work for Condé Nast was to be in.

My principal task was to get out the *Vogue Pattern Book*. Today it is one of the slicks, but then it was merely a pedestrian catalogue. Patterns were known within the company as *Vogue's* stepchild and little money was available for promoting them. I could not even pay for a really good artist although the art work was what sold the patterns.

Sarah was a highly successful woman and she had got where she was because she was bursting with ideas. She had a vision of the poor little pattern book as a fashion magazine. That is what she had hired me for, and she believed in me until the day I left. It was a chance in a million and I muffed it because the situation stirred up old inhibitions. In my childhood it had been presumptuous to have ideas of my own, and I had been obliged to stifle them. Now it was my business to have ideas, but the old pattern was reasserting itself and blocking my mind. No ideas would come.

There was nothing really to be afraid of. I had been sewing for years with little guidance and still had much to learn. I would have had plenty of ideas if I had merely asked myself what information, what advice, I would like to see in a pattern book. I would not even have had to take much responsibility in the beginning. I would have taken my ideas to Sarah and she would have made the decisions until I had proved myself. The project was useful and it interested me. The only difficulty was in my mind, and it was fatal. The only way I could conceal my fear was to defer action. I put out the pattern book essentially as it had come to me and let it go at that.

The days passed pleasantly enough. The offices on West 44th Street, just off Fifth Avenue, were high up with plenty of daylight. The atmosphere was informal, almost cozy. Established employees had great freedom as to where and when they did their work. Sarah was an energetic, outdoor woman from Kansas. When she was tired of the city, she would take her work with her to her cabin in the Colorado mountains. Harry Yoxall, who wrote copy for *House and Garden*, was English, and he was getting his work done for three months ahead so he could spend the summer in England.

Harry had the kind of thorough liberal arts education that is not often encountered in this country, and it sat lightly on him as did his easy jersey suits with Norfolk jackets. When his father-in-law, a physician, gave him a medical encyclopedia in several volumes, he announced that he would have to give away several books to make room for it. Each one of us in the office received one. Mine was Dos Passos' *Rosinante to the Road Again,* and it was inscribed to me "in memory of the many happy days we spent together as missionaries in Conshohocken, Pennsylvania"!

I rented a room on the third floor of the house where Tony Sarg made his puppets, which were works of art. It was on 9th Street in the first block west of Fifth Avenue, where the atmosphere of old New York still prevailed. I had two big windows facing south, that looked out on a back yard with ailanthus trees, where the people who made the puppets worked in good weather. It was pleasant but it was also lonely. The only other roomer was a young woman who worked evenings. I was usually alone in the house except for the caretakers on the ground floor. They were proud West Indian Negroes who didn't even speak to me when I paid the rent—just opened the door a few inches and took my money. It was impossible to stay in that empty house without getting fidgety.

Luckily for me, it was only a short time before Eve came to town to take a position with Montgomery Ward and asked me to take an apartment with her. She had found a charming one in a recently renovated, little old red-brick house on Grove Street. We had two identical rooms with working fireplaces, which occupied the whole top floor. The only building across the street was a public school, closed in the evening. There in the street, Italian children congregated at twilight to play street games. Little girls deposited littler girls on the curb while they sang and wove in and out, to what must have been traditional Italian rhymes, a charming grace note to spring evenings.

That year I greatly increased my knowledge of the city. I discovered Allen Street on the lower East Side, where pawned brass and copper were to be had cheap, and bought a few lovely things, with a little sigh for the misery that brought them there. On Sunday afternoons I often walked across Brooklyn Bridge to see Jeannette and Dorothy Creighton in Columbia Heights, a few doors from where Walt Whitman had lived. They were both writing advertising for McCall Patterns. Dorothy later became my assistant, and my successor when I left.

Dorothy was a handsome blonde with classical good looks. We spent a good deal of time together. I enjoyed her company, but I never felt that I knew her really well. She was very reserved.

She was engaged to a man back home in Ogdensburg, New York, whom she married a year or two later. Sad to say, she died young of pneumonia, leaving three small daughters. Pneumonia was a dreaded, often fatal disease, before antibiotics were available.

A third friend at McCall's was Virginia Vincent. She was the most enterprising of any of us. With a friend, she bought a typical brownstone house on 9th Street, just off Fifth Avenue, which they proceeded to divide into studio apartments and renovate. They had a great time of it and were clever about handling the inevitable mishaps. When the first tenants moved in and there was no heat, the two young landladies threw a party that made everybody feel good, and there were no complaints.

All went well until the Depression set in, after which they just squeaked through for several years. They must have done all right after World War II when real estate prices soared out of sight.

Psychoanalysis was becoming fashionable, and its criterion of mental health was "adjustment." If you were emotionally healthy, you adapted yourself to your circumstances, whatever they might be. It was a perfect concept for a society that had gone all out on an unprecedented getting-and-spending spree. Business had seen visions and dreamed dreams of infinite expansion. If all citizens, not only the rich, could be converted into conspicuous consumers, the possibilities were endless. Advertising was the machinery that was to achieve this happy state. Accordingly, good copywriters were at a premium. All I would have had to do to be a success was to adjust my mind to serving that end. I was not interested.

There was plenty of diversion. Great music and art, fine theater were always available. There were any number of small, foreign restaurants where the food was outstanding, and for special occasions the unpretentious perfection of the old Lafayette Hotel or the old New York atmosphere of the Brevoort. I derived much pleasure from merely roaming the streets and exploring the city with a freedom unthinkable today.

During the noon hour it was sometimes possible to drop into a private art gallery for a few moments. I remember a magnificent Velasquez exhibit that filled two large rooms. The overwhelming impression was the majesty of the artist. He was a Presence more powerful than any of his titled sitters, whose souls he painted in all their bleakness.

And there was always Central Park. On a summer evening it was almost deserted, with just enough light to make it a setting for a Midsummer Night's dream. With an escort it was perfectly safe, and one of the few places where one could escape on a hot night. On Sunday afternoons it was alive with well-behaved crowds, including many family parties: small children sailing their small boats on the pond, and toddlers enjoying the luxury of green grass. It was a fine place to walk any day of the year, with trees and sky and freedom from traffic. New York had its compensations.

In warm weather Eve and I sometimes spent a leisurely Sunday in a remote corner of the botanical gardens in the Bronx with a book and a picnic lunch. Another Sunday pastime was hiking on the Palisades, which were reached by the 125th Street ferry. There it was possible to have the illusion of being in the country with the beautiful river below. The trouble with all such Sunday expeditions was that the feeling of refreshment was unable to survive the ride home on a noisy, dirty subway train. They always left me with a feeling of futility.

Those years saw the beginning of an extraordinary literary renaissance in both England and the United States. New books rolled off the presses year after year by Joyce, Lawrence, Woolf, Huxley, Orwell, Eliot, O'Neil, Wharton, Cather, Faulkner, Hemingway. New York pulsed with an intellectual excitement that I have encountered in no other time and place. It was a fine time to be young, if one were part of it. Rootless as I was, and unsure of myself, that great surge of energy seemed tantalizingly just out of reach.

The strangest experience I had that year occurred on New Year's Eve. On the same floor with Jeannette and Dorothy, lived an elderly woman who was a friend to many young people, and she invited several of us to a small party to see the old year out. A daughter who lived up the line in Connecticut had a small baby and could not get in, but her husband had been detained in the city by a snowstorm, and he came to the party. Since we both had to go back to Manhattan it was natural that he should ask to see me home.

There was heavy snow falling, but the night was warm and pleasant. When we had almost reached the subway station, my companion remarked that this would be a fine night to walk back across the river. Nothing could have suited me better. I said, "Let's do," and we turned around and headed for the Manhattan Bridge, where the pedestrian walks were right next to the railing. There was no one about. The city lights shone dimly through the haze of swirling flakes, and the physical world had vanished. We were wrapped in a luminous cocoon, out of time; nothing seemed real. Our talk turned back to childhood fancies and soon we were laughing like children for no reason except that this magic night had cast its spell on us.

When we reached my door, he held my hand for a moment and left, saying only good night. Words would have been meaningless. I went to bed elated. I hardly knew this man and I was not at all sure that I liked him. I had no desire ever to see him again. Yet something mysterious and profound had happened—a communion as fragile as a bubble and as irrecoverable.

A week later he was dead by his own hand. A strange man, people said; he had never been happy.

In the spring, out of a blue sky, I received a letter from Ralph Yonkers, Hudson's advertising manager. He was the sort of person to whom the grass on the other side of the fence always looks greener. It was just like him to want me back now that someone else had found some merit in me. The letter carried an offer of more money and promises of other benefits to come. Sarah tried to keep me, saying it was always a mistake to go back, which I knew; and still I went. The offer was a face-saving way out of a situation fraught with growing uneasiness. It was the most foolish decision I ever made.

After New York, Detroit was unspeakably dull. Many of the more interesting people had left. The promised benefits did not materialize. To make matters worse, I suffered for many months during the second year with an infected thumb, the result of having a wart removed. Nothing showed but a clean, white bandage, renewed daily by the doctor; but the pain ran up my entire arm, and the infection took a toll of my energy. I suppose my discontent showed. My work suffered. After Christmas I was served notice: I was out, fired. That finished me in Detroit.

There had been a few gains. Anna, who was now a year and a half out of college, had come to Detroit to teach music in the public schools. We took an apartment together and got to know each other better. When she left in the spring of 1924, to go back to Ann Arbor and give private piano lessons, Martha Seeley moved in with me. I had known her in Ann Arbor. She was the second of five daughters of a small-town banker, who had trained her in banking. She had formidable business brains within a small, innocent-looking head, which made her indispensable to a top executive in an industry plagued with intrigue. She worked long enough to put three younger sisters through college before going home to marry a friend of her childhood. She must have been under a greater strain than anyone realized, for she died of high blood pressure when she was only forty.

Those years were also the beginning of my friendship with Clara Moser, another Wisconsinite, who is now the only friend I have left of my own age. She was then writing advertising for Himmelhoch's, one of the better women's specialty shops. Clara was brimming with vitality; she loved people, was open to experience and had an eye and an ear for nonsense. We used to take a bus to the end of the Jefferson Avenue bus line, sometimes on cold winter days, and walk out to Grosse Pointe Farms, where there might be iceboats sailing on Lake St. Clair. Today she lives in Connecticut and is no longer able to travel, but we still share things that amuse us.

There was also Margaret Schnapel, a new copywriter at Hudson's, just out of college, and her fiancé, Sam Breck, who were friends until I left Michigan for good in 1933. Margaret lived at home and had the use of the family car—as yet few single women had their own—and she sometimes invited me to join her and Sam when they drove out to Ann Arbor for football games in the fall. I liked them both and we had good times together.

It was during this time that I read James Joyce's *Ulysses*, which had been banned in the United States. The ready-to-wear merchandise man at Hudson's was, strange to say, a reader. He got hold of a copy and lent it to me. I didn't know what to make of it, and I was not alone. My generation had grown up in an era of faith and hope. How were we to know that this strange book foreshadowed the attrition of both? A true artist knows which way the wind is blowing before the rest of us are aware of anything more than a slight breeze.

By the time I lost my job, my thumb was well. After the doctor decided to try mercury, the infection had disappeared in a matter of days. My spirits took longer to heal.

My first reaction was that I must find a job quickly. Advertising agencies seemed a good place to begin. I wrote to several, and Ayers in Philadelphia responded with a proposal that I meet one of their representatives in Toledo, or it may have been Cleveland, on a certain date. They needed a writer for a Munsingwear account. I believe that was the brand. That was a low point. Had it come to this, I asked myself, to spend my days rhapsodizing over undershirts and unionsuits! I did not make an appointment and I wrote to no more agencies. Suddenly I felt overwhelmed. I had worked for six years and I was nowhere.

One day, in passing, I saw a notice posted in front of the theater to which Jessie Bonstelle had recently brought her stock company. She had moved to Detroit after many years in Buffalo, where she had trained a number of successful young actors, including Katherine Cornell. Now, the poster said, she was about to open a school in Detroit. I walked in and enrolled, with nothing more in mind than that I needed a change and this would certainly be one.

The course was to begin in February. There would be two three-month sessions with classes from four to six, six days a week. They would include calisthenics, fencing, dancing, speech, make-up, and acting technique. Tuition was nominal, and I had saved a little money with a view to going to England the next summer. This I supplemented with a half-time job selling coats at Himmelhoch's. For once in my life I was going to live for the moment. Those months were undiluted pleasure.

The whole company was involved except the leading lady, of whom we saw little. The leading man taught technique. The ingenue was in charge of exercise and fencing. The male character actor, a jovial Irishman, taught make-up and speech. The dancing teacher, who was attached to the company, was a lovely English woman who had danced many years with Pavlova. All of these people were enthusiastic about the project, and they took us seriously and gave us their best. Miss Bonstelle herself took the class in technique occasionally.

Our group consisted of nine or ten women and two men. One of the men was very tight-up, and the other was loose and uncoordinated in his movements; it was interesting to observe their contrasting difficulties. There was a cute youngster of perhaps fifteen who danced professionally; a magnificent Turkish-American high-school girl, a light-weight with too much money, but she was lots of fun; a middle-aged woman with leg muscles wasted by disease, who was back in shape by the time the course was over; a pretty but rather vulgar Irish girl, who must have taken off fifty pounds and put them right back on again. And then there was Katherine Macrae.

Kitty was the daughter of John Macrae, president of the Dutton publishing company. I don't know how to describe her adequately. To begin with, she was a thoroughbred. The first thing you noticed about her was an unconscious natural dignity, unusual in so young a woman. She had just turned twenty-one. When you knew her, what impressed you was her spontaneity. She enjoyed every minute, and her pleasure was as frank as a child's. She was a delightful companion. I had given up my apartment and moved into the college club. Kitty lived there too, and for six months we lived and ate together and talked shop.

Acting was rather fun and I seem to have had some ability. Some of the company were encouraging, and one offered to lend me money to go on. Miss Bonstelle would not comment. She once said, "If you tell an actor what he does well he will never do it unconsciously again." She seemed to carry this opinion so far as to avoid telling a person whether he was any good at all. She was, nevertheless, a stimulating and encouraging teacher who loved to develop new talent. Everyone worked hard to please her.

I had no illusions about having a future in the theater, so I said, "No, thank you" to the offer of a loan and turned back to real life. The exercise had put me in fine fettle and my courage was restored.

Again I headed back to New York, as the best base from which to look for work. This time I looked fruitlessly for three months before

I secured a position with the Joseph Horne department store in Pittsburgh. More copywriting, alas! My funds were low and I had no choice.

I had seen Kitty occasionally during this time, and when I left she came to the station to see me off. It was the last time I saw her. She wrote to me for a year or two; she got married. Then, one Christmas, there was no greeting and I heard from her no more. I don't know what happened. When her father died, his obituary in the *New York Times* mentioned two surviving sons, but no daughter.

Pittsburgh, to use a current inelegant but pithy phrase (and no pun intended), was the pits. The climate was miserable. In winter, soft snow turned to slush underfoot and soot filtered into everything. In summer, all the water in three rivers went up every morning and came down every afternoon at closing time. It was intolerably hot and humid. The "better neighborhoods" were ugly with new-rich money. The wretched slums looked the more wretched for tottering on steep hillsides. The middle-class population was predominantly Scotch Presbyterian, as reticent and as slow to accept strangers as were the residents of a small town.

I was unable to find an apartment, and the College Club was full and had a long waiting list. After looking in vain for several days, I took a room near Carnegie Tech with a family that turned out to be right out of a Charles Addams' cartoon. The unhappy wife dominated her taciturn husband by means of fainting spells that she apparently could bring on at will. These she attributed to a "weak heart." Because of it, she never left the house but spent her days making beautiful clothes for her sixteen-year-old daughter. Horne's frequently sent out bolts of cloth for her to choose from. She was a pretty woman, slim and young-looking at forty, who had been married young to a cousin, the only man she knew in the small town where she grew up. She was eager and vivacious, and her husband was totally inarticulate and inhibited. Her strange behavior seems to have dated from World War I, when she had fallen in love with an army officer and had chosen to stay with her husband out of a sense of duty.

The husband, an engineer, played endless games of solitaire, all evening every evening, friendless except for his affectionate little fox-terrier. The only thing in the world he wanted was to attend the annual dinner of local Cornell alumni; and every year, at the last minute, his wife had a spell. He had never got there.

There were two bright spots in this gloom. Ginnie, the daughter, was charming, light hearted, and amiable; life was never dull when Ginnie was around. The other cheerful human being was the ancient black man who did all the housework on one leg and a crutch. He may have been born a slave. Although he was totally ignorant and alone and poor, and slept in the unfinished attic, he had a gentle and happy disposition. I suppose he felt thankful to have any kind of roof over his head. He went into ecstacies over the paper-white narcissus that grew in my room, and sometimes asked if he might come in and smell them. I became quite fond of him.

The situation became too much for me, however. The weirdness grew upon me as spring came on, and I moved out to Sewickley, where the surroundings were pleasant but there was nothing whatever to do. There wasn't much in the city, for that matter.

At work, the department manager was an ignorant man who had worked up to his position from that of stock boy. He was way out of his depth, with the result that he was continually worried and suffered from stomach ulcers. I tightened up every time he came near me. At weekly staff meetings, and often in between, he harangued us at length on the necessity of loyalty to the company and good grammar. The latter he knew nothing about, but he knew it was important.

The company's rules for employees were antediluvian. Even in the advertising department, we had to wear black or navy blue dresses, except that in the summer white shirtwaists were permitted. The catch was that nobody had seen a shirtwaist since the Gibson Girl era.

My only recreation was a folk-dancing class two evenings a week. For two hours I got an energetic workout, after which I nearly always walked the three miles home in high spirits. The walk took me through downtown, over the railroad bridge, past the hillside slums into a residential district. To the south, the foundries lit the night sky. I don't remember ever meeting anyone; I had the still night all to myself and was happy for an hour. Perhaps I should have been afraid but it never occurred to me. Street crimes were very rare.

Spring brought release. Anna wrote that she had met Mrs. Rankin on the street in Ann Arbor. Mrs. Rankin was a faculty wife who had been kind to me in my undergraduate days. She was on the board of Alumnae House, a small co-operative dormitory, and she was looking for a director. Anna thought I could have the job if I wanted it. I took it for $25.00 a month and my keep.

10

BACK TO THE IVORY TOWER

My new work was to begin in September, and I planned to stay in Pittsburgh through the summer and save a little money, but I made the mistake of telling one of my colleagues that I would be leaving. She had been at Horne's longer than the rest of us, but she had had little schooling, and she was continually worried about being passed over by one of us who had more education. She had to be handled with care. I thought that life might be a little easier for both of us if she knew that I was out of the competition. She went straight to the manager with the information and he was angry. If I was so disloyal as to think of leaving, I might go at once. I think this was about the middle of June. I went home for a few weeks and then to Detroit to fill in for Clara, who was on vacation from her advertising job at Himmelhoch's. Then one day I was back in Ann Arbor again to begin another new life.

I had soon rounded up two other small part-time jobs on campus that brought my cash income up to a respectable $75.00 a month. Then I decided that I might as well get another degree while I had the opportunity. Since I had had no undergraduate major, there was no department I was qualified for; but I was told that I might enroll in the English department if Holley Hanford would have me. Hanford was a Milton scholar with an extracurricular interest in Elizabethan music. In appearance and manner he was a typical New Englander with a long, lean body and narrow, scholarly face, who wore tweeds and smoked a pipe. When I went to see him he leaned back in his chair and asked, "What have you read?" That was easy. I went on until he said, "That's enough. What about foreign authors?" I went on again until he sat up and said, "OK. They don't come like that any more." I was in.

The next two years were the happiest of my working life. I was once more able to come and go freely. My work was varied and I did my own planning. I was exercising my abilities as a woman to make home life pleasant for seventeen eager college girls. My studies were a pleasant pastime. There were, however, two major disadvantages that ruled it out for the long term: a lack of privacy and a subsistence income.

My social life was much more satisfying. Anna was there and so was Jeannette's younger sister, Gretchen, and her husband, Bob Hicks, a freshman medical student. The Hicks's had a whole house, and it was the favorite hang-out of a number of college friends and a few of the younger faculty. Through them, Anna met and married Herbert Sewell, a French instructor. Herbert's sister Harriette and her husband, George Sample, were also part of the group. Another who became a long-time friend was Marion Fisk, whose husband was in the mathematics department.

Bob Hicks was one of those people with energy enough for three or four who seem to function best at the center of a vortex. In addition to being a full-time medical student, he was supporting himself and Gretchen and, a short time later, an infant daughter, with three assistantships, each of which was supposed to be a full load. One of these was in the pediatrics department of the university hospital, and one was in President Little's private cancer-research laboratory. With all this he always seemed to have time for company. Gretchen was also an extrovert, happy in her roles as wife, mother, and hostess. I never saw her flustered.

Music was plentiful. The Detroit symphony orchestra played in Ann Arbor regularly, and a man I was dating took me to all the concerts. There was also a winter series of solo performances. I heard Paderewski, who kept the audience waiting for at least an hour while the auditorium was made warm enough to suit him. By the time he was satisfied I was too hot and weary to know or care very much what he played or how. I also heard Madame Schumann-Heinck, then long past her prime. Her voice was not what it had been, but it was still full of feeling and deeply moving. My favorite singer was Rosa Ponselle, an altogether delightful woman with a very lovely voice. Often Sam and Margaret Breck came out from Detroit for a concert, and sometimes I spent the weekend with them in Detroit. Leone Prochnow, a teacher of home economics who was our dietician, lived at the house, so I was able to get away occasionally.

For the most part, the girls got along well together. There were a few who made a practice of coming to me with trivial complaints about others. "Millie kisses her boyfriend goodnight on the porch where everybody can see her." I summon Millie and suggest that she be a little discreet. She replies, "I don't care who knows that I love my Steve." Millie is mature and sensible, and her Steve is the typical boy-next-door. They can handle their own affairs very well. I let it pass.

A little while later it was Millie's turn to be agitated. She had a new roommate at midyear, an astronomy major whose hobby was taxidermy. When Millie came in from classes the first morning, her Steve's photograph had been moved over to make room for a half-stuffed bird. This was a desecration. Millie fumed. I calmed her down, and until dinner time I thought I had disposed of the matter. Then one of the day's cooks rushed into my room in alarm. There was a dead bird in the refrigerator! Flossie, the culprit, was a gentle soul, who had no idea what the fuss was about.

Two of the girls had serious emotional disturbances. I had been warned that Sally sometimes had catatonic fits. This happened only once during my stay, I am happy to say. On that occasion she was as still and rigid as if she were dead. I was frightened until the doctor came and said, in a tone of authority, "Sally, get up at once," and Sally got up.

Elaine had been devastated when her widowed mother, who had been her constant companion, married again. She wanted attention continually. When she had enjoyed a party she used to wake me up at any hour to tell me all about it. That was all right. But when she decided to take to bed for a few days, demanding service right and left, the whole house was thrown into confusion. Her two roommates, the steadiest girls of the whole lot, were in despair and I could do little to help them.

Alice Lloyd, the dean of women, was understanding and tactful. She suggested that I get Elaine's mother to town for a conference, which I did. It was arranged that Elaine should move, for her own good, to a house where she could have a private room. Elaine agreed—until her mother had left. Then she announced that she had changed her mind. My other problem child came to the rescue. Sally said that she thought she could live with Elaine, and I agreed to let her try. There was no more trouble.

The first spring we had a fire. A small, coal-fired hot-water heater exploded, scattering its contents all over the basement. The firemen responded quickly, and the flames were confined to the basement, but smoke filled the house. Fortunately I was at home, and there were only a handful of girls upstairs, and we all got out safely. The danger was from the smoke, which was dense and hot.

The aftermath kept me busy for at least a month. Every garment in the house had to be dry cleaned; and since the cleaners could take just so many a day, it required the wisdom of Solomon to adjudicate the claims of seventeen young women for priority of service. My own clothes went last. For several weeks, everywhere I went, someone said, "I smell smoke!" All this was time-consuming. My course work got behind and I never caught up.

All of these problems were human problems. When I was able to resolve them the gratification was immediate. My life, in the full sense, was not limited to what little time was left after working hours. All of it was good.

Two of my girls were to be among my best friends as long as they lived. Vivien Bullock, from Waco, Texas, had just turned seventeen when she came to town in a pair of black patent-leather pumps with high red heels. She had a bright, perky face and wavy black hair and the Southern manners that appear to a Northerner, upon first encounter, too effusive to be sincere. Actually her courtesy sprang from genuine kindness. Soon she was everybody's friend. It took her eight years to get her degree, while she served as secretary to Dean Cooley of the engineering college; and she enjoyed every minute of it. We were friends from the start.

Helen Watier of Dayton, Ohio, had transferred from Antioch College and came to Alumnae House as a senior. She was not in need of assistance, but I took her to fill a mid-year vacancy. That year she was just one of the girls, but the following summer when she was a graduate student she sought my company, and I found that I enjoyed her.

A third girl, Marion Lundquist, turned up again nearly fifty years later after my husband and I had retired to Santa Fe, and she and hers to Albuquerque. Marion married Stanley Fletcher, then a music student, who later taught at the University of Illinois. Today Stanley writes music and Marion raises the best tomatoes in northern New Mexico, and they are both lively company.

There was a two-year limit on the directorship of the dormitory, and when my term was up I still had seven hours to go to get my degree. Through Bob Hicks I secured a full-time position as secretary in Dr. Little's laboratory, with the understanding that I was to have three hours a week off for a class. The work was easy, but I thought I should never get used to being tied to a desk all day.

The laboratory operated more like a family than like a place of business. Nearly all of the staff, both the research scientists and the student assistants, were Down-Easterners who had come from Maine with Dr. Little and had worked together for years. Sometimes they got boxes of dried seaweed from home, which they carried about in their lab-coat pockets and munched throughout the day. I was unable to acquire a taste for it.

Occasionally I had to translate and summarize a scientific article from German or French for a national digest. I was not really up to it, but given enough time with a dictionary, I could manage. I used to do this outside of hours so no one would know how long it took me. I made one foolish mistake that I know of. A *Meerschwein* was a porpoise and *"chen"* was a diminutive ending, so I translated it, "little porpoise." Years later I discovered that a *Meerschweinchen* was that staple of research, a guinea pig.

At this time I took over the room that Anna had vacated in June when she got married. My landlady, Mrs. Looker, was an experience in herself. Her father, she told me, had been keeper of the green at Canterbury Cathedral. As a girl she had gone up to London to visit a married sister and had danced and been merry at places that I knew about from reading but have since forgotten.

When I knew her she was a widow in her sixties. For months after her husband died she had been envious of a well-to-do widow who had nothing to do all day but sit by a window and nurse her grief. "An' you know, she's settin' there yet!" Mrs. Looker was not settin'. She was very much alive and her curiosity was boundless.

The excitement that year was a very pretty freshman medical student, a young woman about whom the men hovered like moths. Mrs. Looker was in a high state of agitation because she was unable to keep them all straight in her mind. Every evening when she answered the door-bell, she would say to the caller, "Are you the young man that was here last night?" and he almost never was. She put her foot down about petting in the parlor, so thereafter the young lady and the man she ultimately settled down to conducted their amours on the hall stairs, where I sometimes had to stumble past them in the dark.

The most memorable encounter of Mrs. Looker's life had been with Rear Admiral Richard Byrd of Antarctic fame. He had once rented her garage, which made it something of a historical landmark. She never ceased to be amazed at having been in such close touch with celebrity.

That year I also became friendly with Marion Satterthwaite, of a Philadephia Quaker family, who was working in the Clements Memorial Library. Once on a holiday she took me to the library to look at some of the more valuable acquisitions undisturbed: a Gutenberg Bible, a letter from Columbus to Queen Isabella. Old hand-written documents stir something very deep inside me. There is an immediacy about characters formed by a human hand that brings the writer vividly to life—a fellow creature who lived and breathed and guided his pen to speak for him through the ages. I can see how collecting such things might become an addiction.

The most valuable course I took was that of Professor Reinhard in medieval literature. It covered the whole of western Europe and the British Isles from the time of St. Benedict and St. Augustine through Chaucer. This mass of material was very well organized, and I gained a sense of the unity of Western culture that I had not had before.

A summer course in modern American literature with Vernon Parrington of the University of Washington was as much entertainment as education. Parrington was obviously a man of the world. He had become an overnight sensation in academic circles upon the publication of his history of American literature, in which he attributed its course of development largely to economic influences. I think he was more than a little bored with his class of small-town teachers, and he amused himself by teasing them.

"If Victorianism could be summed up in one word," he said, "That word should probably be 'reticence,' especially reticence about sexual matters. Now, Miss Smith, are you a Victorian?"

It has never occurred to Miss Smith to wonder what she is, and it would seem that she has little to be reticent about, but she knows that she does not wish to be classified as Victorian. She giggles, puts her hand to her mouth in confusion, and manages to say, between convulsions, "Oh, no; oh, no; oh, no!"

This is not to say that the course was frivolous. Parrington was a good teacher. He made us think.

After I received my degree, I ran Alumnae House once more during the following summer session. I was staying on to get the house cleaned and close it up when I received an offer from the University of Wisconsin of a teaching assistantship in freshman English, which I accepted.

I was put up at a senior honor house for a week while I looked for a place to live. With Maggie Duncan, another teaching assistant, who had received her M.A. at Madison that year, I rented a very nice apartment that was being sublet by a home-economics teacher on sabbatical leave. It was tucked away on a short, narrow street just one block below the foot of the hill, where the library now stands.

On the first floor of our apartment house lived three other new assistants, in a larger apartment that became the center of our social activities. One of these was Evelyn Archer, a recent graduate of Antioch College in Ohio, who had been a friend of Helen Watier's. She was a quiet person with a wonderful dry wit and broad sympathies. Another was Jean Dow, daughter of a history professor in Ann Arbor, whom I had not known until this year. Jean was lively and outgoing. She was then engaged to Robert Bacher, a young physicist, who was to be one of the designers of the first atomic bomb.

We were all poor. The women among us taught two three-hour classes for one hundred dollars a month. The men taught three classes for a hundred and fifty. Nearly everyone ate at a so-so cafeteria for about a dollar a day, which left a small margin for other expenses. I had never been able to pass up better food when it was available, and there was plenty in Madison. I economized on breakfast and lunch and ate dinner at one of the many excellent tearooms or, on Sundays, in the faculty dining room at the Union. It took just about every cent I had after paying the rent.

There were about a dozen new assistants, and we were isolated. I seldom so much as saw any regular members of the faculty of my own department except in classes I attended and at monthly meetings of the Freshman English staff. I remember three middle-aged instructors who had offices in our section of Bascom Hall: one man and two women who were working for their doctorates—the sort who live for years on end with their noses to the grindstone, doggedly meeting the requirements for a degree, on a subsistence income. They went their own ways. As a result we had to make our own entertainment.

We had a good crowd, with men and women about equally

divided. We all liked to talk and had plenty to talk about. Those of us who had phonograph records contributed them to the collection in the girls' apartment. On Saturday evenings we rolled up the rug and danced, and on Sunday afternoons, if we had nothing else to do, we listened to classical records.

In the spring, with the lake only a block from our door, we did not lack outdoor activities. There were a swimming beach and a canoe-rental place right back of the Union. Along the lake towards the west, below a cliff, an unpaved, woodsy road ran along the lake past Meiklejohn's experimental college. It was a pleasant place to walk.

The first semester I enrolled in two courses, as I was expected to do, but completed only one of them. Well before the semester was over I concluded that I could not do justice to both studying and teaching, and I chose to teach. This was not the way to commend myself to my superiors, but as usual I followed my inclination without regard for professional advantage.

The best thing about the department, in my view, was that we had complete freedom to teach in our own way. All classes had to study a certain rhetoric text, write a required number of themes, and do required reading; but within that framework we were on our own. I had a "B" group and a "C" group which, as I discovered, needed quite different approaches. I loved the work and gave it everything I had, including much time outside of class, thinking of ways to stimulate interest and looking for suitable reading material.

The "B's" were no great problem. They had come to college willing to learn and hoping to be interested, and all that was needed was to keep the flame alive.

The "C's" were a real challenge, and I am afraid I did not meet it too well. Most of them were farm boys enrolled in the College of Agriculture. For them English was a chore to be got over with, with as little effort as possible. They did not hesitate to tell me that it was a waste of time to learn to write because they did not intend ever to write anything! Discussion was impossible because they had had all their opinions from birth and saw no need for any new ones.

This attitude nearly came to open rebellion when the assigned essay dealt with international relations. I forget the name of the writer, but I remember that she was a well-known New England woman, by no means radical. She had turned the tables on Americans who resented criticism from foreigners, reminding them that their own view of Europeans was often equally provincial. The class was in an uproar. Americans were the only people who were any good and no dumb foreigner had any right to criticize us! This reaction occurred throughout the freshman English sections. By dinnertime it was the only subject of conversation among teachers. It scared me, and it scares me more today. These were the people who supported Senator McCarthy throughout the witchhunts of the Fifties, and it could happen again.

I had told my classes that I would accept their term papers for other courses as their term papers for English, and grade them on the writing. It seemed to me that this was an excellent way to demonstrate that good writing had its uses, and I figured that they would all try harder in the hope of raising their grades in other courses. This was a great success. The students were happy and got their papers in on time, and I got useful insights into their capabilities in other fields.

My own experiences as a student were enjoyable. The course I completed, in Elizabethan literature, was given by Professor Dodge. I was told that he was the last of the full professors in the department who had achieved his position without benefit of a doctorate. He was a gentleman of the old school, formal and crusty, yet somehow likeable. His personality was like good French bread; much of the goodness resided in the crust.

I think he must have instituted the custom of serving four o'clock tea for the English department in a room in Bascom Hall. He was the only senior faculty member who ever attended and he came every day.

One day the tea was being made by a young woman who had never made tea before, Dodge kept an eye on her while she did her best to follow directions. When she poured the water over the leaves into a cold pot, he strode over to where she stood, seized the pot and dumped the contents out of a third-floor window with no concern for who might be passing below, growling, "You always warm the pot first!"

My other course was a seminar on Chaucer with William Ellery Leonard. Leonard was an extraordinary man with a personality that aroused strong feelings in people. He had a somewhat imperious manner that some found offensive. He had, moreover, according to local gossip, offended certain people by the publication of a long, intensely emotional poem about his unfortunate first marriage in which he brought countercharges against those who had blamed him for the unhappy outcome.

All this was history when I came to Madison. He was then, I would guess, in his fifties, strong and virile and, in my opinion, altogether admirable. He was a true scholar, with a prodigious memory, in love with his subject; and he treated his students as equals. Looking around the table one day, he exclaimed, "Wouldn't it be wonderful if the knowledge in all these heads were in one head!" He valued *our* knowledge!

My assigned thesis subject was to determine whether Beothius was a Christian, a question that, it appeared, had troubled scholars down the centuries. Beothius was a late Roman philosopher whose influence was strong in Chaucer's time. Some of the assignments required only a close reading of Chaucer's text. This one required considerable knowledge in fields unfamiliar to me: late Roman history and philosophy. I never got beyond the history.

About the middle of the second semester I was summoned to talk with the head of the English department—I think his name was Lothrop —about renewing my contract. I had not seen him before, but he appeared to know all about me. He told me that I was welcome to come back the next year, but I would have to get down to business about earning a Ph.D., "and I don't think you want to do that." I could only agree with him.

"It would take you five years," he said.

I said, "Better make it ten." I was incapable of the single-minded application he was thinking of.

"You would not be happy in a public school," he went on—the routine, the cut-and-dried methods, the paperwork, the extracurricular duties. I had to agree with that too.

"And I don't know that a private school would be any better. It is no fun to teach girls who are interested only in boys and horses." Clearly, he was telling me that he believed I was on the wrong track. I said I thought I had better not come back next year.

What this adds up to is that graduate schools want doctoral candidates; teaching is subsidiary. I would have made a good teacher, given time, and I would have been happy doing it if I could have done it without being under pressure to get a degree, if it had paid a living wage, if there had been any chance of having any decent sort of life off the job. As it was, I might look forward only to round-the-clock work and a penny-pinching existence, with other relicts for company, while the bright young people came and went. There is a lot more involved in earning a living than the kind of work you do.

When I began to look for other work, I began to realize that the economic depression I had been reading about was real and that it might affect *me*. The only prospect that looked as if it might materialize was a teaching position in an exclusive private school in Washington, D.C., with dormitory duties attached. I had misgivings; but since I had to have work, I decided that I had better pursue the correspondence and see what would come of it. If there was good money in it, I might be able to stand it for a year or two. Money becomes very important when you don't have any.

After some weeks of questions, increasingly detailed, it became evident that the school was looking for someone eminently conventional and circumspect. At one point they were worried about my handwriting; it was too irregular. Was I, perhaps, not entirely dependable? I was relieved when the woman whose place they were trying to fill decided not to leave. She had probably discovered, as I had, that a job was a job. Both the school and I were fortunate.

Nearly everyone in our crowd was leaving. Jean was going home to be married. Archie and two of the men were to go to Harvard in the fall. Julia, the third of the trio downstairs, and Macklin Thomas, both Westerners, were going to Colorado. Maggie was the only one I know of who stayed on in Madison long enough to get her degree there.

One day in early June, jobless again, I took a train for Grand Rapids. Father's troubles had also begun, although he did not yet realize it. For the past several years he had held an executive position in the wholesale office at a considerable increase in pay. Now, the company, already feeling the pinch of the Depression, informed him that he would have to take a very large cut in salary. Father was indignant and quit. Was this the way to treat a faithful employee of nearly forty years!

He was not yet worried. A friend who sold life insurance had assured him that he could make all the money he needed as an insurance agent. I don't doubt that he could have done so in normal times; but when people don't know how much longer they will be able to eat, they are not good insurance prospects. I was apprehensive but I still could not believe that this abnormal situation could go on much longer.

When the summer session at the university opened, I went on to Ann Arbor, where I was pretty sure I could find some way to keep myself going for a couple of months. That would give me time to find something permanent. This was a gross miscalculation. For the next six years my only possible goal was to remain afloat, which I managed to do by taking any and every kind of work that came my way. Chance led me into some strange by-paths.

11

NEVER SAY DIE

The summer passed well enough. Through Dean Lloyd I secured a room free for chaperoning a sorority house. All I had to do was
be there. I rented a typewriter and earned enough typing term papers
to keep myself in food and basic supplies.

Herbert and Anna had set up housekeeping on the second floor
of an old house on Packard Street, with a bed borrowed from Herbert's
mother, a few chairs and a table from a secondhand shop, several
orange crates, and a grand piano that Anna was paying for in small
monthly installments. We often went out with friends for picnic
suppers, sometimes at the older Samples' cottage on Whitmore Lake.

I audited a course in how to teach English in college and wished
that I might have taken it the year before, when it would have done me
some good. Professor Fries, who taught it, was a first-rate teacher and
an interesting person. He had had the distinction of being the only
American to work on the big Oxford English dictionary, only recently
completed; and now he was editing one of the period dictionaries that
were being compiled from leftover information, along with much new
information secured from volunteer readers throughout the United
States. That fall he needed an assistant and he offered me the position.
I would have loved to accept it, but it paid only a hundred dollars a
month, and I still believed that something more remunerative must
turn up soon. I said I was sorry but I had already scraped along for a
year on that income and I could not afford to do so any longer. If I had
only known it, a dependable hundred dollars a month would have
been riches compared to what I lived on for the next seven or eight
years.

Oscar Campbell was now head of the English department, and
I knew that he had spoken warmly of me to Kenneth Rowe, so,
although Michigan was still holding out against women on the faculty,
I applied to Campbell for an instructorship. He replied, "There will
never be a woman on the staff of the English department while I am in
charge."

I asked why.

He said, "Men consider English a sissy subject. I am not about
to confirm that opinion by hiring women teachers." Beyond that I
could get nothing out of him. He was unwilling to be drawn into an
argument.

As the weeks went by and still I had no work, I became anxious. After the summer session ended I was employed in the dress department of Mack's department store as a saleswoman, but there were, alas, no customers. That job lasted two weeks. Vivien, meanwhile, had persuaded her landlady to let me share her bed if I would do the weekly cleaning. I took my meals with Lillian Brazell, who had given up her work at the dormitory temporarily to care for her mother, bedridden with hardening of the arteries. It was a help to them that I paid for my share of the groceries and helped with the cooking.

Helen Watier was also in straits. She was no longer being supported by her father because he disapproved of her taking more graduate work. She was renting a small but quite nice room where she could get herself a light breakfast, but she didn't know how much longer she could afford it. I remember her saying one day, "I refuse to lower my standard of living any further."

It must have been around the first of November when Alice Lloyd came through with another job that would at least keep a roof over my head. Mrs. Adams, who ran one of the oldest approved rooming houses, was in the hospital with terminal cancer, and someone was needed at once to take her place.

It was my duty to clean the three-story house once a week, brush up daily on the first floor, and tend the coal furnace night and morning. For this I received a large pleasant room and kitchen privileges and $5.00 a week. Cleaning day was long and hard, but the rest of the week I had much free time, and I took advantage of it to audit two classes. It cost nothing.

In January, when I no longer expected anything to happen, I was notified by the university placement bureau that a teaching position was open for the second semester at a Southern teachers' college. Since I have nothing good to say about the place, let it remain nameless. I had heard of the "Bible belt," but the expression meant little to me. In my mind the South was vaguely associated with romance: beautiful women, honorary colonels, hospitality—above all, hospitality. I accepted the offer and set out confidently in a smart new outfit, bought in Detroit at after-Christmas prices.

From the moment I arrived, every move I made and every word I said were made known all over campus. Any stranger was under suspicion, and my new clothes were a mistake. As a Yankee I would have done better to arrive looking a little dowdy. Dowdy people were safer. There was nothing overt, which was one of the distressing aspects of the situation. There was no defense against it.

The first night I was put up in the women's dormitory. The next morning, having been roused at five o'clock by a fire-alarm or equivalent, and having had breakfast in the cafeteria, where bedlam reigned, I was given a list of rooms to let, and set out with a senior student for a guide.

At the first place we stopped, the landlady was out but her retarded daughter, a grown woman, answered the doorbell. My escort told her our errand, whereupon she looked me over slowly from head to foot and shook her head, "Not her," she said, "Ma likes them as comes in nights." A fine start!

The next mistake I made was to reject all the rooms I was shown. At one place I was asked, "Do you want me to sleep yuh and feed yuh or just sleep yuh?" At several the only source of heat was a woodstove that I would have to tend myself. A room in a fine new house was just so stuffily vulgar, with landlady to match, that I could not get away fast enough. I do not doubt that the whole town knew before night that I thought I was too good for it.

The next day, by good fortune, I found a really nice room in a comfortable house, with an elderly couple who owned a downtown store. The woman was remarkable. She had grown up in the mountains and been educated by her mother, who had, in turn, been educated by her father, when the family took refuge there after the War between the States. Her education was distinctly superior to that of the people around her, and she was entirely lacking in prejudice.

When she was not helping in the store, she busied herself with making patchwork quilts in beautiful traditional patterns and with reading and gardening. She raised magnificent flowers, which she gathered into a big, deep pail under the kitchen sink, where they sat until they faded. Her whole interest seemed to be in growing them. I used to wish that she would offer me even one.

Three days a week I taught five classes in freshman English, beginning at seven in the morning. Chapel was convened at midmorning. The speaker was invariably the president, an ignorant man, whose discourses were so incoherent that they upset me. I cannot have been the only person who felt that way, but I was the only one who was so rash as to absent myself. I would be leaving in June; let them talk! During chapel hour I bundled myself up warmly and sat in the stadium, the sun on my face, breathing in the merciful solitude, while I waited for the one northbound train a day to come through with its nostalgic steam whistle.

It was not long before I was called to the dean's office to account for numerous remarks I was reported to have made. I had gone to a nearby city one weekend for a little sightseeing, but the weather was too hot for any pleasure. When asked if I had enjoyed my visit, I said something like, "A change is always pleasant." It got to the dean as, "Anything is better than this dead town." I did not try to defend myself. I said, "I am a stranger here. If this is the kind of thing that is coming to your ears I don't know what I can do about it." It was evident that the dean sided with my accusers. His parting shot was, "You certainly don't look like your picture." What he appeared to be saying was that he had not expected the person in the photograph to make waves of such magnitude. I would have liked to say that it did not take very much to raise a storm in a teakettle.

The atmosphere of that college was eloquent testimony to the futility of a system based entirely on repression. Sexual taboos so pervaded the atmosphere that the subject was never out of mind and found release in obscenity. The women's wash room had barnyard-style graffiti scrawled on every available surface, and a three-story cylindrical fire escape had the word, "fuck," painted all over the outside wall in three or four-foot letters. Yet it was newcomers like me who were viewed as sources of contamination simply because we were outsiders.

The social life could not be said to be enlivening. The registrar's wife occasionally entertained the women teachers with an evening of bridge. I attended just one of her evenings, on which occasion I won the consolation prize and the enmity of the star bridge player, who was stuck with me for a partner in the first round.

My work, on the other hand, was a pleasure, thanks to the wonderful students. Most of them came from nearby farms, where their labor was needed almost the year round. Some of them were able to get away for the whole spring semester; others came only for an eight-weeks session in late spring. A few were in school with their parents, who had been coming eight weeks a year for years and years. Their desire to learn was touching, especially in view of their un-preparedness. In my opinion, they would have been poorly equipped for the first year of high school.

First-year English was supposed to be a review of grammar, but we would have had to start from scratch, and it seemed to me a waste of effort. I said so to my department head, and he told me to do anything I liked. What an opportunity!

What those youngsters needed above all else, it seemed to me, was to have a few windows opened in their minds; they were eager for it and they expected to work.

I went to the library, an excellent one, surprisingly, and ferreted out enough material within their comprehension to give each student in a class his own topic for the semester. Each student was to give an oral presentation of his topic and to write a term paper on it. I could have counted on the fingers of one hand the students who could write coherently, but they were all excited about their projects. I like to think that they may have been a little less insular for the experience.

There were two other faculty members who were Northerners: another new English teacher—let me call her Nancy—and a U.S. Army colonel who commanded the ROTC. Nancy was young and pretty and lively, and would, no doubt, have come in for more criticism than she did if so much attention had not already been focused upon me. The colonel was an eminently proper military man with a chestful of ribbons, who had asked for assignment to a small school because of a lung ailment incurred from gas warfare during World War I. He was a bachelor, about fifty, a little stuffy but urbane and a gentleman, old-style, who enjoyed the company of ladies. He was sadly misplaced in a small provincial town. The appearance of two young women from the world outside was welcomed as a gift from heaven.

We three Yankees were allies from the start. For several weeks we ate dinner together in a teachers' dining room on campus that was otherwise deserted at night. The food was the best in town, the quiet was welcome; and it was a wonderful relief, when the day's work was done, to talk and laugh about things that would have irked us if we had been unable to share them. News of this soon got around. The art teacher was the first to join us; she had heard that we laughed a good deal at dinner. Soon, others began coming. Of course, the laughter ceased.

Spring was lovely. The campus had been beautifully land-scaped with a succession of spring flowers: daffodils, tulips, iris; and the air was fragrant with honeysuckle. Charming little Eastern to-whees flitted everywhere. But with spring came my ultimate disgrace.

Nancy was going out with a newspaper reporter; and one Sunday, at their invitation, I had dinner with them and a man I had not met before. We liked each other and I saw him quite frequently until, one day, a student asked Nancy, "Does Miss Broene know he is married?" The perfect finishing touch to my reputation—if any was needed! It seems that the man's wife had come to town with him in the fall, taken one look around and gone home again. He should have told me, and yet I could not blame him much. He must have figured that nothing very serious was likely to happen in the few weeks left, and the temptation was strong to have someone to pass the spring evenings with. He *had* told me to expect nothing beyond the end of the term, and I had assumed that he was engaged, or at least seriously interested in someone back home. If I were to make an issue of it now, all I would accomplish would be to end an agreeable friendship on a sour note. The damage was already done. I decided to ignore the information, and I heard no more about it, but apparently there was talk.

A year later, in Ann Arbor, when I was introduced to a summer student from this town, she laughed, and said, "Oh, you are the one!" Yes, I was the one. It was quite an experience!

When I left at the end of May I had earned $150.00 a month for four months in a town where I was unable to spend more than $50.00, yet I had precariously little money. I had run up small bills with the grocer and the druggist the preceding fall and had charged my new clothes, and the debts were a weight on my shoulders; so I paid them and took my chances.

For a week I stayed with Anna in Ann Arbor and began my acquaintance with Dick, my new nephew. While I was there Vivien gave me a letter of introduction to a friend who was editing textbooks in Chicago, just in case it should be useful sometime. From there I went home, where I found my father and Magdalen in a bad way. Nothing was coming in. Grocery bills were overdue. Obviously I could not stay home long without paying my way, and this I was unable to do. I don't remember that it ever occurred to me to look for work in Grand Rapids. That was one thing I could not do so long as I had any hope for a life of my own. With the letter for an excuse, I said that I was going to Chicago to investigate a job opening. I arrived in that city one afternoon, about the first of July, with $10.00 in my purse. I paid most of it out that same day for a week's board and room at an Eleanor Club on North Wabash Avenue, about a mile north of downtown. By this time the organization had some fine new residences and others abuilding but still retained a few of the old ones in once-fashionable districts, where accommodations were very cheap.

This was the first of several times during the next six months when I was down to virtually no money. This time luck was with me. The Eleanor Clubs did not run an employment agency, but sometimes people left word at the downtown office when they needed help. On the day I went in to see what might be available, I was told that a man would be in that afternoon who needed a maid at his country house for the summer.

Mr. Sinclair (a pseudonym) was a Southern gentleman, perhaps forty, who had grown up in affluence. He was good-natured, easy-going, unassertive, with only one practical accomplishment, as he told me later: the family butler, when he was a boy, had taught him to make fudge. He had not the faintest idea of what qualifications a maid should have and was delighted to have found someone so quickly. He said I should probably know that he and his wife were Christian Scientists, and I told him that they might need their faith when they ate my biscuits. That was all right with him. He hired me on the spot. Now, what had I got myself into! I could not afford to have misgivings, but I did wonder a little at my temerity. I was to have $15.00 a week, a generous wage, with commuting fare to Chicago on my day off; and the job was to last until the house was closed in the fall.

Mrs. Sinclair was less happy about the arrangement. I was clearly not a servant, and it embarrassed her to give me orders and ask me to do things for her. As a consequence, I got off with light duties as such work goes. Much of the time I was alone. Mr. Sinclair went to the city early every morning although there was little business. He worked in a brokerage office. Mrs. Sinclair stayed in her room until noon, reading Mary Baker Eddy, and retired there again after lunch. This program was varied in the evening by reading Christian Science literature aloud with her husband on the screened porch.

My principal duties were to brush up a little downstairs, keep the kitchen clean, prepare a simple lunch and dinner, and clean the house once a week. Meat and groceries were delivered from Evanston, and vegetables were picked young and tender from the garden.

In the afternoon my time was free until five o'clock. My little room was stifling hot, but I managed to sleep for an hour and then read for a while before washing out my clothes and taking a shower and dressing to prepare and serve dinner.

There was one child, a small boy, who spent much of his time with me in the kitchen or followed me round the house, having little else to do, and we developed a firm friendship. On the occasional days when things were hectic, I used to tell him, "You had better keep out of my way today; I am afraid I may be cross and I don't want to be cross with you." He understood.

The gardener was his hero. Every day, promptly at 12:00, when the noon whistle blew at a factory in town, I had to have his lunch ready in a lunch box to take outdoors and eat with his friend. This gardener was a wonderful old man, who had gone to sea and been around the Horn in the sailing days, and he had fascinating tales to tell. Once in a while he would sit in the kitchen and talk. He was always delightful.

On Wednesdays the routine was interrupted. Mrs. Sinclair went to the city early with her husband, and they came back together in the evening after attending the weekly testimonial meeting at church. On that day I had to clean the whole house, and it was a big one.

Thursday was my day off, and I spent it in Chicago looking for work. Week after week there was nothing. Those trips were not entirely futile, however, since they gave me the opportunity to go to the library and pick up a week's reading.

About once a week Mrs. Sinclair entertained friends at lunch, and on these days I was "help" in earnest, complete with uniform. One morning when there was to be a very special guest and I already had enough to do to keep me on the run till lunch was on the table, she decided to dye the large linen tablecloth she intended to use. It was a sight, the dye unevenly distributed in ugly splotches. She brought it to me dripping wet, to iron—a task for a saint under any circumstances. One way or another I got everything done, but in the flurry I forgot to serve the finger bowls that Mrs. Sinclair had painstakingly adorned with freshly picked rosebuds. Her self-discipline was strained almost to the breaking point, but her reproaches were mild. I never knew her to lose control of herself.

On another occasion a couple of dozen guests had been invited to have lunch in the garden. An elderly woman, accustomed to giving orders, was employed to manage the kitchen, and the rest of us had to step around for her. The result was confusion. A former maid, and the gardener in a white coat, were to assist in waiting table. Everything had been planned in great detail, but two hazards had been over-looked. The first was flies. This was horse country, and the food had scarcely been set before the guests when it was black with the pesky creatures. The other was that there was only one kitchen door. With three waiters coming and going, all under pressure, a collision was foreordained. Just before the guests left, the gardener coming in, and I going out, met in the tiny entry way with a terrible shattering of delicate glassware. Again Mrs. Sinclair was upset but she kept her temper.

When the guests and the extra help had gone and frayed nerves longed for quiet, the kitchen was swarming with flies, hordes of them, all in frenzied motion. There was little we could do about it until evening, when most of them settled on the ceiling, more or less drowsy. Then my employers and I went at them with fly swatters for an hour or more. It was a long, hard day.

Towards the end of July, Mrs. Sinclair began preparing me for the visit of her mother-in-law in August, which she evidently dreaded. I gathered that there would be no more easy days for me, but since I was free to quit at any time I decided not to worry. Before the dreaded date, the woman changed her mind and decreed that the family should join her in Atlantic City. I was out of work again after only six weeks.

Now I registered again at my old Eleanor Club. It was only a mile from downtown, so I could walk anywhere I needed to go. Once a small boy approached me, asking for a nickel for carfare. When I asked where he was going he looked uncertain for a moment, then muttered unintelligibly. I said, "Do you know what I do when I don't have carfare? I walk." The child looked at me as if he would like to kill me!

Prospects were poor for any kind of work. Businesses were laying people off, not taking them on. When my summer savings got down to $10.00, I spent five of them for a classified ad in the *Chicago Tribune*. With one exception, the responses came from companies that wanted salesmen to work on a commission basis or from men with personal ends in view. There was a literate and courteous letter from a bachelor in Indiana who was fed up with restaurant meals and would be happy to take me into his heart and home if I would cook for him. There was a note painstakingly written on ruled tablet paper, offering to take me in on trial and marry me if we suited each other.

There was a note scribbled on a small scrap of paper that read only, "Meet me at such a place." The most picturesque offer came from the proprietor of an incense shop who was willing, in part payment, to let me sleep in the back room—whether alone or with company was not clear.

The exception was a letter from a woman who said she was a social worker and asked me to meet her at an El station at a certain hour when she would be on her way home from work. She was a middle-aged widow with a kind, sad face, who was supporting her two or three children on her small salary. She said that she had no extra bed and not much room, but she could give me a roof over my head if I were stranded. "You won't have to sleep on a park bench." Such kindness is, in itself, a gift beyond price. She also told me about a new clinic for disturbed children that had just opened and was still, she thought, looking for office workers.

I made an appointment with the chief psychiatrist and waited a long time before he could give me his attention. When at length I got to see him, he said he was sorry, there were no openings; but when I rose to go he said, "Sit down a minute." Then he began asking me questions about myself and my situation and would not let me go until he had satisfied himself that I could handle it. "You are all right," he said. "You can make it. Just don't ever let yourself think that the failure is yours. It is society that has failed." I lived on those words for the next several years. "You are all right; you can make it."

I didn't think much of Chicago as a city: the endless gridiron streets, so many of them drab and dreary; the railroad yards; the oil-filmed river; the commercial atmosphere; yet nowhere else have I found so much human kindness, so much concern for me, a stranger. I have a very warm feeling for the people.

Just in time I found a weekend job, waiting table at a suburban golf club, that paid enough to keep me for a week in Chicago. On the strength of it I moved to the College Club on Michigan Avenue across from the Drake Hotel beach. The accommodations were much better, the food was beautiful, and the cost was moderate. This luxury was not to last long, however. The golf club manager had other things in mind for me besides waiting table. He seemed a decent sort, quite likeable, but there was evidently a substratum of ruthlessness. He said that if I would oblige him he would give me a full-time job and take me to Florida in the winter with the rest of his staff. He thought he had clinched the deal when he said, "You know that you won't find any other work. There is nothing else you can do."

"Oh, yes, there is," I said. "I can starve," and I took the next train back to the city with twenty-five cents in my purse.

Brief as that experience was, two or three weekends, it gave me an interesting view of a kind of life I knew nothing about. Although the dining room was not open for breakfast, we had to be on hand promptly at eight o'clock to sweep the floor, dust, straighten furniture, and set the tables. After that we worked in the kitchen, supervised by the manager's wife, a grim woman, who took pleasure in pushing us around. Peeling onions is probably not the only thing we did, but that is what stands out in my mind, peeling onions until we could no longer see. If we were lucky we might be sent to the cellar to bring up some peaches, which afforded an opportunity to snitch one and eat it fast. Fresh fruit was one of the items not allowed to us, along with steak and fresh baked goods. The latter we might have next day if there was anything left over.

A convention or a large party always incurred extra work. On one such occasion I was assigned to carry the salad dressing for all the tables into the dining room shortly before lunch was served. We carried large, heavy trays on one shoulder, and we had to go through the swinging doors by pushing with the other shoulder. This day my tray tilted a little; I could feel the load shifting precariously and I thought I was lost. How I righted it I don't know, but I do know there would have been the devil to pay if all the dressing had ended up on the floor!

It was hard work, always under pressure. During my morning and afternoon breaks I used to fall into a heavy sleep for about fifteen minutes, which left me just time enough to press my clothes and wash up before going back on duty.

I shared an extra-large room with a sweet little fourteen-year-old German girl who attended the manager's child. A clothesline, used by everyone on the floor, hung diagonally across the room, where we had to dodge it continually. I used my first morning break to move the line parallel to one wall. Then I went to work on a pile of household linen and transferred it to the linen closet where it belonged. My little roommate was so delighted that she joined me in a general cleanup. She was a neat child but had been overwhelmed by the seeming magnitude of the task.

The first thing I did when I got back to the city was to check out of the College Club and check all my worldly goods at the free checking counter at Marshall Field's. Then I spent five cents on a telephone call to two women I knew who shared an apartment on the North Side. I asked if they could take me in over the weekend, and was told that they would be away but would leave a key for me. A second nickel went for a call to a man I had met through my want-ad. He had seemed very decent and had given me his card and said, "If I can ever do anything for you, let me know." I asked him if he would take me to dinner, which he did cheerfully and later called a taxi to take me to my destination, pressing a bill into my hand at the last minute to pay the fare. Propriety was not a major concern at that moment. It was a five-dollar bill, which left me enough change for several dinners if I was careful.

On Tuesday morning, bright and early, I walked into an employment agency. There it was the same old story: no jobs. "But I can give you a room and breakfast," the woman said. She needed someone to wash breakfast dishes. She also gave me carfare.

The house was in Oak Park, in a good neighborhood, but it was lamentably neglected, and the kitchen was filthy. Two cats, and a litter of kittens not yet housebroken, lived in the basement; and the door was left open into the kitchen so that they could come up and get their food. I was feeling pretty sorry for myself when I made a cup of cocoa the first morning, and when a cockroach floated to the top it was the last straw. Still, I could not bring myself to tell my benefactor what I thought of her establishment. I stood it until Friday, when I knew that she and her husband would not be back until Monday, and left, again penniless except for carfare.

At the last minute it occurred to me that I might have some mail. I did. There was a letter from Helen Watier with $3.00 enclosed! Trust Helen to anticipate a friend's needs. I was in business again.

I had decided to cast myself upon the mercy of the club on Wabash Avenue, where I was well known by this time. They took me in without question; I could eat now and pay later. This was not entirely a free ride, however. I earned my keep by living in a double room with women whom no one else could get along with. The first one was a girl from an Iowa farm, who had come to Chicago to study at the Chicago Art Institute. Now she had no more money and she was unwilling to go home and admit defeat. All day she just sat in the room, saying nothing, doing nothing. At night she used to wake up screaming that her uterus was falling out, and I would get up and give her some aspirin and hold her hand until she quieted down. This went on until the club called her family and asked them to come and get her.

My next roommate was a large, muscular woman from Luxembourg who cropped her hair and wore a long black garment like a monk's. She had lived through the war almost entirely on potatoes, and it had upset her digestive system. This was her only topic of conversation. She had a phobia about germs, and as luck would have it I was washing my musty dresser drawers with Lysol when she first saw me. That was enough to give her a crush on me, and crushing it was.

The top floor where we lived had been an attic, and the plumbing had been installed *ad lib*. Each of the two bath tubs was housed in its own little cubicle, apart from the other bathroom facilities. The other women on the floor understood that I needed a retreat, and they reserved one of the cubicles for me in the evening. There I retired after dinner with a book, which only endeared me the more to my hygienic room-mate. She had never known a person so clean!

I saw a good deal of Lucile Pierce, whom I had met in Ann Arbor the previous summer. She was teaching in a public school, as were her mother and her fiancé; and they were all being paid in scrip, a promise to pay at some uncertain date. Few stores would accept the paper. Marshall Field was one of those that did, and most of what one needed could be found there, but it was no help with the rent or groceries. Lucile was taking it with good grace, and her equanimity helped me keep mine.

It must have been around the middle of September that I went to work at the Merchandise Mart as a stenographer for a food fair. There was a good deal of typing but little dictation, and I got by. My handwriting, however, has never recovered. We had a business manager and a combination social secretary and publicity director. I no longer remember the woman's name. To me she was, from the first, Miss Havisham, straight out of *Great Expectations*, the deserted bride who had grown old in her wedding dress amidst dust and cobwebs. She must have been in her sixties and she was distressingly, painfully homely. Dresses that year were all low necked, and Miss Havisham wore net guimpes to cover her bony throat and chest. When her sister came in one day and told her that her guimpe was out of place, I got the dressing-down of my life. She had not looked into a mirror for years, she told me, and it was part of my job to tell her when her clothes were not on straight!

After she had come to trust me, she told me one day that she had once been engaged to a man in my hometown, who had backed out before the marriage. Miss Havisham, indeed! The breach of trust had shaken her irreparably. From that time she had hidden her hurt being a façade of gruffness and aloofness. I doubt that she had any real friend besides her sister.

The fair was fun. Monsieur Berard, the cheerful chef who managed all four of the restaurants in the mart, proudly showed me through all of them. They were gleaming with stainless steel. A pastry chef showed me the cakes that had won the prizes and the cakes that should have won them. The blue ribbon had gone to the highest and fanciest, which, he told me, was second rate because it was built around an armature. The test of a confectioner's art was his ability to create a structure that would stand alone.

This job lasted six weeks. A couple of weeks later I went on to a second temporary job with the same woman, an annual Christmas event sponsored by the Hearst newspaper. The paper advertised for contributions of used toys for poor children, presumably to be repaired by society women out of the largeness of their hearts. Actually, most of the women came once a week to have their pictures taken looking charitable. A few of them, a very few, came quite regularly and tried to do something, but the real work was done by a man hired for the purpose. Many of the toys were beyond repair.

The regulars were young women who, having nothing to do

that mattered, were trying to do something, anything, that might give them a feeling of usefulness. I developed a real sympathy for one of them; and she, for me, apparently. She must have noticed that I wore the same dress to work every day, for one day she asked if she might give me a new dress that was too small for her. It was made of beautiful woolen goods, very simple and very smart and it fit me perfectly. I swallowed my pride and accepted it, and hated every minute that I wore it. I understood the motive and appreciated the kindness, but that dress made me conscious as I had not been before that I was down and out— a hanger-on at the fringe of the social fabric.

My situation was beginning to affect me in other ways also. When I walked home after work up North Michigan Avenue, I passed a fine Japanese shop where the window exhibits always included miniature carvings of semi-precious stones. Ordinarily I would have enjoyed them and been glad that such beauty existed. Now I asked myself bitterly how such things could be when millions of people were hungry, when someone like me was unable to earn her bread. *I wanted to smash that window.* I wanted it passionately. Our instinct when we are frustrated is to hit out at something. I am glad I have known the feeling, because I suspect it is at the root of much, if not all, violent behavior.

The big event at the office was a tea just before Christmas. The project was housed in a big, empty store building. In the middle of the floor, tables were put together to make one long one. Downtown merchants had been pressured or cajoled into lending us the necessary table furnishings, which included a lace tablecloth many yards long. A young Italian, a protégé of Miss Havisham's, was hired to help in the back room.

He was inexperienced and something went wrong. I no longer remember what it was, only that Miss Havisham, who had been a bundle of nerves to start with, was distraught. When the visitors had left and everything else had been removed from the table, she could no longer contain herself. She and the young man had each picked up one end of the cloth when she began pacing around the table, the man some yards behind her, holding up the other end, like a train. Now she was truly the abandoned bride. The book had come startlingly to life. Then suddenly she stood still. "Well," she said, "I guess that's that!"

After Christmas the world seemed to come to a halt. This is a slack season even in good times. I was nearly out of funds again and had no new leads. I would have to think of something else. If I could find a reason for going back to college, I should be able to get a loan from my *alma mater*. One semester would get me a teacher's certificate. In February I was in Ann Arbor again with a $500.00 loan. I was buying time.

12

MORE DARK DAYS

There were enough of us who had come back to college for the same reason to make a class by ourselves. A few had been in the past year's graduating class, at least one man was over forty, and we were all holding tenuously to the hope that a teacher's certificate might just possibly secure us a foothold in the economic slough.

If I am to be honest, I can only say that I found the course altogether a bore. The aims of education were presented to us as a set of doctrines to be memorized and accepted, not unlike the catechism. The greatest of these was "worthy citizenship," repeated *ad nauseam*. I did what I had to do to get my certificate, nothing more.

I had found a room on Maynard Street, next door to Helen Newberry Residence, that I might have for three dollars a week. I often dropped in at the dormitory at tea time for a chat with my old friend Lillian, who was again at her post. Soon I knew many of the girls; and when one of them who waited table needed a substitute, I was asked to fill in. In this way I earned quite a few of my meals. At other times good meals were available for fifty or seventy-five cents. I was in clover, compared to the year before.

Vivien was still slowly building up credits towards graduation. Marion Fisk had been divorced and was living at her mother's house while she worked for a master's degree in psychology. I was always welcome there. Helen Watier had married Kenneth Rowe of the English department, and they were living in a new development across the river. Ann Arbor was growing. With so many old friends at hand I felt once more at home.

Herbert and Anna had moved into another new neighborhood farther out Packard Street. I saw them frequently and sometimes stayed with Dick when they went out. He was now a mischievous toddler, whose idea of fun was to wake me in the morning by climbing up on my bed and jumping on me! Sometimes I took him out for a walk, on which occasions I was supposed to produce an airplane overhead. This I was usually able to do, thanks to the U.S. mail service. This was something I needed; there had been no children in my life.

For entertainment I could see good plays inexpensively at the new Lydia Mendelssohn Theater. Anna or one of her friends always had concert tickets that someone couldn't use. I also made liberal use of the library. For a few weeks life seemed manageable, until I went home in April or May for six weeks of practice teaching in Grand Rapids. Father and Magdalen were now in real straits. They had got behind in house payments. The grocer was no longer being lenient about bills. And things could only get worse. There was no end in sight, for them or for me or for anybody. Back in Ann Arbor, my course nearly ended, I was overcome by fatigue.

I went to see Alice Lloyd and asked her if I might be put to bed for a week at the Health Service. She arranged an appointment for me and I was referred to Dr. Raphael, the psychiatrist. After questioning me for some time, he was called away for a moment and went off, leaving his notes on the desk. I could not resist looking at what he had written. It read: "Diagnosis: intolerable economic situation." For a week I had nothing to do but eat and sleep.

During the following summer I got on quite well, typing papers for summer-school students and sometimes waiting table for my meals. Once or twice I went to bed hungry, often enough to acquire an understanding of real need. Lucile Pierce was back for another summer session. I had quite a few dates. I made myself a new summer dress from a silk remnant, and when I didn't like the sleeves I took them out, opened them up, turned them upside down, and applied them as shoulder capes. It was quite successful. Necessity is, indeed, the mother of invention.

The end of summer school, however, brought another crisis. With nothing coming in, even my $3.00 a week room was too expensive. Help came through Ann Hill, one of my recent fellow-students, who had got through college as a live-in household helper at the Purdoms. Mr. Purdom was the director of the university placement bureau; his wife, Jemima, was the daughter of Professor Wenley, head of the philosophy department. They lived with their three daughters in a fourteen-room house, which Jemima turned upside down annually for a thorough housecleaning. This she insisted on accomplishing in one week, which required an extra hand.

All three of us worked hard, each cleaning one room a day. At lunch we discussed what to have for dinner and took turns getting off early to prepare it. Dinners were always fun. We enjoyed each other; and the girls, between five and fifteen, seemed to feel that an extra person at dinner made it something like a party. They were uninhibited but well behaved.

When I had to leave, there were still a few weeks before the fall session opened. Anna and her family were away, and I lived alone in their house for a week, with no way to find work except through the classified ads. Answering an ad for a housekeeper, I met a good-looking young widower whose wife had died of tuberculosis two years before, after two years in a hospital. He had come from a farm and built up a successful business as a building contractor, but now construction was at a standstill, and he was stuck with several lots on which he was unable to build. He had had no one to take care of his house and his two younger children except a daughter, then fourteen, who had recently moved out to live with an aunt. He offered me the job at the going rate of $5.00 a week. When I expressed surprise that he had not asked for references, he replied, "I have hired many men in my business; I know a good man when I see one"! I took the job.

This was a highly unconventional situation, I doubted that it could last long, but I had to have something at once. The man was a fine person, and intelligent. If he was willing to try it, I was.

The two children in my care were Mildred, ten years old, and a boy about three years younger. Although they had had little care for four years or more, they were sweet and affectionate. The house was fairly new, but it had not had a really good cleaning in years, to judge by the disarray. For meals, the table was covered with newspaper, and the children's milk was served from the bottles. In a week I had changed all that. The house was clean, and we had a tablecloth and a milk pitcher.

The boy was stand-offish at first, which was natural. I did things to please him when I could and let him take his time to come around, which he did in about a week. Mildred and I were friends from the first moment. She followed me around all day, chattering brightly, like a little bird. Every afternoon I dropped the housework for an hour and took a walk with the children to the playground. It was the high point of their day. They were so happy with so little, they wrung my heart.

Their father went out every morning and came home for lunch, bringing the day's groceries. The vegetable was always cabbage. I like cabbage but within limits. After lunch he went out again until dinner-time, doing whatever it is that men do when they are needed nowhere. He did not drink. Evenings he stretched out on the sofa and lay there, only half alive, a man without hope. I went to my room too tired even to read before I fell asleep.

One day several relatives arrived from the country, apparently to look me over. A few days later, on a Saturday—I forget whether I had been there two weeks or three—one of them came again and took the children with her when she left. As soon as they were gone, I was told to get my things together and leave at once. Obviously I was to get out before the children returned. The reason I was given was that my employer could no longer afford even my small pay. It seemed most unlikely that his circumstances had worsened so much in two or three weeks. The real reason could have been any one of a number of things. He might have found the situation untenable. He might have feared that I was alienating his children with my middle-class ways. More probably, the relatives found the situation scandalous. They had been very cool to me.

I was distressed, knowing that the children had come to trust me and that they might think, or be told, that I had deserted them. Sometimes when I wake up in the night, I still wonder how Mildred took it. That child had wound herself around my heart.

Why did I not protest the manner of my leaving? Why did I not ask, "Do you have any idea what you are doing to your children?" Why did I not say that I would go but I would not run away? The only thought I had in my head was that if I was not wanted I had to do as I was ordered.

The next thing I remember is that I was back in my old room with a $25.00-a-month job, teaching English to foreigners in night school. So much for a teacher's certificate! At four o'clock every afternoon I tutored a girl about twelve years old who was due to enter a private boarding school the next year and was behind in her school work. I don't know whether she made it or not. That unfortunate child was a nervous wreck. She was being prepared for society, with a schedule of lessons so hectic that she had to be chauffeured even short distances in order to get in all her lessons: swimming, riding, French. She could not keep her mind on anything for three minutes at a time, and all she really cared about was horses.

The earlier part of the day was free and it was a godsend to have a fine library available. For many weeks I read Eighteenth Century English diaries and letters. They were written by very clever people, who moved in different circles, literary or artistic or uppercrust. Together they drew a broad picture of English society in one of its livelier moods. It took my mind off the current sorry state of affairs, which I was beginning to need.

For some months, my state of mind, strange to say, had been euphoric. The variety of experience, the unforeseeable changes of fortune, the freedom that accompanied the lack of long-term commitments, had outweighed the anxiety most of the time. But unemployment takes its toll sooner or later. I stopped writing to friends, having nothing to say except that I was still without work. Since they were unable to help, it embarrassed them. At this point I was hanging on not because I had any hope but only because there was nothing else to do.

After Christmas Vivien came to me with an offer of a free room. She was still working for Dean Cooley, who was then acting as executor for an estate. It included a big, old house high above the river, which he didn't want to stand empty. A couple, and the woman's mother, were living on the first two floors; and Vivien had a very attractive room on the third floor. There was one other, which I could have if I liked. It didn't take long to make up my mind. Three dollars a week saved was six dinners. For five dollars I got the walls painted sky blue, and for another five I bought peach-colored voile for window curtains; and that was the end of room expense for the next seven months.

That year was the low point of the Depression. Franklin Roosevelt was inaugurated as president in March, and one of the first things he did was to order a three-day moratorium on all banking activities. I don't know anything about the workings of this, but it seemed to bring to a stop everything that had not stopped already. That month the university paid everybody on its payroll half of what he had earned. Since I had earned $10.00, making an index, I got a check for five.

I had also typed a long report that the university had undertaken for the University of Iowa on the effects of polluted water on fish in the Mississippi. (It was serious way back then.) Iowa was supposed to pay Michigan, which would then pay me, but the money from Iowa was not forthcoming. After several months the director of the project at Michigan paid me the $50.00 or $60.00 out of his own pocket. I was reluctant to take it because few people had such a sum to spare at the time, but I figured I needed it worse than he did. I had been charging my dinners on the strength of it.

During this time a big dish of oatmeal did me for breakfast and lunch. I made a pint of it and ate it with brown sugar and a can of evaporated milk, and it served me pretty well.

This kind of hand-to-mouth living can go on just so long in one place, it seems. For two or three weeks in June I worked in an office in the chemistry department, toting up students' bills for breakage. In July I went to a cottage on Crystal Lake with a faculty wife who wanted a companion until her husband could join her in mid-August; but after a week she got a toothache and we went back to Ann Arbor. I was high and dry again. The typing that had kept me going through two summers did not materialize; I was now living too far from the campus. I could see nothing ahead.

Again Vivien came to my rescue. She said she was sure I could get a job at Macy's in New York if I wished to try it. A sorority sister of hers was personnel manager. So be it. For $5.00 I got a lift from a student who was driving east after summer school, and a few days later I was selling china at Macy's. My pay was $17.00 a week, of which $2.00 was a bonus for having a master's degree. I lasted two weeks. My notice informed me that I was not aggressive enough.

Getty Gunn was now in New York, and I had taken a room where she lived, in an especially nice working women's club on MacDougal Street in Greenwich Village. Three houses had been put together to make one big one with a comfortable and spacious lounge. The back yards had been opened up too, and planted with grass and shrubs and trees. On the next street, the whole block had been purchased by young couples with small children; and their back yards, adjoining ours, had been made into a shady green space, where children played. It was an oasis in the heart of Manhattan. I think I paid

$12.50 for a room and two excellent meals a day.

Jeannette was now Jeannette Moser (I forget her husband's first name) and had a son three or four years old. She was on her way up, as advertising manager at Saks Fifth Avenue.

Eve had married Francis Marks, whom she had met on a recent European trip. They were living comfortably on Jones Street, also in the Village, where the Greenwich Street Settlement House had renovated several attractive old brick houses. I met Francis only once. He died a short time later.

Clara had married Paull Hayden, a Philadelphian. They were both writing advertising and were living in a large, bright, airy, corner apartment in Columbia Heights. Two or three years later they had both lost their jobs. Thanks to Clara's resourcefulness, however, they soon had a thriving business, making and marketing Hollandaise sauce. At College Point on Long Island Sound, they found a spacious old Victorian house where it was possible to carry on the business at home. Over the years they transformed the long-neglected grounds into a thing of beauty. Theirs is the only success story I know of to have come out of those desolate years.

When I lost my job at Macy's I could no longer afford to live at the MacDougal Club. Someone told me that the Women's City Club sponsored a similar residence in the Chelsea area, where the cost was low. There I lived for about a month, until Jeannette offered me a job writing advertising for Saks. She warned me not to expect it to be permanent. It was supposed to be, she said, but Mr. Gimbel wanted a new face about every three months.

Three months was exactly how long it lasted. That was enough to buy one good new outfit, renew my stock of underwear, and save a little money. Jeannette had said, "You will have to wear good clothes to work; employees are expected to dress like the customers"! and she and Eve had let me use their charge accounts to get what I needed. I don't know what might have happened to me without friends during those years.

I had moved back to the MacDougal Club, which was not only nicer but much more conveniently located. I stayed on through January, with only one day's work, shopping for fabrics for a puppet-maker in a chilling winter rain. As I watched my small savings disappear, I began to feel pretty low. Was this vagabond life never going to end!

One night I had a beautiful dream. I was walking down a slope covered with spring flowers, towards a ship that was coming up a river with banners flying. The whole world was ashine. In my dream I was gloriously happy. Only years later did I remember that my mother had always spoken of better times to come as "when our ship comes in." After that I pulled myself together again.

Late in January, through a classified advertisement, I found a job that promised to last a while. I was to begin work at Consumers' Research in Washington, New Jersey, on the first of February. By this time, however, I didn't have enough money to get there and live for a week until I should be paid. I combed the telephone book, without success, for some social agency that might be willing to lend me the fifty or sixty dollars I needed. I had almost given up when I made one more call and was asked to come in and talk about it. I don't remember the name of the organization; it went out of business a few months later. I got $50.00 on my signature, and was off to another small town!

Consumers' Research was an interesting organization. There were about two dozen engineers, writers, editors, and stenographers, nearly all of them from New York or surrounding areas. About the same number of persons in the mailing department were nearly all local girls. The business was run in a very personal manner by F.J. Schlink, an engineer, who saw it as an important contribution to the general welfare. He was exacting, but he was fair. It was a good place to work.

Mrs. Schlink, Mary Catherine Phillips, supervised the mailing room, I believe, but her influence did not stop there. Her likes and dislikes carried weight. I had little to do with her, but when I did there was always a little tension between us. I never felt easy with her; and she was probably not comfortable with me, since these things are usually mutual.

Many of the townspeople resented us. My first landlady, a retired garment worker from New York, took pleasure in sounding off about strangers who thrust themselves upon a peaceful town with their city ways. She was vehement about the shamelessness of women who wore shorts in summer. In such an atmosphere we were isolated.

Whether it was for this reason or from his paternalistic attitude, Mr. Schlink encouraged social gatherings among his staff. The first winter he promoted a discussion group of which the only thing I remember is that I had to present a paper on the Technocrats. These were a group of engineers who proposed that engineers should run the government, as best suited to understand the needs of a techno-logical society. The idea didn't get far. In summer we had frequent picnic suppers at a small lake where there was good swimming and a nice little dance hall. This was better than nothing but it was not exactly a full life, especially since we were a motley crew that hap-pened to have been washed up on the same desert island. At least we got along well together.

This dull existence was alleviated to some extent for many of us by weekends in New York. Several people drove in every Friday after work, and for a dollar apiece they would take passengers. I was always welcome at Eve's apartment, whether she was there or not. When spring came, I made an arrangement with Virginia Vincent to occupy her apartment on weekends; she always went home to New Jersey. What those weekends gave me was principally a change of scene. I had no money to spend and I saw less of my friends than might have been expected. Jeannette had moved out to Bronxville. Eve went away on weekends oftener than not. On rare occasions I indulged myself in a cheap seat at the theater. I saw Eva LeGallienne in *The Master Builder* and *The Cherry Orchard*, and Jane Cowl in *Romeo and Juliet*.

At work I assisted Virginia Alison with the editing of the monthly reports. This was interesting, and I appreciated the opportunity to learn a new trade. It was a severe disappointment when this was cut short after a few months. Virginia left to get married and I took over her work, expecting to inherit her position. Not so. After a few weeks I was informed that a new editor was being brought in from New York. After that I could have no hope of getting anywhere at CR. Mr. Schlink's excuses sounded pretty lame to me. I may have done Mary Catherine wrong but I thought I saw her hand in this. I was replaced by Susan Jenkins, to whom I had to teach the job from scratch before I stepped down. She was embarrassed, but there was nothing that either of us could do about it. We were soon friends in spite of the situation and of wide differences in our views.

Sue was a woman with strong convictions, who felt the miseries of the Depression deeply. She had espoused the cause of unionization as the remedy for economic injustice. There was power in numbers. If all workers could be organized they would be able to assert their rights. Utopia was within reach. Almost immediately upon her arrival, she went to work to unionize CR. I would not have given five cents for her chances of success, but I could not have been more mistaken. She had energy to match her fervor, and her enthusiasm was contagious. As an organizer, she came on like a whirlwind. Persons who had been apathetic for want of anything to do perked up, now that they had a project. Those whose confidence had begun to slip were encouraged to show some initiative. The place began to come to life. Individualists like myself paid our dues and went along with the tide. What difference did it make? By the first of the year we had a full-fledged union.

In February an event occurred that was to change my life. A group of us had adjourned after a meeting to the town tavern, a respectable German establishment, for coffee or a glass of beer. A little later, Herman Southworth, one of the engineers, came in with a new arrival. His name was Robert Rogers and he had been doing graduate work in physics at Cornell University for the past two years. I was attracted to him at once. He had nice eyes and interesting cheek-bones, and his face lit up when he smiled. Just then his cheeks were rosy from the cold. I thought, "If he were ten years older this could be interesting." But he was not, so that was that for the time being. During the time we were in Washington, he paid no attention to me. I had not expected that he would.

Nothing much happened during the rest of the winter or the following spring and summer, so I was greatly surprised when I came back from a vacation in late August to find a strike in full swing. For me it was the last straw. I was not in sympathy with the strike, but all my friends were involved in it. If I sided with the company I would be stuck in that dull town alone, with small prospect of ever getting out of it. It was a prospect I was unable to face. I joined the strikers, salving my conscience by telling myself that my presence on one side or the other could not possibly affect the outcome.

For a few weeks I remained in Washington, taking as little active part in the strike as possible. At the same time, having got myself into it, I tried to convince myself that it might be justifiable. But as the strike progressed and both sides resorted to tactics that seemed to me equivocal at best, I wanted nothing to do with either. But to whom could I turn? Where could I go? I had a roof over my head only because I shared an apartment with Sue. She realized that something was wrong, and early in October she got me transferred to the New York office, where funds were being solicited. At this remove the whole thing seemed distant and unreal, and I ceased to think much about it. I had made my escape sooner that I had hoped, and I would never go back. Today I can only say that I had lived on the edge of a precipice for more than five years, and my store of courage was overdrawn. I was very near the breaking point.

Already the future was taking shape, although I did not know it. I was assigned to a double desk, and whom should I be sharing it with but Bob Rogers! For a few weeks we had little to do with each other except in the way of business. Most of the others were eating at a noisy, mediocre cafeteria, and he ate with them, while I went off to a small tea room on one of the parks—it may have been Gramercy—where I could get a substantial meal at little more cost in a peaceful atmosphere (Those of us in New York were given shelter by strike sympathizers, and received a small food allowance.)

Then, one day, out of a blue sky, Bob asked me, "Would you mind if I went to lunch with you?" After that, things happened fast. We lunched together and we dined together, and we are still together half a century later.

The strike petered out inconclusively. Consumers' Research remained in business. A new consumers' organization, Consumers' Union, was formed in New York, and most of the strikers stayed with it until it got off to a good start. I found work as an editorial assistant at the book-publishing firm of Covici, Friede. Unfortunately it was on the road to bankruptcy, and two years later I was again out of work. At the time it looked permanent. For the first time in many years the future held a promise of happiness.

* * *

Meanwhile the news from Europe grew ever more alarming. First it was wild inflation in Germany, joblessness and unrest. A disturbing novel about the people's plight was translated into English as *Little Man, What Now?* A politically ambitious house-painter who called himself Adolf Hitler was rallying the malcontents under the banner of Nordic superiority. Jews and Communists were the enemy. It was soon evident that he was a man to be reckoned with, a born rabble-rouser. By February, 1933, he was chancellor of Germany.

My friend Stanley Fletcher, a music student in Berlin that year, was sending dispatches home to a Springfield, Massachusetts newspaper. On February second, his last dispatch began, "Something is afoot in Berlin tonight." Hitler's Nazi followers were parading in memory of a comrade alleged to have been murdered by the Communists two years before, and street fighting broke out. The dispatch ended, "Until the March elections anything may happen—the dance is on."

I remember assuring myself that we had nothing to fear because the man was obviously mad. I remember even more vividly the sick feeling that came over me when I realized that this kind of madness was what a defeated and deflated Germany had been waiting for. It would be stopped by nothing short of war.

Stories began to reach our ears of mass persecutions too horrible to contemplate. A little man who looked like a ghost stationed himself every day, summer and winter, on 42nd Street across from the public library, handing out leaflets to passersby. He had dedicated himself to making us, here in the USA, listen. One had only to look at his face to know that the stories were true, that hell was real and he had been there. Yet I never saw anybody pay the least attention to him. I shuddered and passed on like the rest.

In Washington Franklin Roosevelt had taken firm hold of the economic situation. He talked to the country regularly over the radio, and his voice was soothing and confident. "We have nothing to fear but fear itself." The business world was up in arms against his new regulations, but among the people, hope stirred.

13

DO YOU TAKE THIS MAN?

I went to work for Covici, Friede in February, 1936. This was very good luck. The pay was just barely enough to get by, but I had a steady job, the work was interesting, and the atmosphere was peaceful and quiet. Covici was publishing mainly good non-fiction, so the subject matter was varied. Here the wide-ranging curiosity that had kept me from pursuing any branch of knowledge in depth was an asset. The more subjects an editor knows even a little about, the better.

The firm was small. Donald Friede had left before I came. Pat Covici presided over a staff of just nine people. Harold Strauss, the editor, and I were the entire editorial department. After some months Mary McCarthy was brought in part time. Mary was just then beginning to be known for her work with Philip Rahv on the *Partisan Review*. She was an uncompromising idealist who still had a good deal of *Sturm und Drang* to go through before she would be able to come to terms with an imperfect world. At the same time she was young and talented and confident, and wonderfully alive. Amid the gloom of the Depression she was a breath of fresh air.

Early in 1936 Eve went to work for Sears, Roebuck in Chicago. She had asked me if I would be interested in taking over her apartment, since she had fine antique furniture that she didn't want to put into storage. The rent was affordable, so I accepted with pleasure.

Jones Street was fun because it bordered on an Italian neighborhood. Bleecker Street at the end of the block was a street of small shops and bakeries and pushcarts. It was always lively. Sometimes there were small street parades by admirers of Mussolini.

The proprietor of a small vegetable shop in Little Jones Street was not one of them. He had lived in a small room behind his shop for many years while he saved money to bring his wife to New York. Now he had the money but he was unable to get his wife out of Italy. Everyone who entered his shop was greeted with, "*A basso, Mussolini!*"

I married Bob in February, 1938. A wedding was out of the question, but we wanted the day to be a little special. Bob's brother Donald, who was living nearby in New Jersey, lent us his old Ford coupe, and we drove upstate looking for a quiet town that appealed to us. We found it in Warwick, where the county clerk was also the druggist. He was in his old-fashioned drugstore that woke nostalgic memories of my childhood. His upstairs office was a pleasant room opening onto a small balcony that looked out on a rushing brook, black and cold in the snowy landscape. For some reason we had to wait a week to be married, and more than a week before Don was willing to relinquish his car again. He was courting Doris Cole of Jersey City, whom he married the following summer. Eventually the day came. We drove up to Warwick again and were married in the Methodist parsonage. The minister's wife quickly changed into a light blue crepe de chine dress to be a witness, a second one was brought in from somewhere, and we were married in a sunny bay window that might have been my grandmother's, complete with old-fashioned plants and canary.

On the way home I added one more fact to my knowledge of the man I had married. It was impossible to go anywhere with him outside the city without stopping somewhere to look for minerals! It was getting late but we had to go home roundabout to look for serpentine in an outcrop along a small country road. Fortunately there was nothing much to be seen in the fading light. It was now very cold and we were hungry. In a roadside restaurant in a beautiful old house, we had one of the best dinners of our lives. So, all in all, it was a good day. We went to sleep happy.

Why any two people choose each other "to have and to hold" will probably remain a mystery. It has to do with understanding and acceptance below the level of consciousness. Carol Southworth remarked, many years later, that we surprised a lot of people. I doubt that anyone was more surprised than we were.

Bob's father, Job Robert, Senior, was an upstate New Yorker of English-Canadian descent, a civil engineer who had earned his degree at Cornell University. Bob's mother was the daughter of a Philadelphia printer. When Bob was born, the first of five children, the family lived in Buffalo, where his father worked for the state highway commission. A little later he went into business for himself in the small town of Holley.

There was little in the town to broaden a child's interests, but a neighbor once gave Bob a box of books that she had found in the attic. It included, among other things, complete editions of Shakespeare and Sir Walter Scott, which he read off and on for years. When I first knew him he would read anything at hand. As the demands of his work grew, his reading became narrower, but he retained an interest in a wide variety of subjects and developed a strong love of music.

When the time came for college the Depression had begun, but Bob worked his way through Cornell with the aid of state scholarships, majoring in physics. After graduation he stayed on for graduate work, but now, without scholarships, earning a living was becoming too much of a struggle. When a job opportunity came along he took it. His course work for a master's degree was finished but his thesis was still unwritten. He never went back.

After we were married, Bob continued to work for Consumers' Union, which was still struggling to get on its feet and was paying below-standard wages. In spite of our small income we lived in style. We had found a one-bedroom apartment on East 18th Street a few doors east of Third Avenue, where many of the old brownstone houses were still occupied by individual families. This house had recently been made over into apartments, two to a floor, by a sixtyish gentleman with a patrician bearing, who, as we learned later, had spent his life as custodian in the Flatiron Building. Our apartment was on the top floor rear, and large sunny windows looked out upon well-tended grassy back yards that no one ever seemed to use.

We still had Eve's furniture. So, after years of living any way we could, we had a place of our own that was a pleasure to come home to. At seventy-five dollars a month the rent was a bit much for our budget, but we managed and it was worth it. Then, three months after we were married, Covici's closed its doors for the last time and I was out of work again. Our lease ran for another five months.

The sights we saw when we looked for a cheaper apartment beggar description. One of the most surprising was an apartment in the West Eighties that had been a front and back parlor. A bathtub had been installed in front of the fireplace! This might at least have been cozy except that old fireplace chimneys in New York were not to be trusted. We gave up and signed a lease for another year. I was making a little money by free-lance proof reading and manuscript editing, so perhaps we could make it. It would also have been expensive to move, and there was the risk of moving Eve's valuable furniture.

It was tantalizing to live in New York with no money to take advantage of the riches available. We were overjoyed one evening when a woman at the next table in a restaurant asked us if we could use two tickets for a chamber-music concert. I wish our benefactor could have known what a treat she gave us.

On weekends in spring and fall we sometimes went mineral hunting. There were numerous good locations within commuting distance in Connecticut and New Jersey. At first I thought this was a wonderful excuse for getting out in the country, but I learned to be wary. Neither rain nor hail nor hunger nor thirst nor blackflies could dislodge Bob from a good site before darkness fell.

On summer evenings we sometimes took walks after dinner rather than go home to a hot apartment. One evening in Central Park the merry-go-round was in operation, lights on and music blaring, with no one on it and no one in sight. We paid our nickel or dime apiece and got on. Bob chose a horse next to the center pole where he could grab the brass ring for a free ride, and for once I rode until I tired of it. It was a beautiful evening.

One of the things I did with my spare time was to type letters of application for Bob. He had said that if we were ever to get out of this situation he would have to find other work, and the only industry he knew of that was taking people on in considerable numbers was the geophysical industry. So we rented a typewriter and wrote a form letter and I typed about two hundred copies.

After Christmas Jeannette offered me a new kind of job at Bloomingdale's. New restrictions on advertising claims were to go into effect the first of the year, and someone was needed to see that the buyers complied with them, which they were most reluctant to do. No more could they give fancy names to dyed rabbit fur or call Philippine mahogany, "mahogany." It would be my job to read proofs of all the advertising and see the buyer if an ad looked suspicious. The work was not hard in itself. The trouble was that proofs did not come in until rather late in the morning, and I could not go to lunch until they were all corrected. Often it was three o'clock before I could get away for a light sandwich and a pot of tea, or maybe just a bowl of soup. By that hour I was too tired to eat. As often as not the food sat like a rock in my stomach the rest of the afternoon. Sometimes I threw it up before I could get dinner. It doesn't take long for that kind of thing to do serious damage.

In the spring Bob received two offers of jobs from companies we had written to. Later there were two more. It was a toss-up between Houston and Oklahoma City. We chose Houston, knowing nothing about either one. He was offered no more than he was making in New York, but chances for advancement looked better, and the cost of living would be lower.

My leaving caused a flurry of excitement around the store. Since I was out on the floor a good deal, many people knew me. When the word got around that I was leaving for Texas, rumor soon had it that I was leaving to marry a rich oil man! The gloom of the time was so deep, people were so anxious, even those with jobs, that my departure had given rise to a fairy tale. It gave us a laugh on more than one occasion when things looked dark.

We bought an old Ford sedan for fifty dollars from our friend Kate Leers and set out for Houston the first week in May. We stopped overnight at Bob's home in Little Genesee, New York, where we left his mineral collection. By the time we reached our destination he had acquired the beginning of another. We went through Commerce, Oklahoma, in a lead and zinc mining area, and when he saw a sign that said, "Minerals for sale," it was too good an opportunity to miss.

147

The car was about ready for the junk yard. At a country cross-roads in Missouri the brakes gave out, and we narrowly missed a collision that would have finished us. When we reached Alexandria, Louisiana, to which we had been directed in Houston, some boys playing in the street looked at our New York license and shouted, "How did you do it?" Nevertheless, thanks to Bob's persuasive ways with machinery, it served us for another year and many thousands of miles.

The Independent Exploration Company, usually known simply as "IX," was exploring marginal areas, usually unproductive, with the result that the crews seldom remained more than a few days to a few weeks in one place. For two months we lived in Alexandria, Louisiana, a rather pleasant small city but inhospitable to persons with a Yankee accent. From there we went to Eldorado, Arkansas, for three weeks; Morgan City, Louisiana, for four days; Bunkie for a month; Cleveland, Texas, for about two months; back to Sulphur, Louisiana, for one week. Then the firm discovered that Bob had a way with radio equipment and brought him to Houston to work in the repair shop.

While he worked on a crew we lived in whatever quarters might be available and counted ourselves lucky if there was a good boarding-house in town. There were interesting persons on the crews; Bob was not the only one who might have been expected to be doing something better. Two friends we have kept in touch with ever since were George and Olie Garrett from Mississippi. George held a doctorate in physics. He was a crew chief, which was a pretty good position, but it was not one he would have chosen in normal times.

In Houston we found an unbeautiful but clean and adequate furnished apartment in a working-class neighborhood. Most of the women on the street fitted the definition of fat and forty, and Bob took to calling me "the belle of Allston Street." I didn't think it very amusing, but at that time I was not much amused by anything.

I was suffering from intolerable fatigue, like nothing I had ever known. I got through my day's work by dividing it up into fifteen and thirty-minute intervals, telling myself that I could take it that much longer. When I began to think that both Bob and I would be better off if I were dead, I decided it was time to see a doctor whether we could afford it or not. The diagnosis was anemia, liver extract and massive injections of vitamins were prescribed, and gradually my health improved, but it was several years before I was myself again.

There was one remarkable incident during my lowest period. I was lying awake, restless, thinking I had done Bob wrong by marrying him. He was sound asleep beside me. At this point he turned to me, took my hand, and said clearly, "All the people in this house love you. We want you to stay." If this was not extrasensory perception I wouldn't know what to call it.

The Depression was still hanging on. We were barely making it from one month to the next. The day before Christmas the first year, Bob received notice of a raise. Our pleasure lasted only a few hours. On the day after Christmas it was announced that there would be no paychecks that month. Hope went glimmering.

That fall Hitler had invaded Poland, and Russia had swiftly counterattacked. By the end of the year most of Europe was in the fray. It seemed certain that we would be involved again, but anti-war sentiment was strong. The whole country was tense during the years that followed. Half of France was under German domination and Britain had its back to the wall. We lived from day to day.

My father died about two weeks after a heart attack, in December, 1941, the day after the Japanese attack on Pearl Harbor. Fortunately I was able to get home in time to have a few words with him, and I was holding his hand when he slipped quietly away. I was less distressed by his death than by the many bitter years of his old age. He was a good and loving man who had done his best, and he had died penniless and lonely. He could have had some happiness if I had remained at home after I left school. But do children owe a parent their whole lives? My father would have been the first to say no. If we had only been able to understand each other——

Soldiers were already being mobilized when I went back to Texas a week later. The train from Chicago was supposed to make the trip to Houston overnight, but it was thirty hours getting there. Since we had borrowed the money for train fare, I was riding coach. The first night a tired soldier kept falling asleep on my shoulder, and I felt so sorry for him that I couldn't bear to wake him up until my shoulder couldn't take it any longer.

Things moved with incredible rapidity. George Garrett was going to Radiation Laboratory at Massachusetts Institute of Technology, where physicists from all over the country were gathering for advanced research that, it was hoped, would lead to new weapons. George suggested that Bob apply, which he did, and was accepted. The only difficulty was moving expenses. The laboratory said they had already spent more than they should, and they wanted to know how much goods we had to move. Bob replied that we had nothing we could not bring with us in the car. He had reckoned without the weight. He was so worried about the load on the car that we drove all the way to Jackson, Mississippi, at twenty miles an hour.

We were never going to get to Cambridge at that rate, so in Jackson we stopped at a storage warehouse, unloaded the car and left half the stuff there. When we reloaded, there was little difference to be seen, but the car was lighter, and we reached Cambridge on schedule in spite of dreadful weather. We drove from Cleveland to Ashtabula after dinner one night in a blinding snowstorm and put up sometime during the small hours at a hotel that Edward Hopper should have painted.

I loved New England from the minute we crossed the Hudson River near Troy, New York, and drove into the Berkshires on a bitter February afternoon. For nine years I knew the comfort of living in a region where I felt at home. Olie Garrett had found an apartment for us at Garden Court, a quite new group of four-family houses around a landscaped court. It was about a mile out Garden Street from Harvard Square, a pleasant walk. We were told that "everybody" was renting furniture, since everything was uncertain; so we followed suit, rented a bed and a dinette set and moved in. A few other necessities we bought secondhand a little later.

We had not even had time to order a phone when we both came down with the flu, and everything we needed to keep house with was in Jackson, Mississippi—even a can opener! We flipped a coin daily to see who would go to the grocery store and who would prepare the food. One day I came home with a pint of oysters to make a stew. Now when one says a pint of oysters in Boston, it means a pint of oysters, not a pint of fluid with an oyster or two floating in it. Bob went to the kitchen to cook them, and to this day I cannot imagine what happened. I heard a cry of distress and went out to investigate. All the oysters were on the floor, and juice was dripping from the ceiling. For several minutes we were both on the floor picking up oysters and mopping up the mess with paper towels while the juice continued to drip. That incident marked the low point of our fortunes. After that things began to look up.

Robert Rogers, 1938. Nice eyes and interesting cheekbones.

Sidney Green, Boston Public Gardens, 1942. Peanuts for the pigeons.

Hi Suh, Frances and Sang Hie at L.A. airport, 1964.

Robert and Sidney, Concord, Massachucetts, 1942.

Sang Eun, just off the plane from Korea, and Frances at L.A. airport, 1965.

Robert with Sang Hie's children, Kenneth and Ann, Santa Fe, 1975.

Robert and Frances at Tanglewood, 1967.

14

WAR AND PEACE

A war fought entirely in foreign territory is experienced by most of those at home as a terrible anxiety for persons dear to them who are at risk. Since I knew no one in service intimately, I felt it directly only as a few inconveniences: a scarcity of some customary foods and materials, waiting in long queues on the rare occasions when nylon stockings were available, turning shirt collars, getting along without a car. I had a momentary taste of the fear that others lived with when a letter came for Bob from his draft board, ordering him to report for a physical examination. The lab immediately labeled it a "mistake" and got it canceled.

Such seeming favoritism was much resented by men in uniform and their relatives. Actually, men with knowledge that the government needed at home, in uniform or not, hadn't a chance of seeing active service. A colleague at the laboratory who enlisted anyway found himself back at his old desk. All that had changed was the clothes he wore. Such men were serving where they were judged most useful.

My personal life was beginning to be less difficult than it had been for many years. We had an adequate, if modest, income and were paying off Bob's college debts. At the end of the first year we returned the rented furniture and bought our own. Our home was now really a home for the first time.

I am glad I did not know then that the next thirty years were to be almost as changeful as the years past. Fortunately I had served my apprenticeship as a wanderer. I think I managed pretty well to make a life out of what there was to do where I happened to be. But if I had wished to have a career of my own, I would have been obliged to choose between my profession and my marriage, or Bob would have had to make other decisions. This must be a problem with no completely satisfactory solution for many two-career couples.

The first year in Cambridge I had my hands full. Bob's sister Marion was working in Philadelphia and was dissatisfied with the living arrangements she had made for her six-year-old daughter Sidney. In June, a few months after our arrival in Cambridge, we took Sidney to live with us.

She was bright and amusing and seemingly happy, but it did not take long to discover that she was full of anxiety. She had been shunted from one place to another during the past several months until she didn't know where she belonged or whether she belonged anywhere. The anxiety surfaced when I put her to bed. Counting all her adult relatives was a nightly ritual; they were her first line of defense. Then she would ask if I thought her father was safe. Safe! He was flying in France. I said that he was a good flyer and I was sure he had been taught how to take care of himself. That seemed to reassure her for the moment, but the next night she would ask the same question.

For some weeks she was difficult. One minute she would throw her arms around my neck and say, "Aunt Frances, I love you too much," and the next she would make some utterly unreasonable demand and then sulk, deliberately pushing my patience to the limit. There were times when it would have been highly gratifying to be sharp with her, but impatience with children is always a mistake. I knew that much from my own experience. In this instance it would have negated everything we hoped to do for her. As a pediatrician said later, "She has to know whether you still love her when she is bad." As she gained confidence these provocations became less frequent. They were never more than interludes in a truly happy relationship.

On afternoons when we stayed home I insisted on her taking a nap because I needed one myself. When she woke up she liked to come to my room and brush my hair. This led to more lively games and usually ended in a pillow fight or other foolishness that gave occasion for happy laughter. I loved it as much as she did. Grownups don't laugh enough.

I tried to think of things for her to do that could be done in a small apartment. I bought her some modeling clay, and she made a flock of turtles and an enclosure for them, and for a couple of weeks she fed them daily with freshly shredded newspaper. When her interest flagged I told her that the clay could be used over again. If she was tired of the turtles she could make something else. "Oh, no," she said, "Turtles is turtles." For the rest of her stay I cleaned around them.

Most days we went out somewhere. I had served fish filets several times, and Sidney expressed a wish to see a fish "with the head and the tail on." So I took her to the fish market in Harvard Square, where there was a tank of live fish in the window. We told the owner our errand, and he was happy to oblige, initiating his guest into all sorts of mysteries. I think they both had a delightful afternoon.

Once a week we had to go to Woolworth's to spend half of her ten-cents-a-week allowance from her mother. The store still sold a few items that justified its old appellation of Five-and-Dime. There she lingered over agonizing decisions. I was tempted to buy her all her heart's desire, but I decided she was not too young to learn to live within her income.

The other nickel was reserved for peanuts for the ducks and

pigeons in the Boston Public Gardens, her favorite destination. Whoever invented the swanboats should have had some kind of prize for his contribution to happiness. All the children were utterly blissful, circling the pond with the ducks in their wake. One day when Sidney had just got into the boat, a bomb-drill alarm sounded. Tragedy was written all over her face until she was given a rain check.

On Sundays Bob liked to get down on the floor and tinker with his radio. Sidney used to sit alongside him, and he would explain to her what he was doing. She didn't understand a word of it, naturally, but she understood that she was being talked to like an adult, and she would exclaim delightedly from time to time, "Oh, I see." Bob was as pleased as she. I was a much less interested listener.

Such things forge strong ties. Sidney, now a grandmother, still keeps in frequent touch with us: remembers us on holidays, phones, comes to visit when she can, offers to help in any way—and means it. She said to me not long ago, "After I lived with you and Uncle Bob I knew that I would always have a place to go."

When her mother was able to care for her again, I looked about for volunteer work. I sewed for war victims one day a week with a group of MIT faculty wives. Another day I typed letters for the Dutch relief organization. This still left me time to do a few things purely for fun—a luxury I had not had in many years. Olie and I frequently had lunch together at her house or mine. With Kay Gamertsfelder, the wife of another of Bob's colleagues, I took classes in sewing, in wartime cookery, and in pottery making. It was marvelous to be able to plan my own time.

I renewed my acquaintance with Robert and Jean Bacher. Bob was also working at Radiation Lab. I think it was in 1943 that Jean called me one day and asked if I could come over that afternoon because they were moving; she didn't know where. It was to Los Alamos, of course. I found her in a room full of packing boxes, trying to decide what to take with her to an unknown destination.

The most enduring of our new friends were Leland and Paula Wyman. Bob had met Lee at a meeting of the Boston Mineral Club, and we had been friends for some time before we knew that the Wymans were already friends of Bob's brother Arthur in New Mexico. There is little to tell about our friendship because we usually just had dinner together and talked.

They were the most talented people we have known. Lee had grown up on a farm in Maine and attended Bowdoin College. He had a doctor's degree in zoology from Harvard, but one specialty was not enough for him. He had manifold interests and a scholar's mind, and he made himself an authority in whatever field he became seriously interested in. When we first knew him, in his early forties, he was teaching in the Department of Fine Art at Boston University and also teaching physiology in the School of Medicine. At the same time he was on his way to becoming an outstanding authority on Navajo religion. He had become interested in the Navajos on a trip to the Southwest, had spent a year with the tribe and returned for further study every summer for several years.

Paula, a Dane, with the Danish talent for handwork, was a jeweler and silversmith; and her work was exquisite. She taught jewelry making at the Boston Museum of Fine Art and sold silver dishes and tea services to one or two Boston jewelry stores.

The Wymans were also the friendliest of people. Until they died, within the past decade, they maintained contact with many friends all round the world.

After the first summer we had a so-called victory garden in Belmont, the next suburb to the west. A nursery there, unable to get enough help, was renting out plots for vegetable gardens. They kept the plants watered, so attention once a week was sufficient to grow a good crop. We were nearly overwhelmed by Swiss chard and zucchini, both vegetables that I could get along without. The chard I couldn't give away. Fortunately, Arnold, the Italian meat cutter at our wonderful neighborhood market, could use nearly all the zucchini we could bring him.

The market, run by three Egan brothers, was something only to be dreamed about today. At first, as newcomers, we had to take what was left of scarce meat and butter after their old customers had been served. Eventually we arrived at that status and it was like being taken into the family. I went freely into the back room to pick out the freshest vegetables. Eam (sp?) told me to help myself to avocados that might be overripe. "If they are no good throw them away; if you can use them, give me a nickel apiece." Arnold automatically gave us the best cuts of meat. If it was veal scallopini I had in mind he added a bottle of the right wine. On the day before Christmas when they all worked right through without taking time for lunch, just nibbled at sandwiches between customers, I made and took them homemade bread. There was a continuous friendly give and take.

One of the pleasures of Boston was the stores that had been in business longer than anyone could remember and could still be counted on for some of the things that had gone out of fashion. Once, during the war, Eve wrote that a great-aunt who lived high on a mountain in Norway needed heavy black wool stockings. If anyone in this country would have them, it would be R.H. Stearns. And so they did.

Another such company was S.S. Pierce, which sold and delivered top-quality groceries throughout the state. One day on Cape Ann, when we were looking for an old overgrown path across the cape, an S.S. Pierce truck came by and stopped at the only house in sight. We were still within reach of civilization.

The most wonderful enterprise in Cambridge was the Window Shop—a gift shop, bakery, and restaurant in the house of Longfellow's Village Blacksmith, with an old wisteria vine growing over the door. A glass-front wing had been added to one side, for a sales room, and the restaurant occupied the house and patio. It was run by refugees from Germany and Austria, who pooled the profits for the education of their children. The cooking and baking were Viennese and they were superb, and the people involved were superb human beings. I don't believe that any of them had been obliged to leave; they were just decent people who preferred leaving their homelands to living under Hitler. One of them said to me, "When you have seen some things you can't stay."

We met only a few natives. What I know about Bostonians I still know chiefly from books. An amusing incident in Harvard Square bore out the books to the letter. I was in a hurry and was being held back by two women, tweedy Boston women, who were deep in conversation and were proceeding at a snail's pace. One of them had a little girl with her. When I finally managed to pass them I heard the child say, "But Mother, if I don't marry I can carry on the family name." It was perfect!

The city itself I enjoyed greatly. It was slow where New York was hurried. Downtown, where leading department stores looked out on the Common, had the air of a more leisurely era. Across the Common the old rowhouses, the brick sidewalks, the trees, the hilly cross streets, the capitol with its golden dome, were haunted by ghosts, human and fictional, as were Harvard yard and the older streets in Cambridge. I am afraid they have departed today, vanquished by the automobile.

I read much on winter evenings while Bob studied. In the Cambridge Public Library I found a complete edition of Michelet's great history of France. During the better part of one winter I struggled through two volumes with my rusty French. It was fascinating in spite of the difficulty. Michelet understood the passions that drive men and nations, and it gave a dramatic intensity to his writing.

My biggest experience in Cambridge during the war was editing a manuscript for publication by Peabody Museum of Anthropology in 1945. I had applied for work at the Harvard employment office two years before and had forgotten all about it when I received a phone call advising me of this opportunity. I arranged for an interview, and when I came back I told Bob that the job was impossible but I had taken it because I wanted to "help that man."

That man was Dr. George W. Harley, a medical missionary to Liberia. He was also a Doctor of Anthropology, who spent his sabbatical years doing research at the museum. He was looking for someone to edit a manuscript that had been sitting around the museum since 1929 except for a few years when it had been missing. It had turned up in an office in Washington where some secretary had taken it. I gathered that all the secretaries and half the anthropological staff had taken a turn at editing it and had given up.

Now suddenly it had become of the highest importance to rush it into print. Firestone, which had a plant in Liberia, wanted to build roads into the interior. They had heard about the book and wanted to see it as soon as possible. A recent succession of editors engaged for the purpose had all discovered after a week or two that problems at home required their full attention. I was not surprised.

Originally, Dr. George Schwab, a missionary to the Congo, had been commissioned by the museum to spend a year in Liberia and report on tribal customs before they vanished forever. When he had finished his work he turned it over to Dr. Harley, asking him to add whatever he could. To write such a book would have tested anyone's abilities. Dr. Schwab had gathered his information tribe by tribe and had then tried to organize it by topics that cut across tribal lines. Almost inevitably there were repetitions, misplaced material, and many passages where the meaning was in doubt. Perhaps Dr. Schwab himself did not always understand the meaning of things he saw or was told. In such matters I was dependent on Dr. Harley, who spent much of every day with me. I didn't know whether my procedure was legitimate but I knew what I had to do. I cut that manuscript into snippets, sorted them out, and put them back together again. The published book ran to about a thousand large double-column pages. It was like trying to reconstitute Humpty-Dumpty.

I had been working for only a week or two when Dr. Harley reported one morning that he had been ordered back to Liberia, where the United States government was negotiating for an airstrip. Negotiations had reached a stalemate, and Dr. Harley was wanted at once to get them going again. He wired his cookboy to meet him in Monrovia and took off on the next available plane.

If it had not been for Mrs. Harley I could not have continued. Not a day passed that I did not encounter several ambiguities, and there was no authority on Africa at the museum. She kindly came in every Friday to answer questions that I had saved for her during the week. I worked on that book nearly full time for six months instead of the expected half time for three months—at half-time pay. But I finished it, and it was coherent and readable, and that in itself was gratifying. It was also a pleasure to become acquainted with the men in the department. They then included Dr. Earnest Hooton, well known in the field of physical anthropology, and Dr. Carleton Coon, the expert on Arabia. I regret that I cannot remember the name of a younger professor who had an office across the hall from me and encouraged me the most of all. They understood my difficulties.

The big reward was the friendship of the Harleys. Mrs. Harley was, in her way, as interesting as her husband. She held a degree in botany and for many years had supplied Kew Gardens with rare tropical specimens. At the same time she had educated her two sons to meet college entrance requirements in Eastern colleges and had acted as the doctor's assistant. She told me that she sometimes administered as many as two hundred shots a day.

Dr. Harley was a brilliant man, a highly successful doctor, who was also interested in his patients from an anthropological point of view. They trusted him as few foreigners have been trusted, owing, in the beginning, to an inadvertent lucky circumstance. His grandfather had been a blacksmith and, when Dr. Harley was a child, had given him a small anvil which, as a man, he wore on his watch chain. It happened that in Liberia blacksmiths were privileged persons, since they forged certain sacred objects used in religious rituals. Only a blacksmith was able to travel safely outside his own tribe.

Success as a physician confirmed this trust. During his stay the Liberian government was attempting to wipe out the native religion because certain barbarous practices, such as those of the Leopard Society, were difficult to eradicate so long as the old beliefs existed. Initiation rituals, in which young men were taught the proper care of their personal and family masks, had been prohibited; so these objects were now feared. The men were afraid to keep them and afraid to discard them. Dr. Harley solved the difficulty by assuring them that he knew persons far over the sea who would care for them properly, and the people trusted him enough to commit their gods to him. They now reside in Peabody Museum.

* * *

I don't remember when or how I first learned about the atomic bomb. All I can recall is that everybody was stunned. If it had been a bolt from heaven it would have been less shocking. This was a thing of man's own devising for the destruction of his fellows. Its lethal potential was far greater than anything that anyone had ever imagined. It was beyond comprehension. In using it we had given our stamp of approval to what the Germans call *Realpolitik*: in a bid for power anything goes. That a weapon so terrible should have been invented and deployed by the nation that had once been "man's last best hope on earth," seemed to be the ultimate irony.

Developments since that time: the production of bombs with infinitely greater power, the proliferation of nuclear arms, the continued employment of atomic energy for industrial use with its deadly waste that nobody knows how to dispose of, display a total lack of responsibility on the part of governments. I see a direct connection between that bomb and the increased violence and lawlessness in the world today. Sow the wind and reap the whirlwind.

Peace was declared in August, 1945. The mood this time was nothing like the spontaneous outburst of joyousness in 1918. Too much had happened since then. The earlier war had been promoted as "the war to end war," and war was still with us. We had helped to stop Hitler and his brash imitator, Mussolini, and the war party in Japan; but now old fears of Russia were revived. This time nobody expected the millenium to follow. We had survived another crisis, but there was no pleasure in it.

*　*　*

When Radiation Laboratory was disbanded, Bob stayed on at MIT in the laboratory of Dr. Charles Stark Draper, a pioneer in inertial guidance. That eliminated one move but it held no promise of permanence. The men who worked there were expected to move out into industry. We lived from year to year, knowing that we would be moving again sooner or later.

I had seen little of old friends since 1939 when we went to Texas. Train travel by civilians had been discouraged during the war, and the conditions of travel had been discouraging enough in themselves. I was hungry for familiar faces, and as soon as I could manage it I went to New York for a few days, where several friends were still living. I stayed with Paull and Clara at College Point; had lunch with Gertrude, who was living as a companion with an old and feeble cousin and was unable to get away for more than a couple of hours; and went out to dinner with Jeannette, after which we spent a long evening in her apartment reminiscing. It was not until I got off the subway in Queens that I realized I did not know how to get to the Haydens. From a seedy, all-night bar I phoned for a taxi, waited for it on a deserted street corner, and got back shortly before most people would be getting up. Before going home I spent a few days with Don and Doris in New Jersey. It was all too brief but I went home renewed.

In December I went to Toledo to see my sister and her family. Herbert, who was head librarian at the fine new city library, gave me a personally conducted tour. The three boys, between seven and fourteen, outdid themselves to please me. Anna was happy. It was heart-warming after many years of absence.

Now I began to look around again for volunteer work. I do not recall how I happened to meet someone in the school of architecture at MIT. Neither can I remember the man's name or his position. Whoever he was, he was very kind. I was given access to the department library, permitted to audit a senior class in city planning, and referred to the Boston Housing Commission as an organization that could use help.

The director was overjoyed to find that I was familiar with editing. He had been obliged to discontinue a newsletter for lack of funds and personnel, and with my help he could revive it. This looked interesting, but I worked on that project for the better part of a year and nothing came of it. No newsletter appeared.

This was a period when housing was a major concern of governments at all levels. The war had interfered with private building, creating severe shortages. Prices had doubled and families were living doubled up. New regulations were coming from Washington in a steady stream. In his desire to include the latest news, the director put off publication week after week. By the time we got the new news ready to go, the old news was stale. The whole thing was an exercise in futility. This was a profitable experience nevertheless. It revived a long-standing interest in architecture, along with a new concern for the environment; and the time was right for it.

New ideas were burgeoning among building contractors, who had to find some way to cut costs. Postwar houses had been reduced to minimum size and stripped of most amenities, and still the cost was too high. A man named Levitt had built a whole community of houses from a few plans, introducing a new era of mass construction. Cities had become newly aware of the undesirable changes brought about by the automobile: air-pollution, city sprawl, traffic congestion. There was talk of self-sufficient suburban communities, of green belts around cities, and of subsidized high-rise apartments with open space around them for the poor.

Designers of custom houses were experimenting with entirely new concepts. These were the years of "togetherness." The accent was on the family as a unit, the home as a haven. The family room made its appearance. Spaces must be opened up, the outdoors brought in. Some of the new ideas were valuable; others proved to be faddish and impractical. They were all of great interest at the time.

In Cambridge, thanks to MIT and Harvard, we had many opportunities to see the new work. The alumnae organizations of several women's colleges organized house tours as a means of raising money, and we took full advantage of them. Those tours were worth more than all the books for appraising the new trends.

In 1950 Sidney's mother came to live with us for six months. So far as I was concerned, she was our second child; she was twenty years younger than I. She had married right out of high school, and three years later she was back home in Little Genesee with two babies. During the war she had made out all right with a wartime job in Philadelphia, but then she went home again, and in this very small town there were only dull, low-paying jobs to be had. After five years her secretarial skills had grown rusty and she was seriously depressed.

We figured that the best way to help her was to give her an opportunity to improve her skills. We rented a cot and put it up in the living room, brought Marion to town and got her enrolled in a good business school. She had lost confidence and was reluctant to go, but the first week the teacher praised her work to all the class, and her spirits perked up immediately.

In the meantime Bob's brother Art and his wife Barbara took care of Marion's two children, Sidney and Larry. Towards the end of the course Marion wrote to them that she would soon be able to bring them back East.

Larry's response was immediate and forceful. He wrote that she would be a heartless, unfeeling mother if she were to drag him away from what was obviously still God's country. "You can get a driver's license at the drugstore when you are fourteen, you can wear a T-shirt till Christmas and you can shoot horses."

Marion handed the letter to me, saying, "It looks as if I will have to go West." There she found work with Los Alamos Scientific Laboratory and also a new husband.

We asked Art, "What is this about shooting horses?" It seems it was legal in New Mexico, if a neighbor's horses strayed onto your property, to scare them off with gunshots.

We were among the first to be interested when Carl Koch, one of the most interesting residential architects, worked out a plan with several persons at MIT for a new community in Concord that eventually became Conantum. The houses were to be built from a few basic plans, with certain variations, and there would be public land for recreation. We chose a lot and I suppose we made a down-payment—I don't recall. We had even bought a refrigerator when Bob was offered a position in St. Louis that he couldn't afford to turn down.

* * *

A house in Conantum was not the only project that came to a halt. For five years, ever since the summer of 1946, we had spent our vacations, and our weekends during six months of the year, lovingly restoring an old farmhouse we had bought in Jamaica, Vermont.

In the fall of 1945, when gasoline was available in sufficient quantities, we had set out for Stowe, New Hampshire, at the foot of Mt. Washington, anticipating a vacation with fine, fall weather. It rained all the way there, so hard that we could hardly see where we were going, and by the time we arrived it had turned to heavy wet snow. The next day there was more snow; we were house-bound. After more dreary days, unable to get out on foot, we drove on to Bolton, Vermont, where we had once begun a hike up Camel's Hump mountain. There was a beautiful waterfall just off the road. Just as we arrived, the sun came out, making rainbows in the falling water. The woods were glorious. Bob said, "Next year we are going to come back here and buy a piece of this," which we did.

The property consisted of a badly run-down but essentially sound small farmhouse and four of the most beautiful acres in the world. They were high on a hill overlooking the wide West River valley at East Jamaica, and not a dwelling was to be seen. The day we first saw it, a border of mature locust trees and a large old syringa bush perfumed the air. Two hard maples shaded the front yard. There were hickory and butternut trees and a blackberry patch, and a spring bubbling out of the hillside. At the foot of the hill, Turkey Mountain Brook sang its way to the river over a rocky bed. Upstream there were only two houses and Fred Butler's sugarbush. I don't remember ever seeing one human being the whole two or three miles up to the waterfall. For twenty-five hundred dollars all this was ours.

One of the newfound pleasures was watching the changing seasons. In early spring when we turned into Turkey Mountain Road, we were greeted by the exultant piping of the "peepers" in the marsh, just awakened from their winter sleep. In May, violets and trailing arbutus appeared. In June, the lovely wild roses blossomed in the pastures. In August, the streamers of the *aurora borealis* brightened the night sky. The fall woods were brilliant with the colors of beech and birch and maple and ash; and the perfect blue of the bottle gentian outdid the sky.

It was here that we first took an interest in birds. They were so beautiful and so varied, and the days were filled with their song. Bluebirds lived in a picturesque dead apple tree and in a birdhouse beside the spring. A brilliant yellow-throat warbler sang all day from the tip of a locust tree near the gate. A hermit thrush with a nest halfway down the hill, which I discovered by sitting still all one morning, came out at evening to sing at the edge of the clearing. A pair of indigo buntings flashed their colors in the sunlight.

We bought our first field guides to the birds and the wildflowers, and I found the perfect book to help us renovate the house authentically: *Old American Houses and How to Restore Them*, by Ottalie and Lionel Williams. The books we borrowed from the library were anecdotal accounts of the kind of thing we were doing. There were many of these and they were well written and lively. Many people had discovered the pleasures of bringing old houses back to life.

Vermont was still unspoiled. It discouraged tourists. The "city people" were a few like ourselves who had bought some old country place as a base for outdoor living. Native Vermonters had retained a quirky independence and a gift for saying much in a few words. One learned to phrase a question exactly because they answered literally. Bob once asked a man who was working on the road, "Can you tell me where I am?" The man replied, "Looks to me like you're right in the middle of the rud." They were slow to accept newcomers. One word of condescension and you were out. But once you had gained their confidence they were hearty and generous. Bob won his spurs the first spring when he borrowed a horse to drag the rocks out of a new garden plot and harnessed it himself!

The first summer, work on the house had to take precedence over everything else. We camped out in it with army cots and cotton-flannel sheets for cold nights, a kerosene cook stove, a water pail and a marble slab to set it on, picked up in Fitzwilliam, New Hampshire, for a dollar or two. A dropleaf table, chairs, and a butternut chest came next, from country auctions. Until we could clean up the spring we were dependent on the inn three miles away for drinking water. Bob laid a line down from the spring to water his garden, and it also served for bathing when it had lain in the sun all day.

We replaced the old stones around the spring with a large tile, the kind used for culverts. When the work was done we sent a sample of the water to the state health department, and the report came back: no sediment, no turbidity, no color, no odor, no organisms. Just absolutely clear, pure water, the finest we have ever known.

The people we knew best were Arthur and Mollie Gleason from whom we had bought our place. Arthur was a wiry little man, perhaps seventy, with large brilliant blue eyes and a happy smile, topped off with wavy white hair. He was quite handsome. Mollie was a gener-ously built, motherly woman, whose chief interest was in her house. She was always poring over mail-order catalogues, looking for new window curtains and other furnishings. Arthur had made his money buying and selling cattle. He bought them in the fall when poor farmers could not afford to feed them through the winter, and fattened them in the summer on pasture lands he had bought. His key-ring was at least four inches in diameter. Vermont was full of hill farms that had been abandoned when automobiles replaced horses. The cars of those early days were unable to get through the roads in mud season.

Arthur was reported to be the richest man in town, and stories abounded about his stinginess. However that may have been, Mollie never lacked for anything she wanted, but I do know of one occasion when she resorted to subterfuge. We had had supper with the Gleasons one evening, and while Mollie and I were doing the dishes she asked me if I had noticed her new flatware. "Arthur don't know I've got it; I always give him his old ones"!

In the winter Uncle Frank lived with them. Summers he spent alone on an island in the river. He was said to have rigged up a line and a pulley to convey his purchases to the island, including a cook stove.

This would have been possible. A kerosene stove was a light-weight affair. I never knew how he got himself over. He was quite old.

There were two villagers that helped us the first summer. They were both good men and good workmen, but also they were both addicted to alcohol, which sometimes led to complications.

The first, whom I will call Floyd, was a married man with several children, who seems to have stayed sober during the week. But on Saturdays he kept in constant touch with the bottle in his hip pocket, starting early in the morning. We were told that he was the one man in town who could get our foundation stones up out of the cellar, where they had fallen. These were no ordinary stones. They were great slabs of granite, at least four feet long and thick enough to support the house. It took three men and a horse to lift them, and then they had to be set squarely in place.

On Saturday mornings Bob called for Floyd at his house and, as the story was told to me, Bob pulled and Floyd's wife pushed, while gently relieving him of his bottle. His condition seems not to have seriously affected his work. After a few Saturday mornings our house once more stood on a solid foundation.

One Saturday morning the bottle came along. Floyd, having generously offered me a swig, which I refused on the ground that it was a bit early, took a drink himself and set the bottle on the kitchen table. When he had gone out, I picked it up and was putting it in a closet in the other end of the house when I noticed that Floyd was watching me through the window. He winked and I winked back.

Henry was engaged to dig a trench for the overflow from the spring. We were told that he was the best man for digging and the most loquacious. He would stop and pass the time of day with anyone who passed but "he won't charge you for the time he spends talking." Since nobody ever came our way, that was no problem. What nobody told us was that Henry was never to be paid directly. His wages were supposed to be paid to Fred Butler, a selectman and one of the town's most respected citizens, who was Henry's guardian.

We paid Henry in cash and he disappeared for two weeks. When he came to in Brattleboro, thirty miles away, he ordered a taxi to bring him back to Jamaica, saying, "My guardian will pay you."

Welthy Clough was the cook at the inn, where we took our Sunday dinners the first year. The inn was then owned by a well-to-do young man who craved company at all times, the more the better. He and his mother had restored the beautiful old house in great style. Most of the guests were family friends, among them three widows from Bermuda whom the proprietor aptly dubbed, "Yes," "No," and "Maybe." Welthy mingled freely with the guests. A subservient Vermonter would be a contradiction in terms. She was an old woman, a fabulous cook, and an inveterate gossip. She meant no harm; and there was none, really, in relating to a few strangers what the whole town already knew; but the light she shed on the hazards of life in the village was dismaying. Once when I remarked how sweet and pretty one of the waitresses was, Welthy shook her head. She might look that way, but she would come to no good. Nobody in her family ever had! What chance had a child in such a situation?

Miss Edith Clark was a quiet, elderly spinster who lived alone, except for her cat, in the house in which she had been born. In the summer she busied herself with the care of her large and flourishing garden. One day she told me her story. She and a considerably younger brother had been orphaned when Miss Edith was sixteen. She had taught country school for many years and saved enough money to help her brother through medical school. He had only recently begun to practice when a demented woman accused him of rape; and although he had been cleared by the court, his practice fell off, and he committed suicide. She told me about it without bitterness. She had been alone in the world ever since.

These lives that touch ours but briefly, ships that pass in the night, are, to me, among life's most significant experiences. There can be little understanding without moments of sympathetic insight into lives different from our own.

In the spring of 1951 this, too, came to an end. The Emerson Electric Manufacturing Corporation of St. Louis offered Bob a position as consultant for one year at nearly three times what he was then earning, with all expenses paid. Naturally, he took it. The next year he went to the Air Force Research and Development Command in Baltimore, again as a consultant. Between jobs we went to Vermont, expecting to spend a couple of months at the house, but it had rained too much, and we could not get up the hill. Instead we stayed with our friends the Leightons in the valley, and had only enough time at the house to close it up for another year.

In July of 1953 Bob went to work for Minneapolis-Honeywell. It was his first "permanent" job. He had been out of school for eighteen years.

15

A TIME FOR BUILDING

The Fifties as a whole were the most nearly normal decade in forty years, but they began in a wave of hysteria. During the Depression people with any social conscience were looking for something to latch onto that promised a happier society. Large numbers of intellectuals joined the Communist Party simply because it was there, claiming to be ultra-democratic and to have a remedy for all injustice. Most of them soon dropped out, disillusioned. Meanwhile, however, the growth of the party in the United States had worried a good many people. During the war, when Russia was our ally, such fears were played down. But afterwards, when Russia began to act aggressively, refusing to leave Berlin and maneuvering to topple legitimate governments along her borders, those fears were revived and merged with fear of nuclear war, giving rise to what has become known as the McCarthy era.

There was talk of building a vast underground shelter where the federal government could carry on its work if bombs fell. Cities were ordered to make plans for the evacuation of entire populations. Individuals were encouraged to build shelters in their backyards. School children were subjected to regular bomb drills, which sometimes consisted of nothing more than sliding under their desks.

At the peak of this madness a congressional committee chaired by Senator Joseph McCarthy of Wisconsin acted as inquisitor of persons against whom claims of Communism had been brought. It was sufficient to have been at some time a member of a liberal organization or to have been critical of some government action. Such accusations could ruin the career of anyone whose work required access to classified information. When Bob went to Minneapolis he was caught in this net. For several months his clearance failed to come through. Then one day he received a letter from the security board saying that they could not give him clearance unless he could clear himself of certain charges. They were pure fabrication. He had been accused of writing for the *Daily Worker* and contributing to the defense of the heads of the Communist Party when they were on trial in 1949. As a matter of fact, his interest in politics had been confined to reading the papers and voting.

Honeywell was very decent about it. They told Bob that they could not allow him inside the plant, but they kept him on the payroll and gave him work to do at home.

Bob replied to the letter by asserting his lack of active interest in politics and his lack of sympathy for the Communist Party. He went on to say, "Since my college days the only organizations I have belonged to, so far as I can recall, are the New York and Boston mineral clubs and the Windham County (Vermont) Farm Bureau. I have recently applied for membership in the Minneapolis Bird Club." That did it! Actually, what probably saved the day was a highly commendatory letter from Dr. Draper, expressing complete confidence in Bob, and adding, "that every effort should be made to substantiate any allegations before depriving the country of his services." Bob got his clearance. It was a close call.

I was pleasantly surprised to find that Minneapolis was a fine city to live in. There were several lakes within its boundaries, and others nearby. Outdoor activities were pursued with zest summer and winter. The public library, the art museums, the symphony orchestra, the state university were all very good. Civic pride was high. The number of business and professional men and women who worked actively on civic committees was impressive.

I served for a year on a committee to assess the need for a new library. I also served, by request, on a committee to study juvenile delinquency. Since I had never had any experience with delinquents, I was unable to contribute anything, but I was an interested listener. The committee member who interested me the most was the chief of police. He was very much concerned about children with inadequate family situations and had taken several into his own home temporarily when no suitable place could be found for them. It was good to know that such a person directed law enforcement in our town. The results of these studies were a new library and a juvenile detention facility.

Anna and her family had moved to Madison, Wisconsin, where Herbert was an associate professor in the library school. Anna had had her hands full for several years raising her three sons, but the boys were now grown, and she became involved in volunteer work with young children with serious emotional disturbances. She was always good with the little ones. Dick was serving a term as a naval officer in the Pacific before returning to Harvard for a doctorate in history. Bob and Steve were in college in Ann Arbor.

Eve was at her old home in Elroy, Wisconsin, a town of a few hundred people. She had surprised all her friends a few years earlier by going back to the University of Wisconsin and taking a degree in agriculture! Her parents were old and she felt she should be near them. She had taught briefly and edited a farm journal and was now retired. We had several good visits before she died of cancer in the late Fifties.

Her last years were sad. Her beloved father had died. Her mother was the kind of woman whose entire mind is occupied with worrying and fretting. The lack of privacy and of any intellectual life in so small a town had begun to frustrate her, and she knew she could no longer fit into the life of a city. There would not have been much ahead for her if she had lived.

We lived in a rented house in Minneapolis for three years while we looked for a lot to build on. It was pleasantly situated one block from Lake Harriet in the southwest part of the city, where large numbers of migrating birds came through in season.

In the park beside the lake, waterfowl and many varieties of song-birds could be seen. The latter even strayed as far as our back yard. We had a hermit thrush for a few days twice a year. Once I looked out and saw an ovenbird, said to be one of the shiest birds of the deep woods.

On our first New Year's Day we walked over to Lake Calhoun to see what there might be to see on a winter afternoon. There was a great barred owl, motionless in a tree, except that it nearly wrung its own neck watching us as we passed. The fun was a flock of ducks at play. Over and over they circled high in the air, then swooped down upon the ice and skidded several yards into open water—wild freedom in the heart of the city.

We found the building lot we wanted at North Oaks, ten miles north of St. Paul and fifteen from downtown Minneapolis. The property had been the estate of the Nineteenth Century railroad tycoon, J.J. Hill, and was now owned by his grandchildren. One of them, Louis Hill, had built a house for himself at one end and was supervising the development of a new residence community. All business was transacted through his agent, but he personally was the court of last resort in any dispute. I make this point because he later came to my aid in a matter where feelings ran high.

There were eight or nine square miles of woods and open country under development, and as yet only three or four dozen houses had been built, mostly in small groups. It was rolling terrain, studded with lakes and ponds, and it abounded in wild life. Some day it would all be gone, but it would be many years before the whole area was built up. In the meantime we would have nature right at our door. A five-minute walk took us to a woods where deer still roamed, quite tame, because the area had been a refuge. One day a deer with a fawn came right up to the road to look us over. Sometimes a little red fox scurried away as we approached.

I worked for a year on house plans. I had lived in enough houses to know in considerable detail what I wanted and what I didn't. When I asked Bob what was important to him, he answered, "Space. If I have room enough I'll be happy." So I went ahead by myself, though we talked things over from time to time. It was great fun to round up the information for all kinds of details: orientation to take advantage of the sun, the proper width of overhangs for that latitude, the best grade for stairs. All such things are in print somewhere if you can find them.

When I had done all I could, we went looking for an architect who would be willing to work with my plans. The first one we talked to brushed them aside. He would give us a choice of two or three. We continued our search until we found Norman Nagle, a graduate of Cranbrook, who said he thought it would be fun, for once, to work with clients who knew what they wanted. It was a fruitful collaboration. Nagle was good, his houses were pleasant, but they were too much alike. With fresh ideas his sense of balance and rhythm produced a house that everyone seemed to find pleasing.

The specifications for materials and fixtures read, such and such a brand or equivalent. That gave a contractor leeway to use the line that he could buy to his own best advantage. I was having nothing to do with equivalents. Mr. La Belle, our contractor, agreed to let me shop for what I wanted, which occupied me for several months. To look all over town for eighteen-foot lengths of cedar siding and *find* them may not be as great a thrill as discovering the Pacific Ocean from a peak in Darien, but it partakes of the same nature. I have never enjoyed myself more.

The wiring had to be done in midwinter before the plasterers came, so we went out to the house every evening for several weeks. I was needed for a few minutes at long intervals to pull a wire through an opening. Meanwhile I sat in the bathtub in a shell of a house without windowpanes. I thought that tub was the narrowest I had ever known until I realized that I had on six layers of clothing.

In spring it was a pleasure to take a picnic supper out to the house every evening and eat it in the car while migrating warblers flitted like butterflies in the tall grass around us.

We moved in, in November, 1956. The first spring, laying sod had top priority, and nothing else got done outdoors. The following year we put orders in early for shrubs and a few young trees. I was counting on Bob to supervise the planting, but when the time came he was in Europe on business. I would have to do the best I could. I bought a load of manure, hired a boy to help me dig, and waited for results. Everything throve and I was hooked.

Helen Moon and I had taken a course in landscaping at the university that spring, and in the fall I took courses in horticulture and soil and began to collect a library. At North Oaks, a garden club was being formed. As yet I possessed only the most elementary knowledge, but that was more than the other members had, so I was elected president and I held the club together until a more experienced person could be found. The club went on to become a real asset to our village. They planted the children's playground and other public land. I had a very good feeling about having done my small share.

The wild life was engrossing. During migrations the whole place was alive with wings. At all seasons there were birds and small creatures in abundance. A pond at the foot of our hill was a favorite haunt of herons, great blue ones and little green ones. There were teal and mallard ducks on all the ponds, and loons and merganser geese on the lakes. We had many of the finest songbirds: several varieties of thrushes, rose-breasted grosbeaks, meadowlarks. One year a tiny warbling vireo sang all day on her nest at the tip of an oak branch just outside our bedroom window. She kept the robins in their place at the top of the tree, and no bluejay got near it all season. There were many kinds of woodpeckers, including the great pileated that, according to Marjorie Rawlings, the Florida Negroes called "de Lawd God." There were owls and hawks. And there were small four-footed creatures too: raccoons and rabbits, and squirrels that chased each other from treetop to treetop in great leaps.

In winter deer came close to the house. On clear nights rabbits came out to play, chasing each other around in a circle of light from an outdoor lamp. In very cold weather pheasants, a male and three females half buried themselves in the deep snow beneath our oaks. This was never accomplished without elaborate maneuverings on the part of the females for a place beside the male, who remained majestically aloof.

Wild creatures have their share of trouble, but when all is well they appear to live so joyously, so aware of the moment. It raises disquieting questions about what the human race has done with its inheritance. The Golden Ages and lost Edens of ancient mythologies are parables of exile. Today, as never before in history, we have cut ourselves off from the earth. Whatever may be the gain, joy seems to have taken wing.

In the fall of 1960 we took in our third "child." Bob's nephew Eric had dropped out of high school at the end of his sophomore year and wanted to go back to school, but not at home. He asked his mother if she thought Uncle Bob would take him in. Uncle Bob did, and we were substitute parents again for the next two years. Our neighbors seemed to think it was a good joke on us. "The Rogers' have taken on a teen-ager." There was never a shadow of trouble.

We were in a singularly good position to help him get off to a good start socially. Our neighbors the Moons had six children, three of them in high school. They were bright and attractive and they went with a crowd of eight or ten boys and girls who did everything together. Two of the girls were foreign exchange students, one from Ethiopia and one from New Zealand. This was the era of bobbie-soxers, wholesome and happy in their sweaters and flat-heeled shoes.

Eric was immediately one of the crowd, and he spent most of his spare time at the Moon's where there was always something going on. It was a happy year for him.

Then we moved again! Bob received an offer of a position with Aerospace Corporation in El Segundo, California, and decided to accept it. He left in April, and I stayed on with Eric through June so he could finish his school year at Moundsview High School. As a result, the sale of the house fell on my shoulders, and I became embroiled in a controversy that might have taken a very unpleasant turn.

I engaged the services of a real estate agent who lived in the community. One day he brought an Oriental couple, a Chinese engineer who had been studying in the United States when the Communists took over China, and his American-born Japanese wife. They seemed much interested, but I heard no more from them. The next couple to be interested was distasteful to me on sight. I sized them up as brash and vulgar. The woman raved about the house and I got worried. Would it be possible to refuse to sell?

Soon I received a phone call from a woman who said she was a friend of the Oriental couple, the Maos. They wanted my house but they had been unable to reach the agent. I said I would take care of it. Then the agent called to say that the other couple wanted to buy. I said I was sorry but the Maos wanted it too, and they had seen it first. In minutes the agent was at my door in a tizzy. If I really meant to sell my house to Orientals he would have to bow out. He was not prejudiced, of course, but, he said, "I have to live here." Again, I said I was sorry; that was how it was.

Now the president of the residents' association was brought into the picture. He wasn't prejudiced either, but he too had to live there. Besides, if I were to insist on this sale I would be bringing dissension into a peaceful community. I held my ground. The next step was to take the matter to Louis Hill's agent, who took it to Hill; and Hill, to his everlasting credit, said he thought such a deal would be fine. The climate changed at once. The real estate agent decided to collect his commission after all.

The sequel was happy. A year later, Frances Mao wrote to tell me that the roses were blossoming and to thank me for the planting. Pat Young, a neighbor, wrote to tell me that her little girl and the Maos' little girl were inseparable and to thank me for giving them such nice neighbors. All's well that ends well.

Yvonne Bretoi gave a luncheon for me before I left. I was surprised and touched to see how many guests appeared. There were near neighbors, friends from the garden club, and others from an evening discussion group that Bob and I belonged to. I had not realized how many of my neighbors I had become involved with one way or another. I was sorry to leave all this behind.

16

MOSTLY FAIR

We both went to Los Angeles with some misgivings. Bob had been there several times and didn't like it. I didn't much like what I had heard about it. My first view of it was not reassuring. We drove in through Bellflower to Redondo Beach, where Bob had lived for three months in a furnished apartment. It was literally jammed with some of the ugliest furniture I have ever seen. For a month we spent the weekends looking for a house and saw nothing we would consider buying, so we gave up and decided to look at houses for rent. The first one we looked at could not have suited us better.

It was a custom-built house, very well designed in contemporary fashion, with lots of windows and beautiful views, in Crestwood Hills above Brentwood. Hanley Avenue was in a *cul de sac* with only local traffic. A wide deck at the back looked out over a chaparral-covered hillside that sloped steeply down to a street far below, and across the street another hill rose, where pretty little mule deer came out to graze. The area was smog free, and it was high enough to catch the ocean breezes that came up every afternoon around four o'clock. Bob, unfortunately, had to drive a busy freeway to work, but we were only ten minutes by car from Westwood to the east and Santa Monica to the west, where we could buy almost anything we needed, and from UCLA, which provided nearly all the entertainment we could wish.

We had lived there only a month when a forest fire swept down into that area and our entire neighborhood was evacuated. The hill opposite us was blazing, and I was loading the car with what I could think of to save, when a fireman came by and ordered me to leave at once, "and I don't mean go back in the house first." I left, with all the doors unlocked.

Bob was out of town, due back that evening. Eric was at school. As yet I had made no acquaintances, knew little about the city, and was afraid of the traffic. When a policeman at Sunset Boulevard waved me towards Santa Monica, I realized that I had no destination. For a moment I felt completely disoriented. When my mind cleared a little, I thought of Eric and drove to the high school in search of him, only to learn that the senior class had been dismissed to help if they could. An information center had been set up to help people find each other, so I left word for Eric that I would stop in at intervals and he could leave word for me about where to meet him. Then I called Aerospace, where one person referred me to another until I found a sympathetic secretary, Lois Roeming, who said she would meet me for dinner and drive me to the airport to meet Bob. I caught up with Eric just before we had to leave. At the high school, tired children with tired nursemaids or baby-sitters were still waiting for parents to appear. Eric had arranged to spend the night with a friend but was determined to get his car first. He did not yet have insurance, and I had been driving him to school. The area had been sealed off, but I figured he would find a way to get in, so I gave him the key to Bob's car and told him to take his friend with him and bring both cars out, which he did. Bob and I spent the night with Lois, who insisted on taking us home with her.

By morning the fires had been controlled and we were able to go home. The house was intact but dozens around it had burned to the ground, seemingly at random. The fire had spread mostly by burning debris carried on high winds, and where it fell on an inflammable roof, that house was doomed. I was just as glad that day that we didn't own any Los Angeles real estate. Our house and everything in it had to have a thorough house-cleaning. Soot had been forced in even through fixed-glass windows. Under the circumstances, that was trivial. We met a couple at an Aerospace Christmas party who had been on vacation that week and knew nothing about the fire until a taxi deposited them at the site where their house had been!

The first two years, personal affairs occupied almost all of my time. We spent many weekends exploring the state from Capistrano to Morro Rock and vacationed in the national parks and in San Francisco. For Thanksgiving the first year we went to Yuma, Arizona, to see Sidney, now married to Robert Schmidgall, and their three small sons. Al and Lucille Zalon, Minneapolis friends, were living in Woodland Hills. Edith and Charlie were a few hours away in Davis. Uncle Johannes and Josie had retired to Redlands, where we often visited them on Sunday afternoons. I renewed my acquaintance with my cousin Mertie, in a nursing home, and with her youngest sister, Ruth. Aunt Kate had died ten years before.

My most interesting new acquaintance was a tiny, gentle, aging black man who appeared at my door one day and presented his business card. Across the top in bold letters I read, "I love to work for God and man." He wanted to wash my windows. I learned later that he was also a preacher. I could not resist the message, so thereafter, as long as we lived in Los Angeles, he cleaned my windows on a regular schedule. I always prepared a simple lunch for him, which he hardly touched, and afterwards we talked for a little while. I learned that he had grown up on a plantation where his father had been a slave, and conditions in his own time had been not too much different. He and his wife had had one child, a son, who had died, and his wife had never ceased to grieve. Her greatest comfort was an annual visit to her sister in Chicago. I knew we were friends when he came around one day and asked if he might borrow my floor-waxer. A woman down the street did not need her windows washed but she would like to have her floors waxed.

I was worried when race riots broke out in Watts, where he lived. When he showed up again afterwards, he told me that he had been alone —his wife was in Chicago—and had ventured out only when he needed food. The violence had shaken him; he was a man of peace. This was no way to right a wrong.

I felt heartsick about it myself, the more especially since it was clearly only the first skirmish in a new era of turbulence. A hundred years had passed since the blacks had been promised equal opportunity, and it was nowhere in sight. They had served their country in three wars in this century, and now they were subject to being drafted for the new war in Vietnam. They wanted their rights *now*.

Young whites were also restive. They were the generation that had grown up in fear of the bomb, and now they were in danger of being drafted to "save" a country most of them had never heard of.

I was hardly conscious of that war for the next few years. Uprisings against foreign domination had spread like brush fires ever since 1945, almost inevitably followed by civil strife. Old tribal animosities, greed, incompetence, all tended towards chaos. Vietnam, half a world away, was only one more unfortunate nation in the throes of transition. The most disruptive foreign entanglement that this country ever got itself into began almost unnoticed.

An interest that Bob and I shared was extension courses at UCLA. We discovered Walter Starkie and took every course he offered. Starkie was a Dubliner who had grown up during the great days of the Irish Renaissance. He had known Yeats and Joyce, all the literary men of his time. His father had been Commissioner of National Education and taught at Trinity College. Trinity's great Greek scholar, John Mahaffy, was his godfather. He had the kind of mind and education that permit a man to live several lives simultaneously. He was the first director of the British Institute in Spain, and at the same time he was doing important research in ancient music. For years he spent his summers living as a gypsy with the gypsies, interested at first by their music and later by the entire culture. In Los Angeles he gave extension courses in Spanish and gypsy culture, in Joyce, in the Irish theater, in Nobel-prize dramatists, all of whom he had known, enlivened always by personal anecdotes. James Michener has paid tribute to Starkie in *Iberia*.

After a vacation in Mexico we took a course in Latin American literature from Gabriela von Monk Benton. She was a native of Germany, had married an Englishman, studied in Mexico, and was teaching Romance literature in Occidental College in Pasadena and, on the side, translating Aztec poetry into German. We drove all the way to Pasadena one evening a week for many weeks and it was well worth it.

I was beginning to want something more to do when my neighbor, Idella Willson, asked me if I would be interested in an informal tutoring project at UCLA. Newly arrived foreign students, even when they had a very thorough knowledge of English, were often hesitant about speaking it. For such students the university had arranged informal conversation groups with volunteer tutors to help them gain confidence. The wives of visiting scholars and professional men were also welcome. Most of these students were Oriental, as might be expected on the West Coast. They were very grateful for help, and some of them became lasting friends.

Yasuichiro Fujita and his wife Yoko came to the attention of Idella very soon after they arrived in Los Angeles. We were in the middle of the worst hot spell that we were to experience in our whole stay in Los Angeles, and Yoko had come with only cold-weather clothes. It was always a few degrees cooler up on our hill so Idella invited them to stay with her while the heat lasted. She also helped Yoko make a more seasonable dress. Shortly we were all friends.

The Fujitas were both very warm human beings, but beyond that they were a study in contrasts. Yoko was relaxed, outgoing, and usually in high spirits, although she was painfully lonesome for the two-year-old son she had left behind with his grandparents. Yasuichiro was eminently good-natured and amiable but he was wrapped up in his work, and playing the violin was the only diversion he really needed. Left to himself he would seldom have gone out, but Yoko made engagements for both of them, and he went along willingly. He used to say that if he had not brought Yoko with him, he would have returned to Japan knowing no more about Americans than he did when he came.

Yoko Takenouchi attended my group at the university. It was her eagerness that attracted my attention. She was exhilarated by the opportunity to know Americans on their own ground, and she wanted not only to know them but to understand. Her openness to new experience was refreshing.

Both women were products of a Japan greatly changed in a very few years. After they returned home, both of them engaged in the same kind of activities that occupy American women in their position. Yoko Fujita was active in her Parent-Teachers' Association and Yoko Takenouchi taught English in a private girls' school in Tokyo. Twenty years later, her children grown, she is active in volunteer work, her eagerness undiminished.

What impressed me the most about all the Japanese we met at that time was the absence of any animosity. The United States had defeated their country in war and had radically altered their ancient culture; yet we encountered no bitterness, no mistrust. Face to face, it is possible to bridge cultural barriers. It is when we see others as a faceless aggregate and fasten denigrating labels on them that trouble begins.

I met Sang Hie Lee at the UCLA student office when she was in immediate need of a place to live. She had come from Korea to do graduate study in piano and had arranged to live with a family in Arcadia, which was much too far away. I took her home with me to talk over the situation, and by the time I had made tea and she had poured it for me, sitting on the floor beside the coffee table, I had lost my heart to her. Two days later she came to live with us.

Soon the house was full of young people. Sang Hie's brother, Sang In, came often. A friend, Hie Suh Park, who was unhappily situated during the first several months, often stayed overnight, so we came to know her well. Near Thanksgiving Edith wrote that she and Charlie intended to spend the holiday weekend in Yosemite Park and suggested that we come too, which we did, taking with us Sang Hie and another friend, Chong Sook Kim. The weather was fine, the falls were splendid, and we had the place almost to ourselves. On the way home we detoured through the mountains to the coast to show our guests San Juan Bautista. The girls were delighted. We were having more fun than we had had in a long time.

It took a little time for Sang Hie and me to understand each other. At first she wanted to give me a gift every time I did some little thing for her. One day I said, "This is your home. Today I do something for you, tomorrow you will do something for me. We cannot exchange gifts every day."

Her face clouded and she went away, but soon she came back and said, "In my country, when someone refuses a gift we say, 'My face is red.' " She understood, however, and soon we were comfortable together. She liked to take walks with me in the evening, and at these times she would tell me about her family and her school and life in Korea. In the spring she married Kil Sup Lee (no relation), whom she had met at a Christmas party, and went to Indiana where he was teaching mathematics in a private school. Later they both earned doctors' degrees at the University of Georgia. Today she and her children are virtually members of our family.

Before many months we were corresponding with the Korean government about getting the youngest sister, Sang Eun, to the United States to study the 'cello. There were several mix-ups and endless red tape, too much to get her over here that year. She arrived in the fall of 1965. Sang Hie had secured a full-expense scholarship for her at Valparaiso University. Its music department was not one of the best, but Sang Hie said that the best schools all required a personal interview. "The first thing we have to do is get her over here."

Bob and I and Sang In met Sang Eun at the airport and they both came home with us for dinner. She was nineteen and had an air of gentleness the belied her sturdy independence. She was well able to take care of herself. At the moment, however, she was timid in her strange new surroundings. There was a low moment when her brother left and she realized that she was alone with two strangers to whom she would have to speak English. The moment passed, and in a few days she was off to Valparaiso, where she was admitted as a sophomore.

Four months later she was back. The 'cello teacher at the college had died shortly before she came and no adequate substitute had been found. When, towards the end of the semester, she was told that she was not to take any more music courses because she had already filled the requirements for a major, she had decided to withdraw at the end of that term and had simply left without consulting the immigration authorities. Neither she nor the dean understood that her student visa was good only so long as she was at school somewhere. It was impossible to get her into college anywhere during the coming semester. The best I could do was to arrange for her to take private lessons with Gabor Reijto, who was teaching at the University of Southern California, and to apply to USC for entrance the following year.

A week or two later Bob's sister Edith also became part of our household. She was recovering from a severe crisis in her life and took no interest in anything. This was the more difficult because we had no bedroom for her. She slept on a sofa in the living room, where she also spent most of the day. Her doctor had told us that we must not put any pressure on her to recover faster than she was able, but neither were we to let her retire from the world. This was a fine line to tread. A word too much and she got all excited. For a while the going was rough. At one point I took to bed with one of the worst colds I have ever had, letting Bob and my guests worry for a few days about how they would be fed.

When I had pulled myself together I knew that I must take steps very soon to get Sang Eun straightened out with the immigration service. Before I could act, Bob got a phone call at work asking him whether he knew anything about a Korean student named Sang Eun Lee. He referred the caller to me. I greeted him with, "I am so glad you called," hoping to throw him off balance if he was inclined to be accusatory. I was told to see that Sang Eun reported on a certain day at headquarters. We went early in the morning, and after waiting all day we were told to come back the next day. While we waited I observed the interviewers as they came and went; some of them looked pretty formidable. To my relief, we were received promptly the second morning by a fatherly-looking man who immediately put Sang

Eun at ease, telling her that his own daughter had just entered college and inquiring about her interests. The whole affair was settled in minutes.

As it turned out, Sang Eun was just the incentive Edith needed to draw her out of her depression. They began taking walks together, and Edith began to help Sang Eun with her English and to do other little things for her. By spring she was sufficiently herself again to accept Idella's offer of a room. At the end of June, Sang Eun left for a summer music school in Santa Barbara. In the fall we had just enough time to get her settled in a dormitory at USC before we were once again on the move. Bob had accepted an offer from Raytheon in Sudbury, Massachusetts, to head the Systems Engineering Department of their Space and Information Division. We had enjoyed California but New England was home. We had never packed more happily. This time, even the long cross-country trip was a pleasure. Fall was at its best and every day brought us nearer to our hearts' desire.

It is difficult to explain my feeling for this small corner of the earth. In part it is the land; its beauty is intimate, accessible. Deeper down, it is a sense of belonging, of being in tune with the life around me and at peace with myself.

One positive aspect of all this moving about was that we often were able to see relatives and old friends en route. On earlier moves we had almost always been able to stay with Anna in Ohio overnight. That was no longer possible but we stayed one night with Sang Hie in Terre Haute and one night with the Southworths in State College, Pennsylvania. They were about to leave for Korea, where Herman was to be a marketing consultant at an agricultural college for the next six years. Strange to say, we saw them more often during those years than at any other time. Since one of their sons lived near us in another Boston suburb, they always came our way when they were home on their annual leave.

We arrived in Massachusetts at the end of October and found a house in Concord, where we had just missed living in 1951. Until we could get into it we lived at the Concord Inn, once the old Thoreau home. The floors sagged and the beds were not the best, but the food was excellent and the ghosts were friendly.

Of all the places I have lived, Concord is the one I have enjoyed the most. By the time we went there it had become a bedroom suburb, but it had retained the air of the small local center it had once been. There was no fake quaintness. Its old houses were lived in by persons who knew their history and maintained them in their original simplicity.

I have no illusions about what life must have been like there for persons like me in its heyday. The "free thinking" of an Emerson, the idiosyncrasies of a Thoreau, were well within the bounds of a propriety still marked by its Puritan derivation. I would have been stifled. I was no Louisa May Alcott to find relief from my frustrations in writing. Incidentally, anyone who thinks that Louisa May was just one more New England spinster should become acquainted with the stories she wrote under a pseudonym for magazine publication. A free spirit lived in her and managed to breathe somehow in spite of the rarified air.

Nevertheless, that life had its values: a sturdy integrity, a discipline and a strength that helped set this new nation solidly on its feet in a remarkably short time. That spirit still lived in the shady streets and the old stone walls. I never looked upon the old bridge with its bronze minuteman, one legging incompletely buttoned in his haste, and on the touching inscription to the British who fell there, without a thrill. There was a memorable moment one Easter Sunday near sundown when an oriole burst into song, high on a nearby pine, and I knew what the Transcendentalists meant by the imminence of God in nature.

In 1966, Concord was the last of the towns near Boston to preserve the town-meeting form of government. The annual meeting had become three evenings of meetings in two places, but it was still enthusiastically attended. A city manager and a few officials held paid positions, but much of the city's work was done by volunteer committees. This was real democracy and it felt good.

Our house was located in a relatively new development in a slightly rolling area of oak and pine woods, where in early spring the rare pink ladyslipper grew and blossomed profusely. Towards the back of our lot there was a scrubby open area with shadblow and hazel and sweet pepper and a few maples, gorgeously colored in the fall. The woods were thin, since the soil was poor from repeated forest fires, so our first planting was a hundred white-pine seedlings, and seedlings of Andorra juniper and autumn olive on the raw road cuts. Carolyn Heath, who has kept me informed about their growth through all the years since, tells me that the pines are mature and have given her and others much pleasure. There is something very satisfying about that.

A flowering dogwood followed, and wild azaleas and ferns, and English yew and a small wildflower garden.

One of the pleasures of early spring was a visit to the wildflower nursery in Methuen, where an old man had held on to several acres of woods while the city grew around him. In the summer he went to far places like Alaska looking for new varieties. He was a storehouse of information and a charming person. Another errand that I looked forward to impatiently in winter was the visit to the beautiful Weston nurseries in Hopkinton. The drive through farm and orchard country and around the Sudbury reservoir, with buds swelling and the smell of fresh-turned earth, was a joy. Gardening is as near to unclouded happiness as anything I know of.

Again we had birds rare near cities, and they flocked around the birdbath where we could watch them. The robins made a great to-do about bathing. They took their time, splashing about with a great fluttering of wings, drying themselves off and repeating the performance, while the smaller birds waited their turn. A pair of mourning doves built their nest and raised their young in the crotch of a pine just outside our dining-room window. They took turns at sitting on the nest and bringing food, changing shifts night and morning. They sat on those birdlings until they were so big that I would not have been surprised if all three, parent and young, had fallen out.

We lived a charmed life in our small Eden while storms built up around us. Disappointment over the inconclusive results of the Negro-rights movement and mounting resistance to the Vietnam War had reached their peak in the colleges. Harvard Square was a disaster area, all the shop windows broken and boarded up. I went to a meeting at the Unitarian Church, called by some of the people that we later knew as hippies, to find out what was going on. I learned nothing. Their discontent was evident but their discourse was incoherent.

In the summer of 1967 Sang Eun stayed with us for a week before going on to Stockbridge to attend the Tanglewood music school. We woke up every morning to the sounds of 'cello practice under the trees. She returned to Concord just in time to attend the last concert of the season by the Marlboro Festival Orchestra. We drove out to Vermont on a sunny Sunday afternoon in September. The simplicity of the building in which the concerts were held and the closeness of the orchestra made these occasions seem more like friendly gatherings than like public events. Pablo Casals conducted. He was so old and frail that he had to be supported by someone on each side of him when he entered. He conducted sitting down.

From the first chord the music was charged with emotion. Casals was greatly loved and respected, and I am sure every member of the orchestra must have felt that this was his last appearance with them. Traditionally, the last number of the final concert was always Beethoven's choral fantasy. Rudolf Serkin at the piano began singing, then the orchestra. Persons in the audience joined in. As the excitement mounted, Casals slowly rose to his feet and finished standing! It was tremendous, a once-in-a-lifetime experience, the triumph of the human spirit over mortality.

The next summer the Lee girls' mother visited us briefly. Her name was Nak Shin Kim. In Korea a woman retains her maiden name after her marriage. Since her husband's death she had held a position with the Korean department of education and she was in the United States to attend a convention as a guest of our Department of State, which had provided her with an interpreter. Mabel Wright had a cosmopolitan background, she had spent most of her life in the Orient, and she was excellent company. Mrs. Kim was intensely interested in everything American. I don't know who enjoyed her visit the most.

Throughout those years I worked with Patricia Bennett to get out the monthly newsletter of the League of Women Voters. That is as close as I have come to political action. In three places where I have lived I have had friends who were league officers. It apparently has given them much satisfaction. But I do not work happily or effectively within an organizational setting. I am impatient of meetings and committees and adversarial situations. For the same reason I have never belonged more than briefly to the American Association of University Women. I regret that this is so, because such organizations are a useful way of becoming acquainted in a new community.

My principal volunteer activity was a therapeutic-tutoring project at the Adams public school in Lexington. William Gieck, the principal, was a young man seriously concerned about children's emotional needs. He believed that every school child could benefit from having a grown-up friend for guidance and support. Since this was impossible, he had asked each teacher to choose the child in her room who most needed help, and had then appealed, through the newspapers, for volunteers to become friends of those children. We were called tutors for want of a more precise word, but our only duty was to spend a certain number of hours each week with our children in any way we saw fit. The idea was to help them gain confidence.

The volunteers were also required to attend meetings two or three mornings a week, at which we talked over our problems with Amy Lichtblau, the school counselor, or were addressed by someone professionally engaged in work with children. Amy was an extraordinary young woman with an instinctive understanding of children. I think we all gained new insights from these sessions. The project also led me into the literature of many new subjects: child behavior, family life, elementary education, and the special difficulties of my child, a dyslexic.

"Danny," was ten years old. He was a quiet child who gave the impression of being impassive; actually he was outgoing and very well adjusted. His relationship with both of his parents was excellent. His father, who was of Scotch descent, had grown up on a farm in Maine and was now a fireman. He brought home small animals and showed his two sons how to take care of them. One day Danny brought a baby rabbit with him to a meeting and held and fondled it the whole time. It lay perfectly quiet. His father also enlisted the boys' help in projects like building a swimming pool in the back yard. The mother was Irish, and had instilled in the child a great respect for her people. When I asked Danny whether his mother was Scotch, like his father, he replied, "Oh no, she is Irish, *pure* Irish." He made friends readily.

He excelled in sports.

He loved stories, and I had found in the school library a wonderful series of children's books entitled, *My Village is in Ireland, My Village is in Egypt,* and so on. I enjoyed them myself. On Sundays Bob and I sometimes took him and a friend to such places as the Boston Museum of Natural History or a country festival and bazaar. He seldom showed any animation, but he always accepted our invitations with apparent pleasure. I had not realized how many children know little or nothing about what their environment has to offer.

One day when I was in the school library looking for books to read, I looked around for a place to sit. There was just one empty chair, at a table where three boys were sitting. One of them, a very well-brought-up, courteous boy, had been with us the previous Sunday, and he greeted me pleasantly. So I asked if I might sit with him and his friends for a little while. He agreed politely and then said, "We were talking about drugs." Just like that! It was my first encounter with the generation that was growing up in full knowledge of all the evils in the world. I was stunned and I have not got over it yet.

At the end of the term I asked Danny whether he wished to go on for another year, and he said he didn't know. I said, "Oh, come on. You know whether you are having a good time or not." He decided to continue.

The next school year had hardly begun when the sky fell! Raytheon had recently shut down the entire division in which Bob was working. They had promised to find another berth for him, but he was marking time, doing work that did not really warrant his salary, when there was a slump in business, an expected contract failed to materialize, and a certain number of men had to go. Bob was inevitably one of them. He was now fifty-nine years old. This was retirement, ready or not.

Fortunately, my relationship with Danny was already on firm ground. He wrote to me every year at Christmas time until he was eighteen and had finished high school. In his last letter he wrote:

Well, I told you about the farm. . . . I do everything from
buying flowers in the flower exchange to loading trucks.
I am 18 years old. I make $_____ a week which is not bad
for a kid my age. I am going to send you a picture of me.
I would like to hear from you so please write back.

It is so that I think of him: working outdoors with considerable freedom, giving his dog a friendly pat, teaching his children to love and respect the earth and to overcome obstacles, brightening the world around him. May his tribe increase!

17

OFF TO THE RIO GRANDE

The first effect of this unexpected blow was numbness. Obviously we would not be able to remain in Concord long, but where to go and what to do would have to wait until we could think clearly. It was some comfort that Sang Eun had finished college and got married. At least we had no one but ourselves to worry about.

After a few weeks we decided to have the house appraised and find out more exactly how much money we could count on, so we called a real estate agent. In two or three weeks she had rounded up a couple who wanted the house and were willing to wait. This was unexpected good fortune. We sold the place for delivery in May, which left us the whole winter in which to think.

With that off our minds, we felt enough easier to begin thinking about the choice we would have to make. Bob was certain that he could make a living as a consultant if we made the right move. The place would have to be big enough to support a steady flow of work but not so big that a newcomer would be lost in it. It would have to have a not-too-high cost of living and some cultural advantages and be receptive to strangers. Everything pointed to Santa Fe, with which we had some acquaintance. Bob's brother Arthur had lived in northern New Mexico for more than thirty years, and he was the kind of affable person who "knew everybody." That should help.

We called Art and asked him what he thought about Santa Fe as a place to work and what he knew about the housing situation. He said he knew just the house for us; his friend General Sedillo wanted to sell his former home, a good, small house well located and reasonably priced. For the rest, he and Peggy were going to be away for two weeks in March; why didn't we come out and look around? That seemed like a good idea.

In late March we went to Taos. Art and Peggy took off the next day, leaving us their camper, and we drove into Santa Fe daily to learn what we could about it. It had a small-town air, with open spaces and trees on some of the downtown streets. There were pleasant residence neighborhoods. Bob thought the possibilities for work were good.

We were unable to see General Sedillo's house since he was out of town and his agent was unavailable. It looked good from the outside, and it was in a quiet neighborhood of one-third to one-half acre lots not more than a mile from downtown. A couple of days with a real estate agent produced nothing of interest, but our minds were made up. We would take our chances with Santa Fe.

In May we bade a regretful good-bye to Concord and headed west as thousands had done before us. The general's house was just right. It was twenty-five years old, in need of considerable renovation, but the price took that into consideration. It had been designed by William Lumpkins, one of Santa Fe's outstanding architects and had a number of special features, like a window wall in the foyer looking into a shady enclosed back yard, and a wall of built-in bookshelves in the living room. There was even a shop attached to the garage, where Bob could work. The plumbing and heating had to be attended to at once, and the rest we got done as we could.

We moved in on the first of July. At least, we moved in our furniture. We were again house-sitting for Art and Peggy and had to be in Taos at night for a few days longer. Our friends, Lee and Paula Wyman from Boston, had come to Santa Fe for an anthropological convention without room reservations and were unable to find any place to stay; so we set up the beds for them, and they slept gratefully —and, I hope, with pleasant dreams—amid the packing boxes.

Throughout the summer Bob spent most of his time around town, getting acquainted and finding out what projects were afoot. His efforts yielded little that year. For several months during the winter he studied continuously for the state examination for registration of engineers and passed it early in the spring. A year slipped by that way. Business came slowly, over several years, but it grew steadily. Santa Fe has been good to us.

Santa Fe owes its uniqueness to its former status as the capital of the Spanish colonies in North America. I believe that the present population of the whole state of New Mexico is still predominantly Hispanic. This circumstance and the proximity of several Indian pueblos have attracted artists and artisans since the turn of the century; also archeologists, anthropologists, historians, and literary people, with the result that it has an urbanity unusual in a small, out-of-the-way city.

Unfortunately the merchants and the city fathers, always looking for new sources of revenue, have exploited the cultural situation, not always in the city's best interest. The expression, "the three cultures," rolls lightly off the tongues of realtors and publicity agents, with the implication that they exist happily side by side, different but equal. It is simply not so. What we have here is two dispossessed cultures surviving uneasily within the dominant one. Its ways are not their ways, and they have all the difficulties inherent in such a situation. Occasionally some controversial proposal or unfortunate incident stirs up latent resentments. For the most part, however, it seems to me that both the Indians and the Hispanics have adapted themselves to the new conditions better than might have been expected. Bob and I have had the good fortune to become quite well acquainted with a Hispanic family and with an Indian who exemplify all that is best in their inheritance. (The names used are pseudonyms.)

In the fall of 1971 I offered my services to a tutoring agency and was given the name of a young Hispanic woman who wanted to learn to read. Although she had attended school for eight years, she was totally illiterate. Since she had no transportation, I went to her home for the lessons. I will call her Consuela.

She was twenty-six years old, divorced, with four children—the oldest a boy of ten, the youngest a girl of four years. She was a superior person in every way. She was pretty, with a good figure and that something more that makes some persons stand out in any crowd. She was as competent as she was attractive; everything she did, she did well, with no fuss. And she was happy. In two years I never heard her complain about anything. And this woman thought of herself as a failure. She had labeled herself "dumb."

She wanted to learn to read so that she could teach Tommy, the ten-year-old, who was reading only at first-grade level. I didn't want to turn her off at this point by suggesting that this was a rather roundabout way to help Tommy. Perhaps she could be helped, and then we might bring Tommy in. I got nowhere with her. When she looked at letters she fell apart. She was convinced that reading was too much for her, and it was a barrier I could not penetrate. When I proposed that I teach Tommy directly she was greatly relieved. That possibility seems not to have occurred to her.

Tommy had a sunny smile, but he was a very troubled child. I quickly sized him up as bright. He asked intelligent questions and he was witty. But he had fallen behind in his first year in school and had long since given up trying. In school he made a show of indifference. A report from a special teacher said, "He uses his intelligence (which is above average) and his wit (delightful and often sophisticated) to baffle those who are trying to help him."

Yet all the while, this poor child wanted nothing so much as to learn. I think I had a degree of success where others had failed because we were in a special situation. At school he would rather be thought not to care than to be thought stupid. With me he could drop his defenses.

I knew nothing about teaching reading. I had been given a workbook but was appalled by its dullness and its inferior illustrations. How could one hold a child's attention with such unappetizing fare? Textbooks for teachers were little help. *Why Johnny Can't Read* saved the day. It said that nine out of ten words were regular, and it was full of phonetic word lists. Phonetics is not enough, but it is an excellent handle for getting started.

I figured that Tommy needed continuous small successes and that he should have visible evidence of his accomplishments for the inevitable bad days. I bought stacks of colored index cards and cut them in thirds to make vocabulary cards. Then I assigned one color to each vowel sound and typed several hundred one-syllable words. (I didn't do this all at once.) For the first lesson I took with me some two hundred words in a box they just fitted and told Tommy, "When you can remember that an 'e' with consonants on both sides of it sounds like 'pet,' you will be able to read two hundred words. [He knew the consonants.] When you can remember it standing on your head, you may keep the box." Slowly the boxes accumulated. I made up games with words that rhymed, and soon his brother and sister wanted to play, which was all to the good.

None of this was as quick or as easy as it sounds. For a year and a half Tommy lived in fear of failing. I told him the story of *The Little Engine That Could:* "I think I can, I think I can." He would invariably say, "I think I can't." Still, it registered. There were days when he was completely blocked or when he was troubled and couldn't keep his mind on what we were doing. On such days I cut the lesson short as soon as I saw that it was useless.

After a year, with insignificant results, I went to see Mrs. Daugherty, who had run a successful school for young, disadvantaged children for many years, and told her I felt like giving up. She said, "Never give up as long as the child is willing to try." Actually, I couldn't have done it, Tommy knew when I felt discouraged and he would say, "Don't give up on me." I was his last hope.

One day in February of the second year Tommy said he would like to see some of the last lessons in *Johnny,* where, syllables were put together to make long words. He read slowly, "pres-i-dent—PRESI-DENT!!!" He was on his way.

When school closed in June the second year, I decided I had done what I could for him. He now had enough confidence to go on at school. It took him another two years to get his fifth-grade reading certificate, which he showed me with pride.

It was too late to enable him to catch up with all he had missed. He tried high school and found it too hard. He did, however, learn the carpenter's trade and at present is happily engaged in building construction. He has married and is the devoted father of a small son and daughter. His family is proud of him. I call that success.

During those years that I worked with Tommy, Bob and I had both become involved with the whole family, which included the maternal grandparents. They too were persons to be respected, and they were the stabilizing force in Consuela's fatherless family. The grandmother was the kind of woman who mothers everybody and asks no more of life than a constant supply of persons who need her love. Her husband, and his parents before him, had been migrant farm workers. He took a professional pride in such knowledge as how to pick a variety of vegetables most efficiently. Of late he had worked for the city and had recently received a certificate of appreciation for fifteen years of service. He was also handy in working with wood. He had built a camper upon his truck, which he finished inside and out in fine style. The children were very proud of him.

After Tommy began to show progress we were treated like patron saints, and we had to go to all the confirmations and to the grandparents' house for dinner afterwards. What was interesting to us about these occasions was the inside view of a family life that was all glowing warmth: no criticism, no exhortations, no pressure of any kind —just overflowing love and good example. What it lacked was any mental stimulation. When there is nothing to read and questions go unanswered, curiosity atrophies. I am afraid that many of these children enter school already turned off. It is a difficult situation for the schools to remedy.

Our acquaintance with Indians came about through Art. He was in the wholesale Indian jewelry business and had several Indians making jewelry for him in pueblos forty miles or so south of Santa Fe. He dealt with them through an agent in Santa Fe who transmitted silver and stones to the Indians and took in their finished work. When this agent moved to Albuquerque, Art asked us if we would take over the responsibility, and we were happy to comply.

Josefita was a very talented jeweler and she was proud and impatient. I got off on the wrong foot with her by being out the first time she called. When she finally reached me I was greeted with a torrent of indignation. I could not afford to have her angry with me before we ever met, so I pacified her as best I could and went out to meet her at a shopping center way out near the south end of town. The next time I saw her she was a lamb. She and Tony, her husband, were sitting in their car, and she told him to give me an eagle feather that hung in the windshield. It must have been a fetish to ward off accidents, like the figure of a saint that some Catholics use in the same way. It had been embellished with a small orange and black feather attached to the shaft by fine beadwork, and the leather thong by which it hung was decorated with three quite large turquoise beads. I took it to be a peace offering.

I did not know at the time that she was a very sick woman. A short time after I met her she was in the Indian hospital in Santa Fe, terminally ill. Tony came to Santa Fe every evening to spend the night with her, and until he was permitted to go to the hospital he used to come to our house to wait. He was deeply grieved, his woman was dying, and he talked to us as friend to friend about matters close to his heart.

I could not believe my eyes when he drove up one afternoon with Josefita in the truck beside him. She looked like a ghost. She had insisted on going home to die and the hospital had let her go. She had then persuaded Tony to take her to Arizona to see old friends for the last time, and they had stopped off at our house on their way. It could only have been to say good-bye; they had no other business. I did not know all this at the time. She lived just long enough to get to Arizona and back again.

The funeral mass was held in the little pueblo church, and afterwards the whole company walked to the burial ground. There the priest spoke a few words and left, and the Indians took over the ceremonies. Several men picked up their shovels and opened the grave, chanting while they worked. The coffin was lowered in, and the chanting continued while the earth was replaced. That was all, yet it was very impressive: this remnant of a people burying their dead in their own way with ancient hymns.

Thereafter, those evenings that Tony had spent with us voicing his grief were never mentioned, but they were a bond between us. We had shared his sorrow. We received invitations to all the special occasions, marriages and saints' days. Plentiful food, usually very good, was an important feature of every celebration. All day people came and went, seating themselves at the big table when they wished; and all day the kitchen was full of women cooking and renewing the food at the table.

Once Tony's daughter came in from dancing in the plaza, changed from her ceremonial costume to sweater and jeans, and sat down to a game of Scrabble. It seemed to sum up all the incongruities that beset minority cultures.

We saw Herbert and Anna frequently until Anna died in 1985, and renewed our acquaintance with her family, now happily augmented by Dick's wife Natalie, their daughter Rebecca, and Natalie's two children, Debbie and Alan. They brightened Anna's life during her last years, as she did theirs. We also looked up Grace in Denver and found that we had much in common.

For about twelve years I attended a community seminar at St. John's College every winter. It takes two things to make a Great Books discussion worthwhile: a good group and a skilled moderator. At St. John's we had both. The seminars drew men and women of all ages and a variety of backgrounds. I remember three physicians, three lawyers, a sprinkling of engineers, several teachers, an artist and her husband, a composer of music, a writer of detective stories, many wives of professional men. What would I not have given for such an opportunity to bat ideas about when I was young!

We took in our last child in 1980. Robin Slonager had been graduated from St. John's a year before. We met her by chance when she came back to Santa Fe in the spring, not knowing what she wanted to do, only that she wanted to be here. She lived with us for a few weeks until she couuld find an apartment and stayed on in Santa Fe until after Christmas, supporting herself but unable to find worthwhile work for which she was qualified. Like so many young people during those years she felt out of step with the world around her. Ultimately she settled down to working for a doctorate in philosophy at Georgetown University. It was a pleasure to have her with us and it was the beginning of a lasting friendship

In the fall of 1982 I discovered Charlene Stoltz, a granddaughter of Mertie's, and her husband John. She had written to Grace, asking her if she knew of anyone living who could give her information on the Beneker family. Grace passed the letter on to Anna, who passed it on to me. The next spring Charlene and John visited us and began to urge me to write this book. It was the beginning of a cordial friendship that we value the more because new friends are rare in old age. So here I am, trying to sum up a life and appraise the world around me.

*　　*　　*

For twenty-five years after World War II the future looked bright for most Americans. The economy was in high gear. The Baby Boom generation grew up knowing nothing of hard times. What they wanted they got, and they expected this happy state of affairs to go on forever. By the time they were grown everything had changed.

In the Sixties, as I have said earlier, social unrest began to surface. Although race relations and the Vietnamese war were the issues that sparked it, it soon developed into rebellion on a broad front. The movement centered in the colleges, where students demanded "relevant" studies, meaning nothing thought or written longer ago than yesterday. The word "discrimination" was on every tongue, its meaning stretched to include all distinctions. Colleges were discriminatory when they set standards that some students were unable to meet. Protests were accompanied by rowdiness and vandalism. It was mass hysteria.

We had beatniks in weird clothing, then flower children and hippies. Men took to wearing long hair; women, long "granny" skirts, in defiance of convention. Some went everywhere in bare feet. The idea was to start all over again, to be natural and uninhibited—Rousseau's noble savage updated. There was an extensive communal back-to-the-land movement. Society was totally evil; the only honest way to live was to turn one's back on it. As always in troubled times, cults and exotic religions flourished.

By 1970 the sexual revolution was in full swing. Unwed teen-age mothers were becoming a national problem. College students demanded, and got, co-ed dormitories. Men and women were living together openly without benefit of clergy in such numbers that social sanctions no longer had any force. Explicit sexual activities were standard fare on movie and television screens. The consequences were not always as happy as the proponents of freedom had prophesied.

Meanwhile, the deterioration of the environment was accelerating. What Joseph Addison had once ecstatically described as "the starry firmament on high and all the blue ethereal sky" was disappearing over our cities above layers of smog. The national debt was soaring, thanks largely to the exorbitant cost of nuclear armament. Family life was becoming a mad scramble to keep up with the mortgage and the credit cards in the face of inflation. Millions of women joined their husbands as wage earners, relegating the children, of necessity, to the back burner. Violent crime was increasing alarmingly, and the use of narcotic drugs permeated every level of society. Watching television had also become an addiction, and children were forming their conceptions of life from lewd and violent programs. World population was increasing at an unprecedented rate, crowding cities and putting pressure on food supplies worldwide. Refugees from poverty or oppressive regimes, mainly Hispanic and Oriental, were swarming to this country—still the hope of the world in spite of everything—creating new problems of assimilation. And always in the background, the shadow of nuclear war or nuclear accident.

This is, of course, only the dark side. In the pleasant small city where I live and in thousands of others across the country the air is still clean. Many people experience most of these troubles only indirectly. There are still good marriages and happy families and responsible young people. Nevertheless, nearly everyone is living today with anxieties unknown two generaions ago.

Looking back it can be seen that this century has been marked by progressive disregard of authority and rejection of old patterns and old standards in all areas that reflect a society's basic philosophy: the arts, entertainment, popular music, dress, manners, morals; culminating in the rampant individualism of the hippies. Since they had no constructive program they had their day and faded away, but moral chaos remains. The old standards have fallen. Where we shall go from here is anybody's guess, but it seems certain that the years ahead will be critical for the American way of life. If we are to see happier days, it will have to be understood that personal freedom can never be total, and that its price is responsible behavior.

The issue that lies closest to my heart is the plight of today's children and their harried mothers. The two-income family has become the norm. It is taken for granted that a married woman will assume the dual role of mother and breadwinner. It can be done, but not by everyone. For many women, perhaps for most, it is a treadmill. Is it for this that women have been "liberated"? And can society afford the human cost?

I do not know the answer. The financial bind in which the typical American family is caught is a fact of life and cannot be ignored. But surely something is askew when an acceptable standard of living can be maintained only at the cost of family life and the proper nurture of children. Maybe we should be taking a hard look at our priorities.

Another major factor in the present situation is the widespread attitude of arrogance towards nature. The indifference of industry to the consequences of its operations is only the most conspicuous example. The public that leaves a trail of litter in its wake everywhere it goes— even, if a recent account may be credited, at the summit of Mt. Everest —is manifesting the same heedlessness. We are not lords of creation but members of it, as dependent as any other creature on the health of this planet. We would do well to remember that humility becomes us.

This attitude is undoubtedly owing in part to the increasingly man-made environment in which we live. We belong to the earth; apart from it our creatural nature languishes and our view of life becomes distorted. I believe that this accounts for much restlessness, especially in the young. So far as I know, little attention has yet been paid to this subject, although there has been some concern for a long time.

Forty years ago, in *Mechanization Takes Command,*[6] Siegfried Giedion explored the cost of mechanization in terms of human values lost. He concluded that mechanization had created a rift between people's ways of thinking and feeling, which was disrupting the life of both society and the individual, and that a new synthesis would have to be found if our civilization was to survive. At about the same time, in his perceptive little book, *The Twelve Seasons,* a joyous celebration of the natural world, Joseph Wood Krutch asked, "Do we dare to forget . . . that we belong rejoicing by the marsh more anciently and more fundamentally than by the machine or over the drawing board?"[7] It is a question worth pondering.

As I bring this book to a close in the Eighties the tumult has died down. People are tired of worrying. President Reagan enjoys immense popularity because he makes trouble go away. He smiles and waves his hand, and there is nothing to worry about. This may be the greatest danger of all. Of course there are exceptions. Many people are working hard in many organizations to do what they can about individual issues, but it will take an aroused electorate to turn the tide.

I feel a special sympathy for the young men and women who must soon take over the reins. I would like to say to them: Remember that human life began in the wild, where the only goal was survival and the only law was self-preservation. The wonder is not that greed and violence have persisted but that there seems to have been, almost from the beginning of history, a vision of a better world. It has been the polestar of the race throughout the centuries. But the way is long and rough. One day we gain a little ground; another day we lose it again. Paradoxically, the struggle is what makes life worthwhile. Like Hamlet we may choose to rail against the times and bewail our fate, or we may accept the challenge and find life in the endeavor.

I cannot do better than to quote Arthur Machen, a Welshman who was writing in London during the early years of this century. For "the arts," read "life." It comes to the same thing.

> The matter of Wonder—that is the matter of the arts—is everywhere offered to us. . . . And it is utterly true that he who cannot find wonder, mystery, awe, the sense of a new world and an undiscovered realm in the places by the Gray's Inn Road will never find those secrets elsewhere, . . . All the wonders lie within a stone's throw of King's Cross Station.[8]

To understand this is to understand that our lives are what we do with what is offered. The matter of Life is always there for those who will reach out for it. *Give, and it shall be given unto you. Seek, and ye shall find.* This is the message I would leave with those who are setting out in life. With all my heart I wish them *Bon Voyage!*

References and Permissions